D1069288

STEVE McQUEEN
THE GREAT ESCAPE

Steve McQueen strikes a sacrificial pose in Nevada Smith *(1966), replicating an iconic* Giant *(1956) still of his early hero, James Dean.*

STEVE McQUEEN

THE GREAT ESCAPE

A WES D. GEHRING BIOGRAPHY

Indiana Historical Society Press
Indianapolis 2009

© 2009 Indiana Historical Society Press

Printed in the United States of America

This book is a publication of the
Indiana Historical Society Press
Eugene and Marilyn Glick Indiana History Center
450 West Ohio Street
Indianapolis, Indiana 46202-3269 USA
http://www.indianahistory.org
Telephone orders 1-800-447-1830
Fax orders 1-317-234-0562
Online orders @ http://shop.indianahistory.org

The paper in this publication meets the minimum requirements of American National Standard
for Information Sciences—Permanence of Paper for Printed Library Materials,
ANSI Z39.48–1984

Library of Congress Cataloging-in-Publication Data

Gehring, Wes D.
Steve McQueen : the great escape / Wes D. Gehring.
    p. cm.
Includes bibliographical references.
ISBN 978-0-87195-279-0 (cloth : alk. paper)
1. McQueen, Steve, 1930-1980. 2. Motion picture actors and
actresses—United States—Biography. I. Title.
PN2287.M547G44 2009
791.4302'8092—dc22
[B]
                         2009007007

To my mother and father . . .
they made all the difference

"A McQueen Movie . . ."

is often about being "unstuck
in time" . . . a cowboy faced
with time slipping into the future,

is an "escape artist" act, where
an actor as auteur uses pieces of
himself to hide in plain sight,

is a loner's life imitating
art, or maverick art
imitating life, or both,

is a minimalist mask
that can still manage an
Oscar load of personal angst,

is a blue-collar enigma
built upon pragmatic interaction
with objects, from guns to gunboats,

is being born to be unimportant
but living a defiant *Papillon*
credo, "I'm still here, you bastards."

— Wes D. Gehring

Steve McQueen: The Great Escape is made possible through
the generous support of the Lacy Foundation/LDI, Ltd.

All images Wes D. Gehring Stills Collection

Contents

Foreword

Mark H. Massé

At first glance, soft-spoken author Wes D. Gehring has little in common with the subject of his twenty-seventh book, actor Steve McQueen. Gehring had a happy midwestern childhood, growing up as a good student and versatile high school athlete in Iowa. He still enjoys a warm relationship with his parents. By contrast, Indiana native McQueen had a troubled upbringing. He was estranged from his mother and abandoned by his father. While Gehring pursued the life of a scholar and author, McQueen was a high school dropout who spent time in a school for troubled youth. He was an angry young man who enlisted in the U.S. Marines at seventeen. Before securing his first acting roles, McQueen worked in many blue-collar jobs.

"Steve McQueen had a real hard life," Gehring said, adding that the late actor, a heavy smoker and drinker, died from cancer at the age of fifty. Gehring is a health-conscious fifty-eight, blessed with abundant energy and productivity. While McQueen was famous for racing Triumph motorcycles and sports cars at notable venues around the world, Gehring uses his late-model Chevrolet strictly to commute to work at Ball State University in Muncie, Indiana.

Despite their abundant differences, the closer one looks, parallels begin to emerge in comparing biographer and subject. Like McQueen, Gehring considers himself something of a loner and very much a traditionalist. He is proudest of being a father to two daughters, Sarah and Emily. McQueen was a father and stepfather who spoke lovingly of his kids. He was also committed to supporting programs at Boys Republic, a treatment community for troubled children where he had spent time as a youth.

Gehring was raised on a steady diet of Western films and television programs. One of his favorite television characters was the sandy-haired shaggy, dog-eyed bounty hunter Josh Randall in *Wanted: Dead or Alive*.

That taciturn, hardfisted character was played by McQueen, who, like Gehring, had loved watching Westerns when he was a boy.

In writing this biography, Gehring discovered an emotional connection with McQueen. He said his heart went out to the charismatic actor who struggled throughout his life with personal and professional challenges and disappointments: "Like many of his movie characters, McQueen's real-life persona was that of a wounded character who persevered," noted Gehring.

As an award-winning biographer, Gehring peers behind the curtain of fame as he researches the life and times of his subjects: "People are fascinated by how famous individuals deal with the same issues as ordinary people," he said. "In McQueen's case, his life was more interesting than any of his movie roles."

For years, Gehring wrote respected biographies of legendary comedians, such as Groucho Marx, W. C. Fields, and Red Skelton. Critics have praised his scholarship, insights, and unique historical contributions to the film industry. In recent times, Gehring has broadened his focus. One of his recent biographies was of another Indiana native and icon of popular culture, James Dean.

Dean and McQueen were contemporaries. They each lived in Greenwich Village during their early Method-acting days. Though he was two years older than Dean, McQueen shadowed the popular actor and star of such films as *Rebel without a Cause* and *East of Eden*. In the mid-1950s, McQueen hadn't arrived in Hollywood. He was known as an actor on television, a medium considered second-rate by movie buffs. A decade later, however, McQueen ranked among the most popular and highest-paid film stars of his generation. During his movie career, his notable credits included *The Magnificent Seven*, *The Great Escape*, *The Sand Pebbles*, *The Thomas Crown Affair*, and *Bullitt*. Gehring admires that McQueen fought against being typecast, citing how he starred in varied films, including *Papillon* and the William Faulkner comedy *The Reivers*. Gehring added that in researching McQueen's life, he came to admire the actor's fiercely independent spirit: "He was the real person other actors pretended to be," said Gehring.

As a teenager growing up in New York in the 1960s, I enjoyed McQueen's blend of toughness and sensitivity on screen. He was a man's man, but he seemed accessible, even vulnerable. You wouldn't want to mess with the guy, but you felt as if he could be your big brother or maybe a favorite hip uncle who might give you a ride on the back of his motorcycle.

I remember feeling sad in 1980 when McQueen left us prematurely, succumbing tragically to disease. But I am grateful that an author as talented as Gehring has written such a fine biography. As they used to say in the old Westerns, "pull up a chair and sit a spell." Wes Gehring has a tale to tell of a genuine star, the legendary Steve McQueen.

Mark H. Massé, a journalism professor at Ball State University, is a longtime freelance writer, whose books include Inspired to Serve: Today's Faith Activists *and the novel* Delamore's Dreams. *He is currently writing a nonfiction book on trauma journalism, as well as another novel.*

Preface

"When a kid doesn't have any love, he begins to wonder if he's good enough. My mother didn't love me. I didn't have a father. I thought, 'I must not be very good.' So you go out and try to prove yourself. I always did things other people wouldn't do, some dangerous things. I was always kind of a coward until I had to prove it to myself."[1]

STEVE MCQUEEN

In a nutshell, the above quote drives much of what follows in this biography, which explores how a child born to be unimportant could reach the Hollywood heights, yet remain a psychologically wounded individual. Given Steve McQueen's disjointed Hoosier roots, he built his success on a sort of fatalistic pragmatism. I am reminded of an observation from a novel by Nobel Prize-winning author Jose Saramago: "Unless I can see things with these eyes of mine that the earth will one day devour, I don't believe in them."[2] For much of McQueen's life, this self-defensive maxim might have been his mantra.

He even evolved an acting style, a Method approach grounded in minimalism, that was equally protective—not revealing too much of his wounded core, because that would make one more vulnerable. Acting for him was more reacting—building a characterization in the most realistically basic manner as a projection of how he utilized props (especially his beloved mechanical devices) as an extension of himself. That he could also bring an amazing poignancy to these parts effectively denies the famous claim of Mick Jagger's reclusive rock star in *Performance* (1970): "The only performance that makes it, that really makes it, that makes it all the way, is the one that achieves madness." In contrast, McQueen's performance greatness was all about a minimalism that kept the real madness inside, yet almost subliminally made the pain apparent.

During McQueen's 1930s Hoosier childhood, baseball teams in the old Negro Leagues, such as the Indianapolis Clowns, used to perform an inspired warm-up in pantomime with an imaginary baseball. This exercise in entertainment was called "shadow ball." In later years the

phrase became a metaphor for all those African American players not allowed in the Major Leagues whose diamond exploits were as historically
invisible as that imaginary baseball. McQueen's early existence was an
under-the-radar case of shadow ball, too. His rags-to-riches story is all
about fighting that invisibility, such as the line from the long opening
quote that says, "So you go out and try to prove yourself." Moreover, to
come full circle, while McQueen's movie career was the most public of
arenas in which to prove himself, how fitting that he evolved an acting style that was still like shadow ball—a minimalism that strove for a
slice-of-life realism.

As a teenager McQueen spent an extended time exploring America,
roughly paralleling Jack Kerouac's nomadic "research" period for the
novel *On the Road*.[3] Just as Kerouac's book became a bible for the Beat
Generation, the movement helped mold McQueen, from reinforc-
ing his sense of counter-culture outsider status, to effecting his hip,
slangy pattern of speech. The actor's early base of operations was even
New York City's Greenwich Village, the capital of the Beat Generation. Couple this tie with McQueen's dual fascination with motorcycles
and the Method, and one sees another major period influence—James
Dean, who continues to impact the "rebel" mentality today. Of course,
even this motorcycle/Method connection seems circular back to Kerouac's Beats, as best demonstrated by the following pocket definition
of the movement: "The stage-savvy Beats, with their motorbike saints,
were part of the getaway ['on the road'] package."[4]

While all this and more will be explored in the following pages, biography is also a study in angles of vision—neglected takes on a memorable life. First, the text keys on how the actor ironically saw the title
of his film *The Great Escape* (1963) as a veiled reference to what his life
might have been like without the movies. For example, he once stated,
"If I hadn't made it as an actor, I might have wound up a hood."[5] The
book's second angle of vision examines the many nuances of McQueen's
seemingly simplistic, minimalist acting style—elevating the significance
of an approach movingly devoid of extraneous psychological motivation

that he still sometimes denigrated. Third, this biography attempts to showcase a more balanced look at McQueen, beyond the easy-to-anger perfectionist. Yes, the actor was like baseball great Frankie Frisch, well known for his furious reactions to any of the game's bad calls—and he considered any call against him bad. But McQueen often had an innate comic sense, too, even when he was cynically articulating his dark take on life. Here is the actor's tongue-in-cheek justification for questioning people's motives: "Nobody trusts anyone, or why did they put 'tilt' on the pinball machine?"[6] Like his early hero Dean, McQueen was much more amusingly insightful than anyone gave him credit for.[7]

A fourth angle of vision is to elevate some neglected McQueen pictures to classic status—movies that do not conform to his "essence of cool" status, à la *Bullitt* (1968), for which he was acclaimed. Though readers are asked to reconsider the significance of several McQueen films in this text, the two most deserving of a revisionist slant are *The Reivers* (1969) and *Junior Bonner* (1972). The first is a feel-good populist comedy, the latter a sensitive contemporary Western, a cowboy character study. *Bonner*, arguably McQueen's greatest role, also suffered by being a departure from both the actor's standard action fare, as well as the director's, Sam Peckinpah. But whereas a more typical shoot-'em-up collaboration between the two, such as *The Getaway* (1972), values sensation over evolution, *Bonner* is all about the latter—a moving film about introspection.

Bonner is consistent, however, with a basic McQueen tenet that represents a fifth angle of vision—the actor felt like a man better suited to an earlier time and place. This "unstuck in time" component colored everything about him, from his real-life obsession with collecting vintage artifacts, to selecting movie roles with hooks to the past.[8] Thus, McQueen's seemingly diverse title characters of Bonner and Bullitt are linked by being old-fashioned cowboys in a modern world. While the comic tagline for Bruce Willis's John McClane figure in *Live Free or Die Hard* (2007) was "a Timex watch in a digital age," McQueen's adherence to the past was a throwback to America's mythic West; this resonated in everything about the Hoosier-born actor, such as his often quoted line, "I'd rather wake up in the middle of nowhere than any city on earth."

Bonner also represents one of the catalysts for this book. I first saw this movie with my father at the old Iowa Theatre in downtown Cedar Rapids, Iowa. I was then a budding film student at the nearby University of Iowa in Iowa City. We went expecting more of an action flick, but left impressed by both McQueen's acting chops and the bittersweet rapport between the actor and his screen father, Robert Preston. Only much later did I learn how difficult these scenes had been for McQueen, given the fact that the actor's real father had abandoned his family. Since I had the most supportive and compassionate of fathers, I was moved by what a struggle life must have been for McQueen without the parental pillar a good father represents. These feelings helped fuel the writing of this book.

In discussing McQueen with a friend, he ran by me a favorite question he always asks whenever I finish writing a biography: "What should his epitaph be? After throwing out several possibilities, ranging from the flip aforementioned "essence of cool," to the subtitle for my biography, "the great escape," I posited what I felt McQueen might have proposed. Given the actor's modest, often comically self-deprecating style, I think he would have borrowed a line from Clark Gable, a star he greatly admired and who had also suffered an early hardscrabble life. Here is Gable's answer to what his own epitaph should be: "He was lucky, and he knew it."[9]

This study was immeasurably enriched by both the New York Public Library's Performing Arts Library at Lincoln Center, and the Margaret Herrick Library at the Academy of Motion Picture Arts and Sciences, Beverly Hills, California. These archives were valuable resources for McQueen reviews and background material, as were the microfilm holdings of the main branch of the New York Public Library at Fifth Avenue and Forty-second Street. Closer to home, both the Beech Grove Public Library in Beech Grove, Indiana, McQueen's birthplace, and the Indiana State Library in Indianapolis were of additional assistance.

Numerous people helped make this project possible, starting with Ray E. Boomhower, senior editor with the Indiana Historical Society Press. I am forever grateful to his support of my writing, from the pages of *Traces*, which he also edits, to past books I have done for the IHS Press. An award-winning historian himself, Ray is the perfect catalyst for an author with a life to tell. Ball State professor emeritus and film historian Conrad Lane was a sometimes sounding board for the manuscript. Ball State journalism professor and author Mark Massé wrote the book's foreword. As usual, Janet Warner logged time as my copy editor. The computer preparation of the manuscript was done by Jean Thurman. My former department chair at Ball State, Nancy Carlson, was always supportive and assisted by facilitating university financial help. And both Mary J. Betzner and Pat McKeon, of the Beech Grove Public Library, went the proverbial extra mile.

For me, as for most people, my craft ultimately comes down to the love and support of family and friends. Most especially, this support system keys upon my parents, my daughters, Sarah and Emily, and special muse, Cassie Beal. To one and all, let me express my heartfelt thanks.

Prologue
Wanted: Dead or Alive

"Horses can't be trusted. You never know what they'll do.
I don't understand them. I don't like them."[1]
STEVE MCQUEEN

Steve McQueen's trust issues were hardly limited to horses. This iconic antihero screen superstar of the 1960s and 1970s was born into the most dysfunctional of families. After McQueen's father abandoned his young wife and baby son, the actor's mother frequently farmed the boy out to relatives while she followed the most self-destructive of personal paths. Not surprisingly, McQueen soon evolved into a character best described by filmmaker Sam Peckinpah: "Steve was every guy you didn't fuck with."[2]

McQueen comparisons are inevitable with another Hoosier-born legendary actor, James Dean. Both initially traded on a rebellious antiheroic persona anchored in Method acting, though each saw the humor sometimes attached to period spoofs of this new realism. For example, during the 1950s and 1960s the Method was sometimes kiddingly referred to as "the squint-mumble-scratch-and-think school of acting."[3] But there is a basic irony attached to any Dean-McQueen comparison. Dean was a poser in real life. He enjoyed suggesting he completely mirrored the troubled teens he played, but he was *not* the aimless, angst-ridden youth he played in the movies. Dean instinctively realized that for the public, this would add poignancy to his performances; that is, he seemingly replicated his reality.

In contrast, the quiet anger McQueen brought to so many of his young protagonists was anchored in a long history of hurt that will be fleshed out in the following chapters. Dean was every bit as passionate as his screen characters, and the actor suffered neither fools nor phonies in real life. But he had never had to walk the walk and talk the talk that was the train wreck of McQueen's early existence. Even Dean's beloved cousin and surrogate brother, Marcus Winslow Jr., has suggested

"Jimmy" knowingly let elements of this wounded film persona "rub off" on his accepted biography.[4]

If one is looking for a neglected parallel between Dean and Mc-Queen, one could focus on the Western. Dean was fascinated by the genre, especially the famous outlaw Billy the Kid, an interest that went back to the actor's childhood. The unrealized project at the time of Dean's death that he had most looked forward to doing was a film about Billy, which was eventually made as *The Left-Handed Gun* (1958, with Paul Newman in the title role).

Westerns occupied an equally significant place in McQueen's childhood. Part of the actor's youth was spent in the household of his mother's uncle, Claude Thomson. McQueen's great-uncle was a hog farmer in Slater, Missouri, and these periodic stays were the highlight of the boy's youth. As a reward for completing his farm chores, Thomson took his nephew to Saturday movie matinees at the local theater. As the 1930s were the heyday of the B-Westerns, McQueen later recalled, "Westerns were my favorite. I used to bring my cap pistol and fire at the villains."[5]

In 1959, just after the successful completion of McQueen's first television season as a Western bounty hunter on *Wanted: Dead or Alive*, Hollywood powerbroker columnist Hedda Hopper wrote an insightful sagebrush-tinged profile of the actor. McQueen revealed that he had long been a student of one of the Western's signature film stars—Gary Cooper. The young actor also managed to dovetail from his Method training to a Cooper minimalism that he admired more than any technique, noting: "I went to Actor's Studio [home of the Method] three years. . . . The only reason there's so much talk about Method acting is there's no place else to study in New York. Actually, the only 'method' is . . . to find out what you can do as an actor. I admire Gary Cooper, an actor who never studied in his life. He had something; he's gifted with a casual manner I've had to work for. Simplicity came naturally to him."[6]

Wanted: Dead or Alive proved pivotal to McQueen's storied career in seven ways. First, the series established the actor as an up-and-coming star. After years of struggle as a sometimes New York stage actor and

Left: James Dean practices some roping for his twentieth-century cowboy performance in Giant. ***Below:*** *Gary Cooper comforts Grace Kelly in his Oscar-winning role as a lone marshal in the celebrated Western* High Noon *(1952).*

small-screen performer fighting for guest spots, his Western was a hit in its initial season (1958–59). McQueen's star was finally starting to eclipse that of his first wife, dancer/singer/actress Neile Adams, an established stage performer.

Becoming noticed as a television cowboy was, however, no small task in the late 1950s. There were over two dozen horse operas airing in prime time the season *Wanted: Dead or Alive* premiered. Indeed, twelve of the top Nielsen-rated programs that season were Westerns: *Gunsmoke, Wagon Train, Have Gun Will Travel, The Rifleman, Maverick, Tales of Wells Fargo, The Life and Legend of Wyatt Earp, Zane Grey Theatre, The Texan, Wanted: Dead or Alive, Cheyenne,* and *Sugarfoot.*[7]

The path to McQueen's own series started the previous television season, when the actor made a memorable appearance on Dale Robertson's *Tales of Wells Fargo.* McQueen played an outlaw with a secret connection to a robbery. This proved a great showcase for him, since *Wells Fargo* was the third most watched television program that season, trailing *Gunsmoke* and *The Danny Thomas Show*. Ironically, McQueen had not enjoyed the guest spot and even told his wife, "That's the last of these cockamamie cowboy shows for me."[8]

Of course, one should never say never, especially when sagebrush stories were then the number-one genre on television. McQueen's next step toward a cowboy series involved yet another Western program, *Trackdown*. This Texas Ranger show was based on true 1870s stories and starred Robert Culp. The agent for both Culp and McQueen was Hillard Elkins, who found out that the *Trackdown* producers (Four Star) planned a companion series. "The spin-off was about a bounty hunter in the old West," Elkins said. "I immediately knew that McQueen, playing this quasi-heavy lead, wouldn't only be perfect for the part—he'd use it as a launch pad for stardom. . . . I made my pitch to Steve and to Four Star."[9]

Consequently, that same 1957–58 television season McQueen made a pilot that was also broadcast as an episode of *Trackdown*. Titled "The Bounty Hunter," McQueen's tough title character was Josh Randall, the figure he soon played to acclaim on *Wanted: Dead or Alive*. While the young actor waited for the verdict from Four Star (a television production company essentially run by three stars—Dick Powell, David Niven, and Charles Boyer), McQueen made a low-budget science fiction film he assumed no one would see, *The Blob* (1958). To McQueen's embarrassment, this campy B movie—a small town threatened by a huge dose of outer space Jell-O—became a cult hit.

When *Wanted: Dead or Alive* premiered in the fall, the early notices were less than ecstatic. A tongue-in-cheek weekly *Variety* kidded the fact that McQueen's smallish frame had almost super-human powers: "He is lithe and lean and can handle up to six men at a time."[10] The *San Francisco Examiner* criticized the inherent violence: "The man-hunting hero, Steve McQueen, is a trigger-happy James Cagney type. In the first three minutes of the first show he shot a man in the back and broke another man's hand. Later there were two violent on-camera killings. Typical dialogue: 'You make a move and you're open from the scalp down.' For blood and thunder fans, great! For the squeamish, appalling!"[11]

Such comments bring one to the second way in which this series proved central to McQueen's career—it demonstrated to both the actor and the industry how hard work could make a difference. Well before the series started, McQueen spent untold hours becoming a convincing cowboy, "You know, when I first came out here [Hollywood] I'd never ridden a horse," McQueen noted. "But I tackled my role of Josh Randall in the series like it was 'Hamlet' on Broadway. Spent four or five hours a day learning to ride. Even studied how to saddle and unsaddle my horse."[12] Given McQueen's blue-collar background, he always assumed a very fundamental approach to acting: "One of the great dangers of this [entertainment] business is that equilibrium about yourself. You could go off into a never, never land. Acting is a job, like laying bricks."[13]

The only danger to this solid work ethic, given McQueen's new position of authority on his television series, was the actor's inability to both trust people and delegate authority. A few years after *Wanted: Dead or Alive*, he confessed, "I am not easy to make friends with, I guess. I am too suspicious of people. It's something to do with my [dysfunctional] childhood. . . . I have been hit too much and let down too often to trust people much."[14] Therefore, McQueen was often very difficult to work with on this series. Indeed, it was not always a matter of perfectionism or making his character as realistic as possible. Being too tightly wound was a factor, too. For example, the star fired *three* stuntmen on the program's first day of production!

One could argue that two of the pink slips were professionally justified. McQueen believed that neither of the stuntmen looked right to be his cowboy action double. But the third firing revealed a New York stage actor insecure about playing a Western figure. The veteran stuntman was real-life cowboy Richard Farnsworth, decades before his first Oscar nominated turn as an actor in *Comes a Horseman* (1978). "On the set, Farnsworth noticed Steve sitting down, rolling the back of his cowboy hat . . . cowboys didn't do that. 'You're making that hat look like a tortilla,' he teased," one McQueen biographer noted.[15] Farnsworth was soon history.

So who ended up being McQueen's stuntman for *Wanted: Dead or Alive*? The answer, Loren Janes, reveals a more positive side to McQueen. Janes, who became one of the industry's most celebrated stuntmen, won McQueen over with his own degree of tough-guy moxie and a brilliant first demonstration of his skills for the camera. Not only did McQueen ultimately get the best guy for the job, time revealed the fierce loyalty of which the actor was capable, as Janes remained as McQueen's stuntman until the star's death twenty-two years later.

Returning to those aforementioned reviews, *Wanted: Dead or Alive* continued to take criticism for violence. "More than forty years later, rerun episodes of *Wanted* are still saddled with a 'Violence' rating," reported a McQueen biographer.[16] But this did not bother McQueen. His biggest creative push on the series was to give it a slice-of-life quality, and he felt violence was at the heart of the West. In fact, McQueen got in trouble with his cowboy competition when he told the *New York Herald Tribune*: "I have to laugh when I watch some of those [Western video] guys. I've never seen more dandies in my life. In the Old West, a man didn't stay alive by being a sport. They had to be tough, ruthless, and I like to think that my characterization of the bounty hunter in 'Wanted: Dead or Alive' comes closer to what the men of the West really were like than almost anybody else on TV. That's why I accepted the part."[17]

These were fighting words for at least two television cowboys, Gene Barry as *Bat Masterson* and former famed stuntman Jock Mahoney as *Yancy Derringer*. While both of these shows were entertaining, McQueen's comments were right on the money. After all, Barry's Masterson could not have been more dandy-like if he tried, what with his linen shirts, derby hat, and gold-topped cane. Mahoney's Derringer was a clotheshorse gambler in New Orleans, whose only real Western touch was an Indian sidekick named Pahoo.

Regardless, Mahoney challenged McQueen to a wilderness survival test with only a knife for protection. But according to a follow-up

Tribune piece, both McQueen's home network (CBS) and fellow Four Star video cowboy Chuck Connors (*The Rifleman*) advised him not to take it seriously. McQueen's long-winded response to his career's first example of damage control reveals a lot about the young performer: "I've been game for anything most of my life and I must say I was ready to take Mahoney on . . . you strike that out . . . CBS was afraid I would get into something like that. . . . Anyway, Chuck Connors told me not to get so excited but damn it, man, I am upset. . . . He [Connors] said it didn't matter what anybody said about me as long as they spelled my name right. He said it was a publicity stunt and I should recognize it as that and forget it. The sad thing . . . is that 'Yancy Derringer' was one of my favorite TV shows, along with 'Rifleman' and 'Trackdown,' and Mahoney is one of my favorite actors."[18]

McQueen's passion to get his cowboy right brings one to the series' third seminal component with regard to his future career—the ongoing importance of realism. For example, nothing bothered McQueen more than the aforementioned weekly *Variety* comment about his *Wanted: Dead or Alive* character being able to "handle up to six men at a time." When a fighting situation got unrealistic for his video bounty hunter, McQueen's favorite explanation of what his character should do drew directly from real life. It was neither heroic nor fair, but it was real and effective. What follows is his first wife's take on the story: "[When Steve was] in the Marines . . . two toughs had given him a hard time. A fistfight was about to ensue when Steve bowed out, recognizing that he wouldn't be able to handle the two capably. Instead he waited in the latrine and when one of them came in he said, 'Hey you!' When the lone man turned, I punched and kicked the hell out of him. I made my point and was never bothered again." McQueen had anticipated the spirit of the revisionist antiheroic Spaghettis Westerns that soon skyrocketed another television cowboy to international film fame in the mid-1960s—*Rawhide*'s Clint Eastwood. (One minor unrealistic aspect of the series was the oversized shells on McQueen's gunbelt. They were strictly for a macho appearance and would not have worked in the actor's Winchester rifle.)

McQueen's initial reluctance to do a sagebrush series had been tied to his disinterest in the traditional mythic Western hero. But when he was allowed to play it realistically—a variation of himself—the character came alive. "Josh was real to me. I felt that I *knew* him. Lived inside his skin for years," McQueen said. "You do a character that long and you begin to *be* that character. It's like *I* was living in the Old West, chasing bad guys. I'd look in the mirror and see Randall. For a while there I thought I'd never be anybody else!"[19] McQueen also realized that Randall, as a bounty hunter, would have a natural affinity for both a nomadic lifestyle and being attracted to danger. Each of these traits were equally true of the actor, who had spent much of his youth bumming around the country taking chances, not to mention his motorcycle racing. Consequently, McQueen used this common ground to more fully realize the role of Randall.

Early on in his career, McQueen recognized that he did not have a great deal of range as an actor. But by channeling a realistic version of himself into his characters, he achieved a believability that was similar to stars of the studios' earlier golden age. His later director Norman Jewison, who directed McQueen in *The Cincinnati Kid* (1965) and *The Thomas Crown Affair* (1968), explained it this way: "I believed Steve on camera more than I believed actors with more technique. If you put Steve on an empty stage with a choir and a soliloquy to read, he wouldn't hold the audience. That took acting. A Laurence Olivier. But if I asked Steve to walk across a room for the camera, he would be natural and immensely appealing. Olivier would act the walk of the character. Steve would simply walk. It would be so real the audience would believe in him more than they would believe in Olivier."[20]

McQueen's merging of self with the Randall character also further explains why he had to have it his way on the series. But it was a continual battle for the young actor: "I wanted to play him for real—as a guy trying to do a dangerous, unglamorous job with a minimum of fuss. But the Four Star honchos kept trying to turn him into a jaw-busting, sure-shot hero. I had some bad times with them over this."[21] But the battles were not always over major dramatic points. McQueen was also a bear about realistic period costumes that looked lived in, from worn and dirty trousers to sweat-stained Stetsons.

A fourth key McQueen element born during the series was his embrace of minimalist acting—less was better. Western stars such as Cooper were famous for saying very little. They let a look or a gesture do their talking. So did McQueen. In this way, he was a throwback to a classic Western star, even when he was not in a cowboy story. And while he never took on an army of bad guys like a John Wayne character, McQueen did borrow a basic Wayne lesson—"Don't act, react."

Reviewers did not appreciate McQueen's minimalism at the beginning of the series, but they eventually wised up. Here is *Variety*'s first-season take on the actor's character: "[He could] do little else than preserve a wax-like countenance and say the few words (like carbonated water gone flat) he had to say."[22] Two seasons later the same publication found praise for this world-weary approach, noting that "McQueen is a stylized actor, who delivered his lines monotonously but his uninflected style [fittingly] suggested the kind of threatening and intense nature of the scavenging bounty hunter who is the 'Wanted' protagonist."[23]

During *Wanted: Dead or Alive* McQueen also started something that would be repugnant to most performers—he voluntarily gave up lines out of the script. The original catalyst was not always a brilliant insight on his part. McQueen did not receive a formal education past ninth grade, and dyslexia had always hindered his reading. The actor was never comfortable with ten-dollar words and anything approaching a show-stopping soliloquy. Given this background, it was a natural reflex for him to pare down and/or rephrase his dialogue. Moreover, since most of McQueen's characters, starting with Randall, were a variation on himself, this minimalism rang true.

A fifth pivotal component to arise from the series was McQueen's inspired relationship with props. This simply builds upon his minimalist acting. That is, as the actor's screenwriter for *The Getaway* (1972), Walter Hill, observed, "He was wonderful at finding a physical piece of business that would extend his character."[24] While this often focused upon McQueen's professional handling of weapons in his films, his

McQueen as Josh Randall with his signature Winchester "Mare's Laig" rifle for the television program Wanted: Dead or Alive.

winning use of props could be totally generic. For example, *The Get-away* has a brief throwaway scene the morning after McQueen's character has been sprung from jail by his wife. The original script has the barest of details, but the actor makes the scene charmingly real simply through fixing breakfast, being ever so at ease with those kitchen props. McQueen's ongoing realistic motto was always, "God is in the details."

The signature prop for *Wanted: Dead or Alive* was Randall's sawed-off Winchester rifle (sometimes mistakenly called a shotgun), which was named a "Mare's Laig," because it kicked like a horse. But the actor wore it on his hip with a special holster, just like it was a handgun. The idea and design for the piece was McQueen's, possibly inspired by the mesmerizing machine gun-like weapon wheeled by Connors in *The Rifleman* (also produced by Four Star). The young actor so practiced his quick draw of the "Mare's Laig" that this action became, to borrow Hill's line, "a physical piece of business that would extend his character." The sawed-off Winchester became a metaphor for Randall—an undersized "weapon" that packed quite a wallop. (McQueen's small stature gave a certain underdog status to a profession—bounty hunter—not normally viewed with any sympathy.)

Even a much less dramatic *Wanted: Dead or Alive* physical action, such as how McQueen mounted his horse, was practiced for hours. The actor had a patented little bounce to getting into the saddle that was both convincingly real yet distinctively his own. To draw a punning parallel with his Western-like demeanor in *Bullitt* (1968), McQueen also spent hours working on getting in and out of his Mustang automobile.

A sixth central McQueen element brought out by the series, though not fully showcased within it, was the actor's sense of humor. His funny side has often been obscured by his later long-haired reclusive years, when McQueen's public appearances were less frequent than Bigfoot's. His first wife later wrote how influential Hollywood columnists such as Hedda Hopper and Louella Parsons were taken with his comic touch and unusual conversational style, described as "part musician talk, part jive talk, part street talk, and part Steve talk."[25] When McQueen believed someone was toying with him, he had a lifelong affinity for the comeback, "You trying to twist my melon, man?" Or, here is the actor's description of first meeting a future mother-in-law: "It was Hatesville, man. I came on a cycle, in black pants and black shirt and she said, 'Get him out of here.'"[26] It was the beatnik 1950s, and McQueen had, until recently, been living at the heart of the movement—New York. Plus, it was the sort of "hip" speech pattern favored by Dean, whom McQueen had idolized. Indeed, at one point the two men lived in the same New York neighborhood, and friends of both took to calling McQueen "the Shadow" for his habit of following Dean around.[27]

Beyond the colorful language, however, McQueen had a natural wit that first surfaced during his emergence as a Western television star. A popular source of humor, first suggested by the opening of this prologue, was McQueen's ongoing battle with horses, starting with his television series. Just as the actor initially fired several stuntmen, he had a comparable challenge finding a steady mount. The actor told Hollywood columnist Earl Wilson, "They first gave me an old horse you had to put roller skates on to get into the studio. I said, 'I want a fresh horse—one with some fire.' I sure got one. The first time we met, he [Ringo, the new horse] bit me and I popped him right in the mouth and they had to pull us apart. They've now asked me if I want another horse. I've told them, 'Don't take the horse away. He's crazy but I like him!'"[28]

McQueen's misadventures with Ringo soon became an ongoing source of comedy for the actor. The following season the actor told Wilson, "This horse is murder—but I'm going to win. He's been out in pasture all summer thinking up new dirty tricks. He's really a neurotic, that horse. Wait'll he reads that I said that!"[29] Ringo also inspired the following comic riff from McQueen, "I hate horses. . . . I can ride pretty good now [despite Ringo] but I don't have to like it. When a horse learns to buy martinis, I'll learn to like horses."[30] For three seasons McQueen and Ringo battled, with the actor coming out on the short end, enduring a broken toe, numerous bites, and back bruises. But he came to love Ringo's curmudgeonly nature.

Even disregarding Ringo, McQueen still kidded about everything, including himself. He told syndicated columnist Sidney Skolsky, "I became an actor because it was the softest job with the best pay. Get to the theater between 7:30 and 8 at night. Finish at 11. No responsibilities. [Now I'm on TV.] I get up at 5:30 in the morning to be at the studio by 6:30. I come home at 9, dog tired. Somewhere along the line, I got caught."[31]

After making a picture with Frank Sinatra, *Never So Few* (1959), during the production of *Wanted: Dead or Alive*, McQueen palled around with Sinatra's "Rat Pack" set, which included Dean Martin, Sammy Davis Jr., Peter Lawford, and Joey Bishop. But McQueen entertainingly told another columnist, "I never really was a member of 'The Clan.' I shoot off guns at Sammy Davis' once in a while. But I'm well-behaved [as opposed to the 'bad boy Rat Pack']. I even wear shirts with my name on 'em. Look here, see, it says 'Steve.' In case I fall down drunk in an alley [like a Pack member], they'll know whose shirt it is."[32]

Even when McQueen was angry, he could coin a comic comeback. During the aforementioned feud with Mahoney, whose Derringer character was aided by Native American partner Pahoo, McQueen comically proposed a sissy-like duel, telling syndicated columnist Joe Hyams, "You tell Mahoney I'll meet him at [Hollywood's famed] Schwab's Drug Store any morning. Kleenex at thirty paces. The color is up to him."[33] Then, in mock toughness, McQueen topped himself with a smiling final comment, "If he meets me . . . tell him to leave the Indian

The three most high-profile Rat Pack members: (from left to right) Dean Martin, Sammy Davis Jr., and Frank Sinatra.

at home." But McQueen's comic touch was not limited to the early years. Well into his stardom, he was asked what he would be doing in ten years. Laughing, he replied, "I guess I'll be all gray by then and be playing Paul Newman's father." During the same interview McQueen confessed that he still found his wife something of an enigma, but wryly added, "Did you ever know any man who understood his wife?"[34]

While McQueen's Western television series was not the ideal show-case for the actor's wit, *Wanted* did occasionally have its humorous moments. The actor's character was a man of few words, but they could be amusingly sarcastic. In the "Rawhide Breed" episode broadcast on December 13, 1958, Randall is forced to trek across the desert with the most reluctant of companions. When this sorry figure finally asks the bounty hunter why he does not leave him, Randall deadpans, "Misery loves company, and you're all I've got." But on other occasions, after prolonged time on the trail, a more playful Randall could sound like a cowboy kid in a candy store. In the "Competition" episode broadcast on January 31, 1959, a sheriff suspiciously asked him if he is in town on business. Randall, as if mimicking a young Dean Martin, responds, "Oooooh no . . . vacation. I haven't slept in a bed in months. When I catch up on that I'm going to play a little poker, drink a little whiskey [he drums the bar—a visual pun à la a "whiskey drummer"], might even talk to a girl or two." Moreover, some episodes completely em-braced comedy, such as the first season's Christmas show, titled "Eight Cent Reward," which was broadcast on December 20, 1958. This was the amount a child (Jay North, later television's Dennis the Menace) gave Randall to find Santa Claus. After several misadventures, including McQueen's character hiring a substitute Saint Nick that turns out to be a lush, a sort of frontier Father Christmas puts in a poignant surprise appearance.

Given Randall's often quiet nature, however, *Wanted* sometimes recycled a comedy component seemingly borrowed from a then cel-ebrated series of Western feature films starring the iconic Randolph Scott and directed by Budd Boetticher. Between 1956 and 1960, they collaborated on seven comic-noir Westerns. Like the existential film noir private eye pictures of the 1940s, they have minimalist Scott speaking in an entertainingly laconic manner, à la Will Rogers. In contrast, the typical Boetticher villain is charismatically loquacious. This is best illustrated in *Ride Lonesome* (1959), in which Pernell Roberts's character goes on and on about the stunning sexuality of the heroine. His comments culminate with the observation, "I guess she's about the best all over good-looking woman I ever seen." To this Scott has the most comically concise comeback, "She ain't ugly."

The *Wanted* episode that most closely replicates this Scott-Boetticher model is "Reunion for Revenge," broadcast on January 14, 1959. Ralph Meeker, probably best known now for his film-noir turn as Mike Hammer in *Kiss Me Deadly* (1955), played a desperate, yet charismatic, villain holding Randall and several others hostage. His verbal tour-de-force performance is only interrupted by McQueen lines such as, "I don't plan to make an undertaker happy . . . until I die of old age." The Scott-Boetticher connection to *Wanted* is doubly interesting because Scott often plays a bounty hunter in these pictures, and McQueen was a big fan of the veteran cowboy star. Indeed, to prepare to play Randall, McQueen had even studied some of Scott's pre-Boetticher roles where the older actor played a bounty hunter.

Unfortunately, like McQueen's fellow Hoosier hero Dean, neither actor's comic side has been much recognized by biographers. Dean's friends and family especially enjoyed both his imitation of Marlon Brando doing Charlie Chaplin, and Chaplin impersonating Brando. In fact, during the production of *Rebel without a Cause* (1955), Dean stated, "Come 1956 . . . I wouldn't be surprised to find myself with [Nick] Adams doing a two-a-night [comic impersonation] nightclub routine."[35] Coincidentally, at the end of McQueen's first season as Randall, a *Los Angeles Times* columnist revealed, "Steve tried out for me a few imitations he's going to use in a nightclub act he's working up—one of Walter Brennan [a frequent actor in Westerns], Cary Grant, and Marlon Brando doing a speech from *Julius Caesar* [1953] through [Method] clenched teeth."[36]

A seventh seminal aspect to McQueen's cowboy series was the ongoing significance of the Western to his career. His Randall character was the catalyst for McQueen being cast in the epic John Sturges's horse opera *The Magnificent Seven* (1960). Based upon Akira Kurosawa's acclaimed *The Seven Samurai* (1954), McQueen's sixth film (and first cinema Western) made him a movie star. He periodically returned to the genre in such underrated outings as *Nevada Smith* (1966), *Junior Bonner* (1972), and *Tom Horn* (1980). But there are definite cowboy overtones to several of McQueen's other pictures, especially *The Getaway* and *The Hunter* (1980), an unofficial modern homage to *Wanted: Dead or Alive*, where McQueen's last role has him playing a contemporary bounty hunter.

Wanted established McQueen as a star, provided him with a vehicle where hard work could pay off, underlined to him the importance of realism, encouraged the actor's minimalism technique, first demonstrated his gift for using props as an extension of character, briefly provided a window to his private quirky comic tendencies, and forever underlined the ongoing significance of the Western to him. But a simpler take on the whole process might have been Hopper's two-word description of McQueen as a young Western television star, "*He* excites!"[37] For most film fans, that never ceased to be true.

Dysfunctional Beginnings

"My life was screwed up before I was born."
STEVE MCQUEEN

As an adult, Steve McQueen often quoted the line from *The Merchant of Venice*, "The sins of the father are to be laid on the children," but he sometimes substituted the wording "of the mother," too.[1] Both parents tragically failed him. The actor was born Terrence Steve McQueen on March 24, 1930. (He later named his first child and only daughter Terry.) The setting for McQueen's birth was Beech Grove, Indiana, now an inside-the-beltway city surrounded by Indianapolis. McQueen's mother was pretty, blonde, nineteen-year-old Julia Ann Crawford, later Julian to friends. Her parents, Lillian and Victor Crawford, lived in Saint Louis, Missouri, which is where Julian met William "Red" McQueen in 1929. Seven years older than his young bride, the senior McQueen was everything a naïve teenager looking for adventure could want. Red, or more often Bill, was a handsome hooligan who doubled as a county fair barnstorming pilot and sometimes gambler with a gift for swashbuckling stories. He soon had more than her attention. Julian's pregnancy led to a hurry-up marriage, but Bill was gone forever within months of the baby's birth.

McQueen biographical material normally treats Julian as a teen runaway (with her extended family all in Slater, Missouri), who resurfaced in the Indianapolis area solely upon the whim of her new husband. But when one goes to the International Genealogical Index, which also taps into the U.S. Federal Census Records, one finds that Julian's parents were living in Indianapolis on North Bosart Avenue at the time of their grandson's birth.[2] Plus, Bill and Julian were actually married in Indianapolis, with Julian and her baby already listed as residents of her parents' home when Steve was only one month old—making Bill's abandonment of his family even earlier than the six months normally cited.

Given the senior McQueen's interest in gambling, his actor son later made the funny/sad admission, "I didn't know much about my father, except that he must have had a weird sense of humor, naming me after Steve Hall, a one-armed bookie pal of his. Not many fathers name their sons after one-armed bookies!"[3]

The actor later poetically described this exit as "[my father] just flew over the rainbow," adding, "He was a sky gypsy. Between air shows he'd hedge-hop the States, crop dusting a farm for his gas and the price of a meal. Always on the move. I heard he was with Chennault's Flying Tigers during the Second World War. For a long time I hated him for leaving us but later—after I had kids of my own—I got to feeling sorry for him because he missed seeing me grow up. He never had the special kind of kick that being a father can give you."[4]

This is a telling quote for three reasons. First, it underscores the actor's lifelong commitment to children. Besides rearing a beloved daughter and son, he later invested a great deal of time and money into the California Junior Boys Republic (Chino, California). Sort of a Boy's Town West for neglected and troubled youth, the institution (then known as the Boys Republic of California) had turned around a teenage McQueen headed for juvenile delinquency. In later years he frequently credited Boys Republic for keeping him from being a criminal.

Second, while his father was a charismatic cardsharp flyer (who briefly operated "Wild Will's" casino in the same building with a brothel on Indianapolis's wild Illinois Street), the actor's quote documents an embellishing tendency on his part. His first wife, Neile Adams, later confessed, "[By 1959] Steve had created, with his unrestrained imagination, a role for his father that portrayed the old man in a romantic and virile light. Steve had him alternately flying with the navy or the marines, depending on which came first, and finally had him die with General Chennault's raiders in China."[5] (McQueen's father actually died in the United States, years after World War II.)

This creative flair for the dramatic about a missing father is hardly unique to McQueen. Indeed, several Hoosier entertainers have practiced the same poetic license. Vincennes-born comedian Red Skelton lost his father months before birth and later fabricated a story about the senior Skelton being a world-famous clown. Madison-raised actress Irene Dunne lost her father as a young child and later turned him into a Will Rogers-like crackerbarrel figure of innate wisdom, going to great lengths to cite him in 1930s interviews.[6]

One should add, however, that McQueen did not limit his biographical embellishments to just his father. *Look* magazine essayist George Eells noted early in the actor's career that he had "an aptitude for inventing colorful detail to replace uninteresting fact. For instance, he customarily speaks of the Boys Republic in California, where he spent part of his childhood, as a 'reform school' instead of a home for neglected boys."[7]

As a biographer, one needs to reframe a problematic action by one's subject. Thus, veteran biographer Marc Pachter offers the challenge: "How much can be learned about an individual from the facts he invents about himself?"[8] Granted, a common phenomenon of profiling any personality is wrestling with that most human of traits: "Like most people, he gave different accounts of what he believed at different times."[9] But McQueen, and especially Skelton, had a propensity to reverse reality to mold a personal mythology that went beyond the natural changes and/or little white lies most people create to get through the day.

Red Skelton in his greatest film, A Southern Yankee *(1948).*

The greatest catalyst for mythomania is quite simple—the need to tell a better story. With McQueen being in the storytelling business, what could be more natural? Moreover, his wife suggests that these fatherly tall tales seemed to be born full blown, precisely at the time when her husband had become an overnight success with his television series *Wanted: Dead or Alive*. How appropriate that the new storyteller in town would see fit to punch up his own story, or that of his father.

Of course, with both McQueen and Skelton, there was another major factor pushing the embellishment trait. Each of these Hollywood Hoosiers had the most dysfunctional of childhoods, with no memory of their fathers. When one is dealing with such an autobiographical black hole, romantic tweaking (such as a dashing flyer or a famous clown) seems very natural. But this brings one to a third reason why McQueen's quote about his father was significant, embellishment, or not. This wandering romanticized loner that the actor sketched early in his career might have doubled as a thumbnail description of many of McQueen's later roles, starting with his *Wanted* bounty hunter Josh Randall. This antihero list included such signature McQueen parts as his cowboy drifter in the star-making movie *The Magnificent Seven* (1960) and his "Cooler King" (solitary confinement) prisoner of war in *The Great Escape* (1962).

More specifically, given the senior McQueen's obsession with flying, gambling, and women, it is difficult to watch the young actor in either *The War Lover* (1962, in which he plays a womanizing pilot), or *The Cincinnati Kid* (1965, a cardsharp torn between two women) and not think of the performer's father. One might further push the parental addendum with the assumption that Bill must have been good with engines, since barnstorming pilots, by necessity, had to double as their own mechanics. This interest in all things mechanical also described the actor, who raced motorcycles and automobiles and eventually collected and flew vintage biplanes—the same sort of World War I aircraft owned by his father. McQueen was also fond of using his mechanical interests as the badge of still being a regular guy: "[Success and responsibility] hasn't really changed my way of life. I'm still hung up on machinery—you know."[10]

In addition to McQueen's expert weapons-as props handling, he also periodically applied this character-defining interaction with objects to motors. Prime examples varied from his Oscar-nominated character in *The Sand Pebbles* (1966, in which his sailor is obsessed with the gunboat's engine), to his underrated comic turn as the small-town hell-raiser in the adaptation of William Faulkner's autobiographical novel *The Reivers* (1969, with McQueen equally engrossed with how the county's first automobile runs). Consequently, the actor's broadly romantic description of the father he never knew manages to provide greater insight into the son, as well as demonstrating an unusual degree of influence for a parent seemingly forever out of the picture.

If Bill's abandonment made the actor a better father and advocate for troubled youngsters, Julian is probably the source of Steve's often ongoing problematic relations with women. A desertion before birth/memory is one thing, but Julian's periodic abandonments of her son (such as shipping him off to relatives or placing the child in Boys Republic) were even more devastating. In addition, while the actor's mother was fond of denigrating her ex-husband's lifestyle with the alliteration "butch, brawling, ballsy," her conduct and habits soon sank into an equally self-destructive pattern, including periodic prostitution. As McQueen biographer Christopher Sandford observed, "Steve came to hate his mother even more than his runaway father. Every night he wandered among the drunks and rat-infested garbage while Julian turned tricks in their bedroom."[11]

Not surprisingly, McQueen grew up with little respect for women. Married three times, he could be physically and psychologically abusive. His insatiable sexual appetite made him a constant womanizer. Though partly fed by his later fame and a nonstop stream of women who threw themselves at him (further fueling his lack of esteem for them), this loveless sexuality was McQueen's world from the very beginning. While Julian would later knock Bill's bedroom axiom to her son, "They're [sexual partners] all grey in the night," is not that a motto even more appropriate for a prostitute?

For all these negatives, Julian also had a certain sexual charisma that sent a mixed message to her son and the people around her—that a libertine life is somehow excitingly admirable, too. McQueen biographer Penina Spiegel effectively described both Julian's ability to almost ooze eroticism, and included a period quote that indirectly links the actor's mother to the late 1920s symbol for sexuality or "It"—Jazz Age iconic silent film star Clara Bow: "[Julian] had an attractive figure and a sexy walk and favored flapper-style dresses and the spikiest of spike heels . . . when she walked the fringes on her dress would swing and sway. . . . On her infrequent visits to Slater [Missouri], to see her son or to drop him off, the young girls would watch her 'and go Ooooh,' recalls one of them. They thought she was 'IT.' There were rumors going around that she'd been caught in a fire in New York City and she'd run out of the apartment 'Stripped stark naked, with just a sheet around her, and she weren't alone, neither.'"[12]

As this titillating tale suggested, Julian was a character who could elicit a myriad of emotions in people. Even years later, after she had lived a very hard life, the actor's first wife (and rare female friend) found Julian "charming, bright, and friendly. . . . But Steve always kept her at arm's length. He didn't want her unhappiness to spill onto us."[13] Given this multifaceted figure of a mother, with casual sexuality a given for both parents, McQueen evolved into a womanizer allergic to using the word love. His countless one-night stands were decidedly unromantic. To recycle that old chauvinistic cliché, the actor was strictly a "slam-bam, thank you ma'am" sort of lover. Any satisfaction the woman achieved was strictly tied to having bedded a celebrity. But given McQueen's sad and loveless childhood, one might further defend him with an old populist axiom, "You can't give away something [like love] you never had."

One Julian positive, however, given her son's later memorable movie career, was the fact that she was a huge film fan. The best times with her son were those days she took him to a movie in downtown Indianapolis.

Besides the B-picture cowboys his great uncle had introduced him to during Saturday matinees back in Missouri, the boy's favorite star quickly became tough guy Humphrey Bogart. Decades later, McQueen recalled, "I first saw Bogie on screen when I was a kid. He nailed me pronto, and I've admired him ever since. He was the master and always will be."[14]

McQueen's favorite Bogart picture was the same movie that made the older actor a star, *High Sierra* (1941). It is a revealing choice for the then eleven-year-old McQueen to have made. The film has a wonderful pedigree, from having been written by John Huston and gifted crime author W. R. Burnett (from his novel), to being directed by gangster auteur Raoul Walsh. Though ostensibly yet another Bogart gangster story, the movie has Western overtones, matching young McQueen's love of cowboy movies. Indeed, Walsh later remade the picture as the Western *Colorado Territory* (1949, with Joel McCrea). Fittingly, both movies' climactic shoot-out takes place high in the mountains.

Humphrey Bogart as a soft-hearted killer in High Sierra *(1941), McQueen's favorite film.*

Even more of a *High Sierra* revelation, with regard to McQueen, is the poignant vulnerability of Bogart's character. While saddled with a grossly inappropriate, though standard, gangster name, Mad Dog Earle, Bogie is a killer with a soft heart. On the lam for a robbery caper, the mobster's ultimate demise is the result of abandonment and a pet dog. Bogart's character has romantic feelings toward a girl (Joan Leslie) who needs major surgery for a deformed leg. Once his money corrects the problem, she deserts him for boys her own age. But his lingering interest in Leslie has put him at risk, as has the easy-to-identify dog in the care of Bogart's nominal girlfriend, played by Ida Lupino.

McQueen undoubtedly would have identified with Bogie's abandonment victimization. Moreover, the gangster's slip in professionalism, with regard to allowing the dog along on the getaway, would also have struck a responsive chord with young McQueen. After spending rare happy hours on his great uncle's Missouri farm, the boy had more faith in animals (especially dogs) than people. Throughout McQueen's life, stray mutts always had a safe haven in the actor's household. The actor would have appreciated the similar sentiments of another Hoosier antihero (James Dean) on the plusses of farm creatures: "There are a lot of things I learned from animals. One was that they couldn't hiss or boo me."[15]

The duality of Bogart's *High Sierra* character also brings to mind a tragic dichotomy equally applicable to young McQueen. Like Bogie and other gangster film figures of that era, whose tough childhoods were often sketched out in cinema prologues, "[McQueen] was constantly fighting between 'I'll prove I'm somebody,' and 'I'm not worthy; I'm going to destroy this.'"[16] In either case, it was all about anger— something the actor fought his whole life. How sadly fitting that, even at eleven, he could connect to world-weary Bogie's cruelly touching ambivalence. Of course, as his *Tom Horn* (1980) costar Linda Evans stated, "[While] I don't feel he was at peace with his past . . . he did a hell of a lot with it. He used it [in his acting]."[17]

As a final sidebar on McQueen and his special connection with Bogart's *High Sierra*, the young actor also became a longtime fan of Bogie's gun moll in the picture—Lupino. That undoubtedly had something to do with getting her cast as McQueen's no-nonsense screen mother in Sam Peckinpah's masterpiece *Junior Bonner* (1972). Interestingly, the name for the television company that produced McQueen's Western series, Four Star, was a veiled reference to Dick Powell, David Niven, Charles Boyer, *and* Lupino, although the men (especially Powell) seemed more directly involved in the organization's day-to-day operation.

Hoosier author David Hoppe probably coined the most hauntingly poignant take on the youth of this Bogie fan when he wrote, "There are apparently no childhood snapshots of Steve McQueen. That was the kind of childhood he had."[18] Young Steve spent his first three difficult years in Indianapolis. Because Julian was trying to deal with her own abandonment issues (a missing husband) and the onset of the Great Depression, being a mother was not a top priority.

Previous profiles of McQueen have Julian returning to her extended family's hometown of Slater, Missouri. The year is 1933, and, so the story goes, her mother and father (Lillian and Victor Crawford) raise the child while Julian attempts to find herself (or lose herself) back in Indianapolis. The only catch here is that the recent revelation of period census records have Julian and young Steve already living with the Crawfords in Indianapolis within a month of the child's birth.[19] (The Crawfords and a young Julian had earlier lived in Slater, Missouri.)

McQueen and Linda Evans in a quiet scene from Tom Horn *(1980).*

A better "reading" of McQueen's early days is that the only reason his mother probably kept him for the first three years is that her parents were no doubt doing much of the child rearing. Plus, the 1933 exit to Missouri was possibly precipitated by Victor losing his position as a traveling salesman. That is, it was not just a matter of Julian shipping young Steve to Uncle Claude W. Thomson's (Lillian's brother) Missouri hog farm to be raised. Thomson took in his sister and brother-in-law after Victor lost his job. Since they were seemingly already surrogate parents to Steve, Claude's generosity simply included his great-nephew.

Things would have been stressful for the adults in this new blended family household. Lillian had long been estranged from her brother, with their differences probably tied to her overly pious Catholicism and his more earthy dictatorial ways—an independent hog farmer untouched by the Great Depression. Family charity, given this backdrop, would have been wrought with friction.

Despite these circumstances, McQueen blossomed during this country respite. His great-uncle was tough, but fair, and the boy bonded with him—the closest thing he would ever have to a father-son relationship. The boy's chores had built-in rewards, from his own room to those Saturday Western matinees. But there was also discipline if one did not pull his weight. Years later McQueen was fond of crediting Claude with the most basic of life lessons: "You work for what you get." One might also attribute his fascination with speed and/or competition to a red tricycle, a fourth birthday gift from his great-uncle. McQueen matter-of-factly later observed, "That started my racing fever. There was a dirt bluff behind the farm and I'd challenge the other kids in the area. We'd race for gumdrops. I usually reached the top first. Got some skinned knees, but I sure won a lot of gumdrops."[20]

McQueen's love of the land, from fishing and hunting to a pure embrace of wide-open spaces, was born from his days on Claude's Missouri farm. This later surfaced in various ways in the actor's life, from a special affinity for the Western genre to selecting homes and getaways away from cities and people. McQueen was most poetic on the subject when discussing a favorite charity, the Navajo Indians: "Every so often I

A grim and grimy McQueen prepares for battle in the World War II film Hell Is for Heroes *(1962).*

drive to the reservation with vaccines and antibiotics. I really dig those
Navajos. They have a phrase—'A land where there is time enough and
room enough.' That's what I want, too."[21]

The only obvious downside to Missouri, besides a mother that
seldom visited and a stressful household (though Lillian and Victor
soon moved out), was McQueen's struggles with school. His lack of
interest in books was probably fueled by dyslexia and a hearing loss in
his left ear. The year before he started school in 1935, the youngster had
suffered a mastoid infection (an inflammation in the temporal bone
behind his ear). In the years before antibiotics, the infection spread to
the middle ear and resulted in a hearing loss (acerbated by a later diving
accident) of unclear severity. I add this qualifier because his first wife
later shared that her husband often used the deaf, hand-to-ear gesture as
"nothing more than a play to give him time to think [over a reporter's
question] or just plain tune out when he became bored or annoyed."[22]
As sort of a real-life Huckleberry Finn type, McQueen would undoubtedly have mastered early such a con-man trick—a huckster nature also
synonymous to Mark Twain's greatest figure.

Still, even a resilient Huckleberry Finn could be brought low by
a mother who treated him like a yo-yo. One of Claude's neighbors
remembered seeing the boy at a particularly down time: "Steve was just
a poor, sad, fatherless, mixed-up kid. I don't think it's possible for a human being to look as absolutely beat as he did at that moment [Julian
had returned to Indianapolis without telling him] . . . Steve slumped
there on the [railroad] tracks and wept his eyes out."[23]

Sometime in 1938 Julian remarried and decided to again play
mother.[24] Eight-year-old McQueen, however, was justifiably angry
about being torn from his rural existence to a more hand-to-mouth
world in a rough section of south-side Indianapolis. McQueen's great-
uncle was crushed at losing the boy but respected the rights of his
mother. He did, however, give the child a gold pocket watch with the
inscription, "To Steve . . . who has been like a son to me."

Unfortunately, McQueen's new "home" was also marred by the
fact that the alcoholic, good-time Julian was seemingly attracted to

hard-drinking, abusive men. Her second husband, a Mr. Berri (only his surname survives), found it necessary to beat the boy for any transgression, real or imagined. Partly as an escape from this man, and maybe partly as a self-fulfilling prophesy to this stepfather who had nothing but negatives to say about young McQueen, he fell into a life of gangs and petty crime. The actor alternately described it as a "bad scene" or "doin' a little stealin'," before more fully fleshing it out: "I feel I was in a neighborhood in Indianapolis where one inevitably grew up with gangs. We would break into locked-up shops . . . that kind of thing. It wasn't that we did this in terms of money . . . because we were never short of money . . . but as a relief from boredom."[25] He was also fond of simply reducing his Hoosier legacy to a typically cynical McQueen joke: "[My Indianapolis education was limited to learning] how to steal hubcaps and shoot pool."

In a 1963 article written by McQueen, something of a rarity, the actor assumed a more lyrically thoughtful position on these early troubled times: "Man, I can't get used to it [my success]. I could just as easily have wound up behind the eight ball. When I did 'The Great Escape' for producer-director John Sturges . . . I kept thinking: 'If they were making a movie of my life, that's what they would call it, 'The Great Escape.'"[26]

With young McQueen out of control and/or Julian exercising no control, the boy was again shipped back to Uncle Claude's farm. After a few years, McQueen's mother relocated to the Silver Lake area of Los Angeles. It was the early 1940s, and sources differ on just which man was now in her life, though the aforementioned Berri is most often cited.[27] The International Genealogical Index even has Julian first marrying Berri in 1938. But in all likelihood, there were several Julian men before this second tenure with Berri. California was probably their starting-over destination.

This time McQueen's mother had him come to Los Angeles. But things proved even more violently volatile on the West Coast, largely because of Berri, whom McQueen later described as a "prime sonuvabitch." Once again McQueen was sent back to Missouri. But by now

Uncle Claude's world had become a bit dysfunctional, too. The boy's grandfather Victor had died of cancer, the increasingly bitter grandmother Lillian had become unglued and been placed in a mental institution, and virile over-seventy Claude had married a woman half his age. Eva Mae, formerly the hog farmer's housekeeper (and prior to that a Jazz Age hootchy-kootchy dancer) was a fun-loving gold digger who soon had her illegitimate teenage daughter ensconced on the farm, too. But because Eva Mae had given birth so young, the child was diplomatically referred to as her "niece" when there was company.

With all this change, and presumably a sexually distracted great uncle (probably further painting women as mere objects and/or erotic toys to the boy), the farm now held less charm for young McQueen. When a traveling carnival/circus came through Slater, Missouri, in 1944, fourteen-year-old McQueen joined up. But unlike the earlier romantic allure to be found in Hoosier poet James Whitcomb Riley's "The Circus-Day Parade," an innocent elixir that caught the spirit of such midwestern funnymen as Kin Hubbard, Red Skelton, and Joe E. Brown, McQueen's carnival/circus experience was just an escape route out of town—a means to an end.

Ironically, the teenage McQueen eventually worked his way back to Los Angeles and the love-hate relationship with his mother and stepfather. When the beatings continued, and a young but tougher McQueen found he could give as good as he got with Berri, the parent-child conflict had reached an impasse. The Missouri farm no longer represented a safety valve, so Julian enrolled her son in the aforementioned Boys Republic in early 1945. The school for neglected boys is on a San Bernardino County ranch about thirty-five miles outside Los Angeles. While attending the accredited high school, boys had a variety of chores, such as caring for a herd of cattle, working in the dining room and campus-style houses, and preparing the institution's now famous Della Robbia Christmas wreaths. These decorations, a fixture of the White House and other public venues since the presidency of Calvin Coolidge, remain Boys Republic's chief fund-raising tool. Such crafts and basic work assignments for the boys also underlined the school's motto: "Nothing Without Labor." Despite all this discipline and duty and the mistaken moniker of being a lockup for juvenile delinquents, Boys Republic had no exterior walls and operated on an honor system.

Still, the placement was not an immediate hit with McQueen. He believed his mother had sentenced him to a reform school, like his film favorite Bogie being sent up river to the "Big House." The anger from what seemed like one more Julian rejection fueled a now celebrated McQueen show of rebellion—he attempted to escape on one of the Boys Republic tractors! Paradoxically, Boys Republic turned out to be Julian's greatest parenting move. While the main catalyst for her signing the papers was protecting McQueen from an abusive stepfather, Boys Republic really reached her son.

At first McQueen's rejection of the school resulted in punishments that only made the situation worse. After a second runaway attempt, a sympathetic counselor, who reminded the boy of Claude, tried a different approach. This Mr. Painter convinced McQueen that he could rechannel his energy into something positive: "He said he saw that I had something special, that I could really be *somebody* in the world if I gave it a real shot. No one else in authority had ever talked to me like that. No one else had seemed to give a damn about my future life as an adult—but *he* did, and it meant a lot to me."[28]

For the first time McQueen began to feel a certain sense of self-worth. He managed to fit in at Boys Republic, making friends and even being elected to the school's self-governing board. He found that he was good at working with wood and metal in shop class, as well as making the institution's Christmas wreaths. He had successfully completed the ninth grade by the time of his April 1946 release, which concluded his formal education. The future movie star never forgot being saved by the school. The year after McQueen's death (1981), Boys Republic director Max Scott noted: "He seemed to come back to get his batteries recharged. He'd go up to his old cottage. . . . He just wanted to be with the kids—shoot pool, play ping pong. He never tried to convey a tough guy image . . . . He always asked them what they were doing, what they planned to do when they got out of here. He never focused on himself.

Kids used to write to him. Steve, to the best of my knowledge, always answered these letters—and always answered in his own handwriting."[29] Besides his time, the actor donated hundreds of thousands of dollars to the school over the years. To paraphrase a line from novelist Eudora Welty, "McQueen's awe and delight over what Boys Republic represented to him remained forever cloudless."[30]

McQueen had made great strides during his eighteen-month term at Boys Republic and was now prepared to apply these practical lessons to the real world. McQueen would soon be thrown, however, into yet another challenging arena. The abusive Berri had died, and Julian had moved to New York City, where she was living with movie cinematographer Victor Lukens. His mother sent cross-country bus money for her sixteen-year-old son. Another challenging chapter to McQueen's life was about to begin.

2

New York, on the Road, Back to New York

During Steve McQueen's days as a struggling actor in New York, he "spent a lot of his time at the mirror, running through lines of Brando's. He looked at himself and said, 'I've gotta make it, man; I've gotta fucking make it.'"[1]
A FORMER STEVE MCQUEEN GIRLFRIEND

Despite Steve McQueen's past disappointments with his mother, including her failure to visit him at Boys Republic, he found the idea of starting over with Julian in New York exciting. So while a more prudent path would have been to finish high school in California, he gladly accepted his mother's bus money and headed East. One more time McQueen allowed himself to be guardedly optimistic about Julian. But this would be the last time.

When McQueen disembarked from the bus on what was then a tough area of New York, near Thirty-fourth Street, the actor later said he felt like Li'l Abner, the title character of Al Capp's popular newspaper comic strip about a naïve young country boy. When Julian picked him up, she had been drinking, but then that was par for the course. Unfortunately, things only became worse at his mother's flat in Greenwich Village, an area of the city synonymous for the arts and Bohemian lifestyles. Mother and son were soon in a bitter argument with two possible catalysts—either Julian's boyfriend or the sleeping arrangements.

His mother was paying for her son to share a flat with a neighbor in the same building. But when the youngster went to check out this new address, he found his roommate in a romantic embrace with another young man. Whatever the cause, the donnybrook that ensued between

Julian and Steve effectively ended any hope of the two ever reconnecting. She told him if he left, "Don't come back!" McQueen took Julian at her word, and it was over. Though he was later civil to her and eventually took care of his mother when he became a star, he never again allowed her to be emotionally close enough to hurt him.

Ironically, this final fiasco by Julian was not without some potential prophetic signs for McQueen. Although the youngster was about to embark on a year of vagabond wanderings, Julian did introduce her son, albeit briefly, to the then cultural capital of America. After McQueen's picaresque proverbial "days in the desert," which would also include a hitch in the U.S. Marine Corps, he returned to New York, lived in Greenwich Village, and tried to become an actor.

Before McQueen found himself as an artist, however, he had to find himself as a man. Just as his future screen persona was defined through action, the teenaged McQueen soon set out on a personal odyssey. Years later, he sometimes downplayed the differences with his mother and painted a romantic explanation of what possessed him to suddenly take off: "[Julia and I in New York] didn't stay together for long. I had a yen to cut loose, to see the world."[2]

Like the street kid Julian's lack of love had forced McQueen to be, from running with gangs to simply killing time in tenement hallways while his mother turned "tricks," being suddenly on his own in New York's mean streets was not as devastating as it would have been for most teenagers. Between hustling money with his pool-hall skills and an easy rapport with street people, including Greenwich Village prostitutes who were happy to put up a cute California kid, McQueen got by.

This first New York sojourn then briefly assumed a sort of nineteenth-century romance of the seas slant, à la Richard Henry Dana's *Two Years before the Mast* (1840) or Herman Melville's *Typee* (1846). McQueen met two storytelling sailors at a bar in New York's tough Little Italy district. Under the influence of several drinks and these amateur maritime "poets," McQueen soon found that he had joined the merchant marines. His ship was the SS *Alpha*, bound for Trinidad. Unlike Dana and Melville, whose nautical disillusionment took time and was often frightfully colorful, such as *Typee's* cannibals, the easily distracted McQueen simply became bored and jumped ship in Santo Domingo after one week.

For approximately the next year, the young man was like a leaf in the wind. His vagabond life became an ongoing geography lesson. While there is no question that McQueen relished being a modern-day Don Quixote, he also had a gift for embellishing the facts. As *Look* magazine author George Eells later wrote, "[The actor had] an aptitude for inventing colorful detail to replace un-interesting fact."[3] So as the teenaged McQueen's travelogue is briefly sketched, readers are welcome to "treat" their perusal with more than a grain of salt. In McQueen's favor, however, the provocative biographical travelogue that follows remains more creditable than the tall-tale tendencies of another older Hollywood Hoosier, Red Skelton.[4] The younger star had apparently absorbed a basic lesson later turned into an axiom by *New York Times* author/critic Terrence Rafferty: "That's the trouble with [made-up] stories . . . they have to be believed."[5] In other words, too much myth making strains one's credibility.

Regardless, the romanticized take on McQueen's first safe haven after his sudden departure from the merchant marines has him landing in a Santo Domingo bordello, probably on a tip from a fellow sailor. He earned his keep with a plethora of odd jobs, from general maintenance man to resident tough guy if a customer was slow to pay. In McQueen's first wife's autobiography, she revealed, "The [prostitute] perks that came Steve's way were plentiful. He said to me with a twinkle in his eyes, 'I was one happy fella!'"[6] Because of these special benefits, he lingered in Santo Domingo for nearly three months.

McQueen next turned up at a Port Arthur, Texas, brothel. After all, he had references. Once again, he played at being the house's man Friday, though history has not recorded any sexy dividends. From there the teenager became an oil field "grout" (common laborer) near Waco and Corpus Christi, Texas. McQueen followed this up as a traveling carnival "barker" (front man for various acts inside the tents). When not so employed, the teenager also sold pen-and-pencil sets on the midway. By the time the carnival reached Ottawa, Canada, he decided to become a lumberjack. Naturally, the young McQueen signed on to the craft's most dangerous position—the "tree-topper," who cut off the topmost branches before bringing the tree down.

Sandwiched into the nomadic résumé of jobs, McQueen also found time for some prizefighting and the occasional petty crime. As one of his biographers comically noted, it was as if the actor anticipated a future "audition for the role of Jack Kerouac," author of *On the Road.*[7] With a few spare dollars from playing Canadian lumberjack, McQueen took a vacation at the lovely resort town of Myrtle Beach, South Carolina. The actor later claimed, "I was an old man by the time I was seventeen." This loner, nomadic teen with a taste for danger later put these traits to good use in his acting career, starting with his roving television cowboy bounty hunter, Josh Randall.

Along related loner lines, there is a funny/sad anecdote peppered throughout the McQueen literature involving a gargantuan appetite predicated upon a youth spent going without sufficient food, either from neglect or from living on the run. The story has been replicated by countless friends and family members and goes something like this: The actor is dining out and he orders double of everything—two steaks, two baked potatoes, and so on. Since McQueen would not always be able to finish all this food, a dinner companion who had witnessed this phenomenon before asks, why not just request single portions, and then, if you're still hungry, order again? The movie star who could not get used to being a movie star would reply, "What if they run out?"

During McQueen's stay in Myrtle Beach, he had his first traditional boy-girl romance with a young lady named Sue Ann. He celebrated his seventeenth birthday with her family, and though they were relatively well off, especially compared to the young ragamuffin, they became as enamored of this world-weary boy as Sue Ann. Maybe because the young man saw normalcy staring him in the face, he enlisted in the U.S. Marines in early 1948, prior to his eighteenth birthday.[8] During McQueen's three-year tour (1948–51) Dean Martin and Jerry Lewis made a film called *At War with the Army* (1950). With a little military branch tweaking of that title, it might have described McQueen's time in the marines.

Seven times McQueen was dropped from PFC (private first class) to private for various infractions. He also spent over a month in the "brig" (military slang for guardhouse) for going absent without leave in 1949. McQueen had stretched a weekend pass to see Sue Ann into a two-week visit. Worse yet when the shore patrol came calling to Myrtle Beach, McQueen resisted arrest. Years later the actor drew upon his bread-and-water incarceration for his prisoner-of-war role in *The Great Escape*, and his title character convict in *Papillon* (1973).

Despite all this friction, McQueen ultimately came to greatly appreciate his time in the marines, though he remained rebellious. Here is his later comic take on being put behind bars: "That session in the brig didn't really tame me down much. But it got one message across to me loud and clear. When you're in the Marines, Uncle Sam calls the shots. What you *don't* do is go running off to see your chick."[9] Still, like McQueen's time at Boys Republic, the marines gave him more discipline and increased the young man's coping skills.

In addition, the marines allowed McQueen to more fully embrace what became one of his defining components—his interest in all things mechanical. By becoming a mechanic in the tank division he had fun and even found an outlet for his sense of humor. McQueen's new goal was to create a hot-rod tank! After much tinkering and a blown engine, McQueen found that a souped-up tank was beyond motor pool parts, but it made the marines more entertainingly real to him, like a kid working on his car.

Sometime the comedy, moreover, was totally spontaneous. When McQueen's unit was sent to Labrador, Canada, for cold-weather war drills, food rations were reduced to simulate a battle situation. This was more than McQueen could stand. Luckily, he was assigned to an unloading detail for the mess. Drawing upon his petty larceny background, he managed to liberate several large cans of beans.

Later, McQueen and a buddy fired up the engine of an amphibious landing craft so he could warm-up his bonus beans in the hot exhaust.

Unfortunately, he did *not* first open the can. McQueen later remembered, "Suddenly there was this tremendous explosion. It blew beans over everything—tents, jeeps, radar equipment, everything. And for about the next week I'd go by an officer and salute him and he'd have a bean stuck on his helmet. I had a lot of trouble keeping a straight face . . . in Labrador."[10]

Not all of McQueen's marine experiences involved fun or fighting. Again, like a character from his later movies, the young Hoosier displayed bravery, too. During the aforementioned Canadian deployment, a transport ship accident during landing exercises sent several tanks and their crews into the ocean. Tragically, there were numerous drownings. But through McQueen's quick, cool action during an emergency amphibious rescue, he was personally responsible for saving the lives of five marines. No doubt, this heroic action (for which he won a special commendation) contributed to the distinction of his being appointed to an honor guard overseeing the protection of President Harry Truman.

The actor's blue-collar background and military service later made him a conspicuously old-fashioned patriot in the liberal, antiwar Hollywood of the 1960s. As a typical period article reported, "A supporter of the American effort in Vietnam, McQueen can explain the domino theory of world politics—if Vietnam falls, then all of South East Asia goes—as well as many high-domed hawks."[11] Along related lines, McQueen's marine background and his hard-knock résumé of macho activities, from Texas oil fields to Canadian forests, sometimes made him question the manliness of being an actor. This was a perspective consistent with some past iconic film stars with whom he was compared, such as Clark Gable, who had also worked in the oil fields before Hollywood. Thus, when McQueen was later polled by the 1960s media about broader questions of the day, such as the proclivity of actors entering politics, the young star could be self-deprecatingly articulate about his profession: "Everyone has the right to express his opinion on politics. But because actors seeking office are sometimes merely 70 per cent delivery [acting]. . . . You know, actors as such are not the great people. The great ones are the philosophers, the writers, the scientists."[12]

Of course, in 1951, the year McQueen was honorably discharged from the marines, such issues were years away. The young man's immediate thoughts were about that pretty girlfriend back in Myrtle Beach. His military tour, even his brig misadventures (caused by loyalty to Sue Ann), had made him an even bigger hero to her family. With a marriage obviously looming in the near future, Sue Ann's father went so far as to offer the nomadic Hoosier a promising job in his business.

McQueen was tempted by this promise of a real family, or maybe it was just Sue Ann's big, beautiful green eyes. But ultimately a suffocating feeling overcame the former marine, and he walked away from this first chance at normalcy. McQueen, the escape artist, was back in business. Returning to his premilitary vagabond ways, he worked his way up the East Coast from Myrtle Beach. Once again there was an assortment of odd jobs, including driving a taxi in Washington, D.C. The lonely emptiness of his past that seemed to drive (haunt?) him was later described by his first wife as a "black hole" at his core.[13] One is reminded of an insight by Friedrich Nietzsche about how one can overdo remembering. To paraphrase the German philosopher, "Without forgetting, it is impossible to live at all." McQueen never got over all that childhood hurt. According to the actor's later friend, Pat Johnson, who knew the star during the good times, "[The idea that] you can never trust people— that's [still] what he lived by. Life was a scam. It was always, 'What does this person want from me? They're acting nice but what's behind it?' He couldn't accept people at face value."[14] Given McQueen's sense of humor, he sometimes defined distrust in comic terms, such as suggesting the "tilt" factor on pinball machines suggested big business did not trust anyone either.

Eventually, McQueen found himself back in New York's Greenwich Village in a nineteen-dollar-a-month cold-water flat, with a bathroom down the hall. There was not, however, a sudden eureka moment about being an actor. McQueen continued to sleepwalk through an assortment of meaningless sales jobs, hawking everything from homemade sandals to encyclopedias. But pitching reference books made him feel guilty, since most of his potential customers could not really afford them. He was also an apprentice tile setter and flirted with becoming a plumber's assistant.

Along the way, there were countless one-night stands and many girlfriends. But these liaisons were not just about the sex. His blond boyish good looks and those piercing blue eyes contributed to his con-artist skills. The more responsible of McQueen's pretty young conquests had food in the icebox and money to lend, at least at first, to their charming new lover—someone who never carried cash or cigarettes. (This mooching trait continued into his movie star days, too, with the actor often joking, "I throw pennies around like manhole covers." But to his defense, many born-to-privilege types, such as John F. Kennedy, also conveniently neglected to carry cash.)

After McQueen struggled to make a living for several months in New York, one of his girlfriends suggested he try acting. Flattered, yet hardly convinced, he weighed other issues, but no "art" as a motive/goal never came up. As implied earlier, he was impressed that New York stage work meant he could sleep in mornings, with just a two-hour workload in the evening. More importantly, acting was a great way to meet more girls, from interacting with them in classes to impressing them afterwards with one's sensitivity. Moreover, it was slowly dawning on this former marine that he had always been an actor; he had played so many parts through his short but troubled life, whether it was surviving a dysfunctional family or all those mean streets. But the clincher came when he thought back to his main line of "work" as an Indianapolis gang member—"acting beats stealing hubcaps."[15]

Interestingly, references to hubcaps remained a metaphor for reality for the rest of McQueen's life. When a number of critics at a press junket praised the actor's performance as the sophisticated title character of *The Thomas Crown Affair* (1968), McQueen graciously replied, "Well, thank you. But I think I do better playing hubcap roles than doing the Phi Beta Kappa thing [à la Thomas Crown]."[16] One could also link this hubcap/reality connection to McQueen's aforementioned tangential feelings about being an actor. Here is the performer's take on just wanting to be perceived as a real person: "Somebody once said something about me that I liked. It was, 'The one thing about Steve McQueen is that he's not like an actor.' A lot of actors have the idea that they're really important. They've got to be able to give a little."[17]

McQueen's hubcap/reality mindset also explains why he would often preface his man-of-the-people perspective with the opening, "I'm just a guy from the Midwest."[18] Granted, there is a degree of con man posturing here for the press, as the actor polishes an "aw shucks" persona. Plus, there is also irony to the Midwest references, given his bitter memories of a childhood often spent shuttling between Indianapolis, Indiana, and Slater, Missouri. But despite this modicum of hypocrisy, the actor frequently and sincerely waxed poetic about the Midwest's inherent sense of right and wrong and fairness—values in which he wanted to believe, though he invariably struggled with executing them.

In 1951 McQueen's midwestern penchant for a straightforward reality/practicality met the perfect mentor in New York's Neighborhood Playhouse drama coach Sanford Meisner. The same McQueen girlfriend who suggested he had a certain stage presence took him to one of Meisner's classes. If the young man had assimilated nothing more than the quote with which Meisner always opened his class, it would have been a tutorial for the ages. The veteran teacher said, "The foundation of acting is the reality of doing."[19] This, in an arty nutshell, is the essence of McQueen's style/stardom. With only modest range, the actor effectively inhabited a character by nailing the details—an authenticity of movement and clothing married to an interaction with signature objects that were also defining extensions of his character. Method acting, at least for McQueen, had never been distilled so purely.

When the young man read for Meisner, the instructor was impressed: "He was an original, both tough and childlike—as if he'd been through the wars but preserved a certain basic innocence. I accepted him at once [as a Playhouse student]."[20] Beyond Meisner's perceptive anchor in "the reality of doing," McQueen was impressed by the drama coach's tough directness with him: "You can either be a fine actor or no good at all. It all depends on you." This appealed to the former marine. McQueen later remembered thinking, "I know I wanted to be something more than a farm boy, so I worked hard to be an actor."[21]

Though there was a certain logic in a multifaceted con artist becoming a professional performer, *Vanity Fair* author James Wolcott has
more recently posited an amusing take on McQueen finally finding
a career: "Acting was a strange choice of a profession for someone so
dead-set on hooding his emotions. In [1962's] *Hell Is for Heroes*, [direc-
tor] Don Siegel was unable to elicit tears from McQueen for a tragic
scene despite the use of onions, chemicals, and sad stories; he even
smacked his star across the face, hoping the stinging sensation would
make his eyes water, but McQueen couldn't/wouldn't cry."[22] While such
minimalism might have elicited critical knocks about wooden acting for
someone else, McQueen's meagerness often translated as troubled mystery, with maybe a sense of Henry David Thoreau's haunting refrain,
"Most men lead lives of quiet desperation."

Though McQueen's Playhouse enrollment was made easier financially by his use of the GI Bill, he needed a full-time job to cover all
his expenses. This resulted in driving a post-office truck all night, after
which he went directly to classes. He also supplemented these wages
with weekend poker games and motorcycle racing at Long Island City.
(There would later be a partial scholarship, but his need for part-time
jobs persisted.) Although McQueen seemed to have made an immediate connection with Meisner, he could often be an initial challenge for
other instructors. Voice teacher Carol Veazie observed, "In the beginning he was openly skeptical about acting and about any talent he
might possess. He had a 'show me' attitude, was short-tempered and
would prove his contempt by going to sleep in class."[23] But through
patience and forcing McQueen to study one of his flawed readings on
tape, the young man came around.

Julian still lived in Greenwich Village, and McQueen had intermittent contact with her, though sometimes with embarrassing consequences. Since his mother often frequented bars favored by performers,
her son saw and/or periodically heard about various drunken episodes.
Paradoxically, while Julian provided no encouragement for McQueen's
new career in acting, Victor Lukens, her boyfriend when McQueen first

came to New York, seems to have assisted the young man. While it is now unclear whether Julian and Victor were then either still together, or if they had ever married, McQueen's application to the Playhouse listed Lukens both as his stepfather and as a professional contact (someone who had used the youngster in film work).[24] This probably constituted application padding on McQueen's part, though cinematographer Lukens also doubled as a director of documentaries and industrial films. So maybe the actor's real cinema debut has yet to be correctly identified! Of equal significance, however, is the fact that this suggests that Lukens and McQueen must have patched up any differences they might have had initially.

Whatever the length of Julian's relationship with Lukens, both individuals were free spirits. Colleagues described the filmmaker as a "middle-aged beatnik" who assumed the look of what now might better be described as a hippie—long hair, sandals, and a consciously unkempt appearance. Fittingly, McQueen's first wife often described the then hippie-like Julian as the "first flower child." Moreover, Julian and Lukens had the perfect backdrop for such Bohemian beliefs—Greenwich Village.

Even when McQueen more fully embraced his Playhouse activities, he struggled with what seemed, to him, the unmanliness of acting, which he kiddingly called a "candy-ass" profession. Given that background, one can imagine how the reluctant actor felt about wearing leotards for dance class; for anyone that cared to ask, McQueen's answer was, "damn clown." Another comic twist for McQueen was his first professional acting job. Hired by a Jewish repertory company on New York's Second Avenue, his only line was, "Nothing will help," in Yiddish. It might have described this modest debut; he was fired after just four performances. McQueen was later fond of offering the kidding explanation, "I guess it was my lousy Yiddish."

McQueen's English-language stage work soon developed, including a summer stock production of *Peg o' My Heart*, which had been a popular film in the early 1930s with Marion Davies. The old-fashioned story centers on an independent Irish lass taken to a fancy English

manor to fulfill an inheritance requirement. McQueen's version of the
work (staged in Fayetteville, New York) starred 1940s child star Margaret O'Brien. One cast member was so down on the Hoosier's acting that
this amateur critic might just as well have recycled the aforementioned
Yiddish theater line, "Nothing will help." This criticism, despite the fact
that *Peg* was hardly close to what would become known as McQueen
action-adventure material, made the play a pivotal production in his
early career. He seriously considered moving on to something other
than acting. But once McQueen made the commitment, things slowly
improved.

Getting back to Greenwich Village might have helped, too. A few
years later, McQueen confessed that this art colony of lower Manhattan
might have mellowed him a bit. "For the first time in my life I was really exposed to music, culture, a little kindness, a little sensitivity. It was
a way of life where people talk out their problems instead of punching
you," noted McQueen.[25] Although his post-*Peg* days of struggle demonstrated a new commitment to performing, McQueen forever remained
a maverick. Indeed, during his Greenwich Village days his nickname
was Desperado. As a later author described the then major star, "Acting,
though his living, is not his life."[26]

McQueen continued to embrace the James Dean-like reckless youth
scenario, continuing to race motorcycles at Long Island City (and on
the streets of New York), spending his first real acting money on a red
MG sports car, and taking impromptu road trips. One of these brief
getaway vacations resulted in a punctured eardrum. Skin diving off the
coast of Florida, he came up too quickly and did further damage to an
ear already affected by a childhood infection. Veazie later read him the
proverbial "riot act" for not taking care of himself, but that was just
McQueen being McQueen. Ultimately, he stayed with acting (other
than a late-in-life lull) *much* longer than anyone thought he would.
After several early successes on television and film, McQueen observed,
"Man, after I've gotten my sugar out of this business, I'm going to take
off—and run like a thief."[27]

McQueen demonstrated more acting talent in a stock company production of *A Member of the Wedding*, which showcased the pioneering black actress/singer Ethel Waters. The veteran performer poignantly re-created a role she had played both on Broadway and in the 1952 screen adaptation. The story was about a young girl (Julie Harris in the movie) prodded into maturity by a brother's wedding. Waters's character helped facilitate that metamorphosis. While this woman focused, coming-of-age tale was still miles from McQueen territory, his modest supporting part was memorable to him for two reasons. First, he managed to handle himself professionally, with no "Nothing will help" cracks from fellow cast members—a modest step forward. Second, he was amazed by the way Waters connected with an audience. He had never experienced something like this up close. Though a young man then known as the Village's Desperado would never have admitted to being inspired by Waters, her performance gave him a kind of benchmark toward which to shoot.

Persistent practice at his craft took McQueen from the Neighborhood Playhouse to the Uta Hagen-Herbert Berghof Dramatic School. Impressively, this was followed by admittance to the prestigious Actors Studio—heaven for disciples of the "Method" and the school of acting made famous by such McQueen heroes as Dean and Marlon Brando. A joke then going around New York claimed that if God were so inclined to go on stage, the Actors Studio is where he would be found—if he could pass the audition!

This early 1950s comic blaspheme was only a partial exaggeration. Of some two thousand auditioning actors, McQueen was one of only five to be accepted into what was normally just referred to as the Studio. (His entry into this hallowed hall was the same year as Dean's death, 1955.) The Studio was the place to be if one were a young actor on the make. At the time it was heavily associated with its leader and central teacher Lee Strasberg, as well as director Elia Kazan, a founding member (1947) of the Studio, and his protégé, Brando. The latter duo had become the proverbial toast of both Broadway and Hollywood, with their most high-profile joint project being the stage and screen productions of Tennessee Williams's play *A Streetcar Named Desire*. These hugely influential works, particularly Brando's animalistic characterization of Stanley Kowalski, helped to redefine the parameters of naturalistic acting. Dean, who entered the Studio in 1952, also cast a huge shadow. His greatest film was also directed by Kazan—*East of Eden* (1955). And his premature death later that year, in an automobile accident on the way to race his sports car, forever made him into a freeze-frame hymn to youth itself. Martin Sheen later paid homage to both Dean and Brando when he noted, "When I was a young actor in New York, there was a saying that if Marlon Brando changed the way actors acted, James Dean changed the way people lived."[28] For much of McQueen's time in New York, he tried to be like these two actors, from persistently repeating Brando lines in the mirror to racing his sports car around Manhattan like he wanted to replicate a Dean tragedy.

McQueen's early stage work is said to also sometimes reveal a vulnerable demonstrativeness truer of Dean, and to a lesser degree Brando, than his later more minimalist style. In fact, this sympathetic excess, at least for McQueen, is still apparent in his first starring role, the cult horror B movie *The Blob* (1958). But as film historian and critic David Thomson has observed, "[McQueen] was in the Dean and Brando tradition, except that he [ultimately] rejected their self-pity and neediness. Like many people psychically damaged, McQueen hated to show weakness."[29]

With McQueen's offbeat sense of humor, he later sometimes separated himself from pioneering Method types in a comic manner. For example, the actor's uncouth habit of, to borrow an old colloquialism, "scratching where it itches" in public, sometimes compelled people to compare him to the naturalism of Brando acting. Here is McQueen's tongue-in-cheek take on the subject: "All this ratchin' and scratchin' jazz . . . I don't think Mr. Brando is really like that; I think he uses it as an actor, which is great. But I come from a [real] world of ratchin' and scratchin,' and I'm trying to get away from it. I don't want people staring at me in a room like I'm some long lost [uncivilized] bird."[30]

When McQueen entered Actors Studio, Method's Valhalla, there was a great deal of public misunderstanding about both the school and the technique. In Foster Hirsch's history of the Studio, *A Method to Their Madness*, he insightfully reminds readers that many of Hollywood's top movie stars of the time, including Clark Gable, Gary Cooper, Jimmy Stewart, and Spencer Tracy, were much praised for their naturalism, too.[31] They seemed instinctive; their dialogue delivery and physical movement was without self-consciousness. With no distracting technique, they seemed to be playing variations of themselves. Though this is a simplification, their art was about making things look natural. The Method, quite simply, more fully embraces this sense of naturalism by being a "total immersion system," with the actor drawing upon personal experience. Ideally, this provides a sense of freedom that Strasberg further fleshes out in his own book; crediting the Method as not having "the time to worry whether [the actor] will be able to act his part or what the audience will think of him or how awful it feels to walk on

Dean in the role that made him famous, Cal, the troubled son in East of Eden *(1955).*

the stage where everyone can see and criticize."[32] Consequently, there is a greater intensity to the Method actor than what one expects from a Gable or a Cooper.

Often the Actors Studio performer is an antihero—a stark contrast with the dynamic leader-of-men type synonymous with Gable and the other old-school actors mentioned previously. Because of this, the stereotypical Actors Studio antihero is more inarticulate and/or vulnerable. Not surprisingly, such imperfections of speech, such as mumbling

Director Norman Jewison (in sunglasses) prepares to roll the cameras in a scene from The Thomas Crown Affair *(1968).*

or stumbling over one's words, soon became the gist of comic impressionists—something McQueen even did privately among friends. Ultimately, McQueen did tap into his private demons to play a litany of loners, mavericks, and misfits. *But* he toned down his histrionics (as compared to Dean in *Rebel without a Cause*, 1955), playing everything much closer to the metaphorical vest, as suggested earlier by David Thomson. Intuitively, McQueen recognized his lack of range compared to a Brando or a Dean, and wisely embraced Playhouse instructor Meisner's central axiom, "The foundation of acting is the reality of doing." Using assorted props as a defining extension of himself, his minimalism revealed a personal magnetism that connected him with the movie stars of his youth, such as Gable, Cooper, and McQueen's favorite, Humphrey Bogart. Such unique charisma maybe did not translate into great theatrical acting, but mesmerizing movie presences made them beloved pop-culture icons. Norman Jewison, who later directed McQueen in *The Cincinnati Kid* (1965) and *The Thomas Crown Affair*, put the young actor in the same class as the previously noted macho male stars of Hollywood's golden age, adding, "[they] were personally more important than the characters they portrayed."[33]

McQueen, the self-described "greatest scammer [con man] in the business," was now close to a breakthrough in the only legitimate trade—acting—for which he showed any talent.[34] McQueen was also about to meet the closest he ever came to a soul mate.

3

Neile Adams, Broadway, and Beyond

*"I live for myself and I answer to nobody. The last thing
I wanted was to fall in love with any broad."*[1]

STEVE MCQUEEN

Milestone accomplishments are great for the scrapbook, but they do not always pay the bills. Such was the case with Steve McQueen's acceptance into the Actors Studio. He was not suddenly inundated with job offers, but he was honing his skills. McQueen continued to appear in summer stock and to play minor parts in television at a time when New York was the small-screen capital of the world.

Eli Wallach, who later costarred with McQueen in *The Magnificent Seven* (1960), first met and trained with his Hoosier friend at New York's Neighborhood Playhouse and the Actors Studio. Wallach later recalled in his entertainingly named autobiography *The Good, the Bad, and Me* (a title spoof of the 1967 film that made him an international star, *The Good, the Bad, and the Ugly*, where his character was the ugly): "Even then [mid-1950s], McQueen had the raw skill. His greatest talent lay in being observant. He could always find what in an earlier scene had led logically to what he was doing just then. In *The Magnificent Seven*, McQueen once asked [director John] Sturges to cut some of his dialogue. 'Please,' he said, 'movie acting is reacting. Silence is golden on the screen.' Nobody quite grasped the poetry in the flow of film like he did. What McQueen had learned to do was what separates the true artist from the ham—to watch and, above all, to listen. McQueen was the best reactor of his generation."[2]

Unfortunately, this intuitive sense of what was right for the television and motion-picture camera did *not* serve McQueen well on stage, where the playwright's words tend to be the star. This became clear during his first major acting job, replacing Ben Gazzara on Broadway in the lead for *Hatful of Rain*, which originally opened November 19, 1955. This was a pioneering play on the subject of drug addiction that drew upon a wealth of young Studio talent: actors Gazzara, Shelley Winters, Tony Franciosa, and *Hatful of Rain* author Mike Gazzo. Anchored in an Italian family, with lead character Johnny Pope as a junkie, and generously peppered with slice-of-life sex and violence, *Hatful of Rain* was a major critical and commercial success.

Given the hit play's Studio foundation, when several of the stars eventually jumped ship for greener Hollywood pastures, replacement players with connections to the celebrated Method school had a distinct advantage. While this was a plus for McQueen, he also had several strikes against him, starting with inexperience. There was nothing in his modest résumé that suggested he could carry a high-profile Broadway drama. As a blonde, blue-eyed WASP, McQueen was the wrong ethnic type. Indeed, his middle-America appearance had earned him the Studio nickname Cornflakes. The part of the Italian junkie called for a dark Latin look. McQueen eventually dyed his hair black, but given the Studio's large number of Italian members (sometimes referred to as the Mafia), many felt it was inappropriate to cast McQueen. A final challenge for McQueen was simply all the competition. The part of Pope, even as a replacement, still had career-making potential. The frontrunners who went on to long successful careers included George Peppard and John Cassavetes, who later became more famous as a pioneering writer/director of independent films.

Ultimately, McQueen just wanted it more. He also had an ally in playwright Gazzo. Borrowing a page from director Nicholas Ray, who the previous year (1955) had James Dean hanging out with real gang members prior to shooting *Rebel without a Cause* (1955), Gazzo facilitated McQueen meeting actual junkies in a tough section of New York called Hell's Kitchen, an old Irish ghetto. But beyond this research and support from the playwright, the actor simply pulled out all the stops, from constant rehearsal of the part to sending a steady stream of cards and positive past notices to the producers. He also was not above ordering flowers for the wives of the production's backers. McQueen even offered to defer his salary if he won the part.

Frank Knox, a McQueen acting acquaintance from *Somebody Up There Likes Me* (1956, both were unbilled), best put the Hoosier's drive to win the *Hatful of Rain* lead in perspective when he comically observed, "Short of some shtick involving a horse's head [à la the *Godfather* scene] it's hard to think what more Steve could have done."[3] Like a classic American success story, McQueen's persistence paid off. Come July 2, 1956, Broadway had a new lead in *Hatful of Rain*.

At this point, however, one might recycle that old folklore axiom, "Be careful what you wish for, because you might get it." The part often seemed to overwhelm McQueen, especially as he later confessed, in terms of a basic technical facility, such as voice projection and effectively handling lengthy dialogue passages. He further revealed, "I had this one big scene where the character, who's a dope addict, gets delirious—and it really spooked me. I mean, each night, doing that scene I got more and more depressed. Got so I couldn't eat [a McQueen rarity], and I began losing weight. I felt lousy. There was so much about acting I still didn't know."[4] Among the major publications covering his Broadway debut, only *Variety* found him "effective" as Johnny Pope.[5] Coupled with this, maybe the push to get the part resulted in a letdown, which was further exacerbated by the repetitious nature (never a McQueen strong suit) of being a Broadway performer. This is the implication of Marshall Terrill's seminal McQueen biography: "The [*Hatful of Rain*] crew's consensus was that Steve had become progressively worse in the role of Johnny Pope. He wasn't as fresh as he was at the beginning."[6] Not surprisingly, McQueen was dropped from the part after six weeks, with the play closing a month later (October 13, 1956). Ironically, the young man eventually won some vindication by later briefly touring in a *Hatful of Rain* road company.

Though this Broadway credit figures prominently in later McQueen television and motion picture company press kit material (and the resultant articles drawn from these publicity-directed profiles), his brief run on Broadway was a bittersweet experience for him. A great accomplishment, getting there, followed by a sense of inadequacy. Paradoxically, even the great achievement of getting into the Actors Studio had been followed by a letdown. The central Method guru at the Studio, Lee Strasberg, was brilliant but bullish. McQueen's first wife, Neile Adams, wrote in her memoir, "Strasberg . . . had a way of dissecting and criticizing an actor's work that Steve found intimidating and frightening at the same time. [Steve would say] 'I would rather take my chances with the paying public.'"[7]

McQueen still learned a great deal at the Studio, but more and more it was about watching others present special scenes. Like so many of his later signature cinema loners, he sat back and observed. McQueen was later a big Beatles fan, especially of the band's designated smart aleck, John Lennon. Had McQueen lived long enough to hear Lennon's *Double Fantasy* solo album (1980), the actor would have greatly appreciated the musician's number, "Watching the Wheels Go By," because McQueen enjoyed stepping outside the rat race while still taking it all in.

The Beatles in their groundbreaking first film, A Hard Day's Night *(1964). From left to right: Paul McCartney, George Harrison, Ringo Starr, and John Lennon.*

Fittingly, both this perspective and a fear of Strasberg's merciless criticism, was something McQueen shared with fellow Studio actor Dean.[8] Shortly before McQueen's time at the Studio, Dean had adapted a scene presentation for Strasberg from a novel called *Matador*—a wordless piece about an aging bullfighter preparing to enter the ring. Like Dean's later often criticized scenes as a middle-aged Jett Rink in *Giant* (1956), Strasberg did not find Dean effective outside the security blanket of playing his own troubled age. Worse yet, the Studio master saw Dean's presentation as merely an exercise piece and not a legitimate sketch for consideration. Strasberg savaged the young man, which was the teacher's style. Why would he be that way? I am reminded of the comic line to the vaudeville sketch explanation by someone with an equally ogrelike nature: "That's what I do." Behind Strasberg's back he was affectionately, and sometimes not so affectionately, known as the "high priest."[9]

Never one to take criticism well, Dean was devastated by Strasberg's slashing response. Something along these lines appears to have also happened to McQueen, another Studio student hypersensitive to even the most valid of faultfinding. Of course, any disapproval/humiliation at the Studio seemed greatly amplified by the high-profile audience invariably in attendance, from special guests to the many talented students on the verge of stardom. People whose association with the Studio might have put them in the audience for a scene presentation by either Dean or McQueen would include: Marilyn Monroe, Winters, Carroll Baker, and Wallach.

Dean was so hurt by Strasberg's criticism he threatened to leave the Studio. His vulnerability was later revealed when he confessed, "I don't know what happens when I act—inside. But if I let them dissect me, like a rabbit in a clinical research laboratory or something, I might not be able to produce again. They might sterilize me."[10] This admission seems curiously naïve, given that the Method is all about tapping into past experiences for current acting assignments. But on a broader level, Dean's statement simply articulates a typical, almost superstitious, belief held by many performers, including McQueen—over analysis of any

Neile Adams and McQueen dressed in their best for an awards program in the early 1960s.

gift might make it go away. Indeed, McQueen felt so lucky about his stardom, given his troubled youth, that his concerns about losing everything went beyond just too much critiquing. He had an unfounded but real fear he could lose everything at any time. Regardless, though both Dean and McQueen avoided presenting Studio scenes after run-ins with Strasberg, they each opted to continue attending and learning from participants.

Though McQueen's time as a Broadway star was painfully brief, it paralleled the birth of the most significant relationship of his adult life—the woman who would become the actor's first wife, dancer/actress/singer Neile Adams. Three years younger than McQueen, she was starring on Broadway in *The Pajama Game*, an exuberant musical comedy about a pajama factory grievance committee and an unexpected love affair. Little did Adams know that a truly unexpected love affair was about to unfold in her real life.

The term "exuberant" perfectly described the young Adams, a long-legged, petite beauty whose exotic good looks were a product of a Spanish mother and a father of English, Chinese, and Filipino background. While her soon-to-be delineated biography was comparable to the roller-coaster ride doubling as McQueen's life, Adams embraced the good and the bad with equal laughter and a philosophy inherent to a popular song showcased that same year in Alfred Hitchcock's remake of his *The Man Who Knew Too Much* (1956), "Que Sera, Sera."

Adams's knack for rolling with life's punches was in direct contrast to McQueen's mercurial moodiness—the quick wit suddenly side-swiped by suspicion and anger. Once past these differences of personality, however, their two profiles were unusually similar. Neither knew their fathers. Adams's mother, a Spanish dancer in Asia named Carmen, married her lover only to later discover he already had a wife. Like McQueen's mother, Julian, Carmen was more interested in men than motherhood, so Neile (again like Steve) was largely raised by others. While McQueen periodically found himself in strict disciplinary settings, such as California's Boy Republic and the marines, Adams endured a Japanese concentration camp in the Philippines during World

War II. Both of these young lovers also suffered from dyslexia. Neile later poignantly summarized the situation when she observed, "Steve had a heart as hard as steel but inside was a great yearning to be tender. We both hungered for the same thing: someone to love and be loved by and never to feel left out again."[11]

Most McQueen literature treats his summer 1956 courtship of Adams as yet another example of the actor's cocksure machismo, such as tooling around Manhattan on his motorcycle. But one senses some vulnerability in McQueen here. Did the fact that he was slowly being overwhelmed by his Broadway role contribute to him inexplicably opening up to Adams? Or even more inexplicably, look at how suddenly he got serious about her, moving into her studio apartment within a week. After all, McQueen was normally the king of one-night stands, who had once even turned down a pregnant Greenwich girlfriend's request for abortion money with a "heart as hard as steel" (to recycle Adams's line), because he could not be sure it was not someone else's baby. Adams's autobiography ultimately makes a convincing case for these two misfits becoming soul mates. Yet timing is just as important in life as in the arts, and for McQueen, a sexy, grounded person was just what he needed. (For Adams, who had also spent part of her youth in a convent school, McQueen probably represented the temptation of the dangerous yet exciting "bad boy.")

Still, given McQueen's womanizing ways and a career on the verge of a nosedive, Adams's friends and colleagues were adamant that he was just out to use her, as he had used so many other women before. Moreover, with Adams's career in fast-forward mode—a Broadway star (part of the Bob Fosse-choreographed "Steam Heat" number in *The Pajama Game*) and Las Vegas courting her singing and dance skills—what did she need with an iffy actor about to get his Broadway pink slip?

While there is no explaining love, Adams was willing to make compromises for McQueen from the beginning. With regard to her future husband's philandering, even during the early days of their passionate relationship, she made this startling admission: "I instinctively knew there were other girls lurking around. He didn't strike me as the monogamous type. But I didn't ask and he didn't volunteer anything. I figured what I didn't know wouldn't hurt me."[12] While this tacit agreement does not justify McQueen's ongoing promiscuousness during their marriage, it does suggest there was an unofficial green light from the beginning. In fact, as a performer herself, aware of show business's many temptations, Adams later reluctantly accepted her husband's philandering, as long as he was discreet. Eventually, he could not even do that, and their marriage, with additional baggage to be addressed later, ended in 1972. But in 1956, they were like most young couples—living for the moment.

What made this "moment" a professional challenge for the chauvinist McQueen, however, was that while his career had stalled, Adams had the entertainment industry banging at her door. As she prepared to leave *The Pajama Game*, Adams was approached by Hoosier-born director Robert Wise, who invited her to Hollywood to test for a part in *This Could Be the Night* (1957), an offbeat comedy about a proper teacher doubling as a secretary to a gangster. Wise was a few years away from his multiple Oscar wins for *West Side Story* (1961, as codirector and producer) and *The Sound of Music* (1965, again winning as director and producer). Though these were big-budget musicals, Wise's long career revealed a filmmaker equally capable of creating classics in multiple genres, including horror, *The Curse of the Cat People* (1944) and *The Haunting* (1963); science fiction, *The Day the Earth Stood Still* (1951); biography, *Somebody Up There Likes Me* (1956); war, *Run Silent Run Deep* (1958); and action/romance, *The Sand Pebbles* (1966). Couple these memorable movies with the aforementioned Academy Award-winning musicals, and one has an amazingly diversified résumé.

I belabor this Indiana director's background because of his several special connections with McQueen, beyond Adams's eventual appearance in *This Could Be the Night*. Wise directed the boxing biography of Rocky Graziano *Somebody Up There Likes Me*, with Paul Newman in a title role. But this was also McQueen's debut film. While his unbilled gang member role was modest, McQueen had made an impression with Wise during their first meeting: "He came in, in a sports jacket, kind of gangly and loose and he had a little cap. A little bill around the top of his head. I guess it was his cocky manner somehow, not fresh but just nice and cocky and a bit full of himself that just caught my eye and I cast him in this small part. It was the part of some kid on a rooftop fighting back in New York."[13]

Though *Somebody* was seemingly just a blip in McQueen's career, the picture had a three-part effect on his life. First, while Wise was in New York City shooting the film during the winter of 1955–56, he saw Adams in *The Pajama Game* and thought about using her in *This Could Be the Night*. At least one major McQueen biographer believes that Adams's ultimate casting in that movie was catalyst enough for the actor to propose: "He couldn't get a job in a movie but he could get the girl."[14]

Second, *Somebody* opened in New York almost simultaneously to McQueen's Broadway debut in *Hatful of Rain*. Although his stage turn was as a lead, versus an unbilled screen appearance in Wise's film, even then the young actor could intuitively sense that movies were the medium for him. Ironically, Method's "high priest" also seemed to have recognized this film fact. That is, "Lee Strasberg had once remarked to him while Steve was still studying at the Actor's Studio, 'With that [cinematic] face, you've got to be something in acting'"—a statement that implies the dream-factory magic of the camera to capture and magnify the physical persona, a face on screen forty feet high.[15]

Third, *Somebody* was undoubtedly the source for McQueen's later one-sided rivalry with Newman. New York's new golden boy after the death of Dean, Newman now represented the antihero bar for young actors. Being an unbilled player to Newman's star turn made McQueen set his goal on eclipsing this other blue-eyed, soon-to-be superstar. McQueen later accomplished this goal, for a time, during the 1960s. Yet, McQueen's fierce pride paid a price, too. For example, he later had an opportunity to costar with Newman in the now celebrated *Butch Cassidy and the Sundance Kid* (1969), but only if he received top billing. Generous Newman, who was responsible for bringing the property to McQueen in the first place, was willing to go the standard star compromise route of a cobilling, but negotiations broke down when McQueen was adamant that he would have to be number one.

Along related lines, there is also an apocryphal *Somebody* story that gives McQueen's rivalry with Newman a more pointed cause. This tale has McQueen feeling slighted by the young star during exterior work in a bitterly cold East Coast winter. Newman had a heated car to double as a mobile dressing room, but the unbilled players just had to deal with the elements. McQueen, for whom the word chutzpah might have been coined, managed to keep warm by appropriating Newman's car. When a representative for the film's star, however, became aware of this impropriety, McQueen was summarily evicted. So, the story goes, through no fault of Newman, McQueen had his catalyst for a grudge.

Though the tale's hyperbolic nature makes one question its historical accuracy, it does ring true on two counts. McQueen *never* forgot a slight, whether real or imagined. And Newman was *always* the actor he had to beat, including McQueen's request for more lines than Newman when they both appeared with an all-star cast in *The Towering Inferno* (1974), a film in which McQueen received top billing. The bottom line is that McQueen was a kid from the streets who did what he had to do to survive. He brought that same take-no-prisoners mentality to acting. One might best demonstrate that philosophy by his cutting comments upon the death of Dean, a performer whom he both admired and aped in some of his early roles. McQueen, astride his motorcycle when appraised of Dean's fatal car crash, said: "I'm glad Dean's dead. It makes more [acting] room for me."[16] *Hollywood Citizen News* journalist Peer J. Oppenheimer offers a similar, though more sympathetic, slant on McQueen's fisticuffs philosophy: "To Steve, life is black and white. He believes in an eye for an eye and a tooth for a tooth . . . [but] he will fight for his friends with the same vigor as he does for himself."[17]

Returning to McQueen's multifaceted connection to Wise, the performer went from an unbilled player in the director's *Somebody*, to an Academy Award-nominated Best Actor in *The Sand Pebbles* (1966), his only run at an Oscar. Wise recalled during the latter shoot, "After I gave Steve that walk-on in *Somebody* . . . I never dreamed I'd be working with him here in the Orient as the star of a multimillion-dollar production. But the truth is, he's a perfect choice for the part of Jack Holman. I've never seen an actor work with mechanical things the way he does.

He learned everything about operating that ship engine, just as Holman did in the script. Jack Holman is a very strong individual who doesn't bend under pressure, a guy desperately determined to maintain his own personal identity and pride. Very much like Steve."[18]

Interestingly, though a decade had transpired between *Somebody* and *The Sand Pebbles*, with McQueen going from a relative unknown to an international star, the distrustful street kid still remained. Candice Bergen, his admiring costar in *The Sand Pebbles*, later recorded this poetic profile of McQueen during the production: "He seemed to trust

Director Robert Wise gives some advice to actress Marayat Andriane on the set of the film The Sand Pebbles *(1966).*

no one and tried constantly to test the loyalty of those around him, to trap them in betrayal. Yet for one so menacing, he had a surprising, even stunning, sweetness, a winning vulnerability. But he seemed to live by the laws of the jungle and to have contempt for those laid down by man. He reminded one of the great outlaws, a romantic renegade; an outcast uneasy in his skin who finds himself with sudden fame and fortune. One had the sense that it came too late and mattered little in the end. And that he tried to find truth and comfort in a world where he knew he didn't belong."[19]

This "sudden fame and fortune" was still years away when McQueen flew to California in 1956 "to make an honest woman" of Adams (then shooting *This Could Be the Night*). The duality of Bergen's portrait of McQueen—from "menacing" to "vulnerability"—probably helps explain Adams's surprising acceptance of his proposal. Still, being a kept husband, due to a less than robust career, was difficult for a man Adams affectionately called "chauvinistic." But one should not judge McQueen harshly for his less-than-feminist perspective. The time was the conservative 1950s. More to the point, this was the view of a boy/man whose childhood dream had simply been to have a mother at home. Long before the McQueens had children, Adams had to constantly play mother to her husband.

While Adams was an "A" star for Wise and had an extended Las Vegas run after shooting *This Could Be the Night*, the best McQueen could do were a series of quickie B movies starting with *Never Love a Stranger* (1958, in which he plays a Jewish lawyer in a modest part). While this picture sat on the shelf for two years before its limited release, McQueen's next B assignment, the science-fiction horror movie *The Blob* (1958), generated more notoriety. Bad acting and a limited budget transformed this unintentionally funny movie into a campy cult classic. Assuming he could just take the money and run, as he had done on *Stranger*, with no fear of *The Blob* being seen by many viewers, Steven McQueen (his billing) had miscalculated. For cult fans, the movie has never gone away. Indeed, it was even remade thirty years later. McQueen had also miscalculated on his payment for *The Blob*. The producer offered him either 10 percent of the gross or a straight three-thousand-dollar salary. The actor played it safe by taking the salary. But the film's instant cult status made it a sleeper hit, meaning McQueen missed out on an eventual paycheck of more than a million dollars.

Losing a fortune on *The Blob*, however, made him a much better businessman on his future movie contracts. And while it took McQueen years to live down the fact that his first starring role was in what another generation would label a "golden turkey," he eventually developed a sense of humor about the film. When dining with a studio executive at Warner Brothers years later, the by then icon kidded that a framed picture of him from *The Blob* would look right at home among all the stills of stars showcased in the Warner commissary. Late in life McQueen also occasionally telephoned his grown children when *The Blob* was playing on late-night television, inviting them to steal a laugh at their father's expense.

McQueen's B movie work during 1957–58 concluded with *The Great Saint Louis Bank Robbery* (1958). Shot on location in Missouri, this low-budget quickie had a top-billed McQueen playing a robbery hostage. But as with *Never Love a Stranger*, the movie had a negligible impact on the young actor's career. Worse yet, with his wife's career anchored in Hollywood and Las Vegas, McQueen's assorted odd-job roles kept him away, at various B movie sites and on to occasional television work back in New York City. But the actor's small-screen work, particularly in a 1957 two-part episode of the dramatic anthology *Studio One* titled "The Defenders," helped end their bicoastal marriage.

This *Studio One* script had McQueen playing a contemporary killer. The actor recognized this could be a breakthrough part but had no idea how to make it uniquely his own. His wife, who would be his best adviser throughout their marriage, made two simple but effective suggestions. Adams convinced him to tone down the lingering influences of his idols—Brando and Dean—and let McQueen's real character come through. Next, given the comic side of the actor, Adams wanted her husband to, as she said, "Smile a bit." This would not only encourage McQueen to draw upon himself for the performance, a smiling killer would also give the character a multifaceted complexity. This resulted in a memorable performance that was the catalyst for a series of television parts where he played "smiley tough" guys. How appropriate that the boy who grew up idolizing tough-guy killer Humphrey Bogart, especially the more vulnerable Bogie of *High Sierra* (1941), should first find himself as an actor with a similar persona.

Ironically, while McQueen's dream to become a film star bigger than Brando was not being realized through B movies, the small screen was about to make that goal possible. Television successes in 1957 and early 1958, particularly in Western programs shot on the West Coast, would give McQueen both a platform for eventual screen stardom and an opportunity to settle down in California with his wife and start a family.

McQueen as George Fowler, the driver for the criminals in The Great Saint Louis Bank Robbery *(1958).*

The difference maker was his popular Western television series *Wanted: Dead or Alive* (1958–61). For three seasons McQueen starred as the charismatic bounty hunter Josh Randall, crisscrossing the West in search of outlaws. Adams's earlier advice to tap into himself and play that "smiley tough" persona had direct links to the Randall character. *Wanted* was then perceived as the first series where a nominal "heavy" (a bounty hunter) had the lead. But that bad-man stereotype had to be softened somehow in the casting. McQueen's size, or lack of it, and his blond boyish looks were the perfect antidotes. Being undersized translated into being an underdog. And the boy/man appearance helped embellish the antihero perspective that complemented this new type of cowboy. Plus, McQueen topped off his Randall characterization by filtering that "smiley tough" persona through his own nomadic mean-streets background. As he pointed out: "I liked Josh Randall. He was a lot like me—a loner who played his own games, made his own decisions. He was no hero strutting along with a badge pinned to his chest; he was a hired man doing a hired man's job for the money it paid him. I could identify with Randall, and I think the audience sensed that identification and responded to it."[20]

Like the standard comments of his cowboy character, McQueen's modest statement, "I think the audience . . . responded," is an understatement. After a slow start, the Nielsen television ratings for 1958–59 had *Wanted* ranked an impressive sixteenth among all programming, and the series climbed into the top ten the following season.[21] While these numbers translated into millions of fans for McQueen, one particular Randall devotee, director John Sturges, ended up being more important than all the rest.

A John Sturges Trilogy

"The film [Never So Few, 1959] may provide a catapult to stardom for Steve McQueen, hitherto known principally as a television actor. He has a good part, and he delivers with impressive style."[1]

VARIETY

Through the years Steve McQueen worked with a series of significant directors, including Henry Hathaway (*Nevada Smith*, 1966), Norman Jewison (*The Cincinnati Kid*, 1965, and *The Thomas Crown Affair*, 1968), Sam Peckinpah (*Junior Bonner*, 1972, and *The Getaway*, 1972), Don Siegel (*Hell Is for Heroes*, 1962), and Robert Wise (*Somebody Up There Likes Me*, 1956, and *The Sand Pebbles*, 1966). But the director most responsible for transforming McQueen into a superstar was John Sturges, who directed the actor in three pivotal pictures: *Never So Few* (1959), *The Magnificent Seven* (1960), and *The Great Escape* (1963).

At the time of *Never So Few*, Sturges was considered an action director of note whose specialty was the Western. This was the heyday of the genre, when fully 25 percent of all American films being made were "horse operas," with the format also dominating the small screen. Bob Hope joked at the time, that before he turned on his television he had to brush the hay off the top of the set. McQueen's popular *Wanted: Dead or Alive* series was, of course, part of that video sagebrush movement.

Seminal Sturges pictures prior to *Never So Few* included *Bad Day at Black Rock* (1955, a contemporary Western with Spencer Tracy in an Oscar-nominated performance), *Gunfight at the O.K. Corral* (1957, with

Burt Lancaster and Kirk Douglas respectively as Wyatt Earp and Doc Holiday), and *Last Train from Gun Hill* (1959, with Kirk Douglas and Anthony Quinn in another tough lawman story). As this mini-résumé suggests, Sturges worked well with major stars, a skill that served him well on *Never So Few*—a Frank Sinatra vehicle about a maverick World War II American commander directing guerrilla operations near the Burma-Chinese border.

Sinatra was at the apex of his career as an Oscar-winning actor (*From Here to Eternity*, 1953), music-defining recording artist, and major stage presence in nightclubs, such as the then burgeoning Las Vegas scene. Thus, Sinatra used his clout to dominate any production in which he was involved, though he invariably surrounded himself with quality people such as Sturges.

To increase Sinatra's comfort level on a shoot, which was not his favorite artistic effort (compared to recording and live performances), he often had his close circle of Rat Pack friends cast in supporting roles. Consequently, Peter Lawford played a fellow officer, with Sammy Davis Jr. set to be a comic army driver pressed into fighting service. But Sinatra and Davis had a falling out shortly before *Never So Few* started production. The friction was over a Chicago radio interview in which Davis claimed to have eclipsed the proverbial "old blue eyes." Lawford recalled, "That was it for Sammy. Frank called him 'a dirty . . . bastard' and wrote him out of *Never So Few* . . . the part [originally] created so that Sam could be in the movie."[2]

Suddenly, this high-profile picture had a vacancy in a strong supporting part. Sturges, an established Western auteur with an eye for young talent, was already a fan of McQueen's Randall character, and he became the director's choice to replace Davis. But Sinatra needed to sign off on the decision. So the director showed his star several episodes of *Wanted*; Sinatra was equally impressed. McQueen now had a plum part. Not only that, this Hoosier in Hollywood hit it off with the mega-star. McQueen likened their connection to a common mean-streets background: "Frank and I are on the same wavelength. We both grew up the hard way."[3]

There was, however, one potentially shaky early moment for Mc-
Queen with regard to his remaining as part of the cast. Sinatra was a
practical joker, and during some downtime on the set, with McQueen
studying his script, the *Never So Few* star placed a firecracker in the
young actor's ammo belt. McQueen later recalled: "The thing went
off and shot me about three feet into the air. So I grabbed one of the
Tommy guns we were using and jammed in a full clip. Frank was walking away from me, laughing it up with some pals, when I yelled at him.
He turned around looking plenty startled when I let him have the full
clip, zap-zap-zap. . . . Of course, the thing was loaded with blanks, but
the effect was wild. I figured that evened the score."[4]

McQueen might have thought that "evened the score," but after
his burst of gunfire there was a deathly silence on the set. For Sinatra's
entourage, the newcomer had stepped over the line. One always let the

Above: *Director John Sturges (far left) on the set
of* The Great Escape *(1963) with McQueen on
the far right and costar James Garner in the center.* **Left:** *Frank Sinatra (left) and two fellow Rat
Pack members Dean Martin (center) and Peter
Lawford on the Las Vegas strip, circa 1960.*

man later nicknamed the "chairman of the board" make the first move. Without thinking, McQueen's knee-jerk response had jeopardized his newly won, potentially breakout part. But after a pause, Sinatra's explosive laughter was the ultimate validation for McQueen. Indeed, the superstar was soon encouraging Sturges, "Give the kid close-ups."

The two men got along so famously that McQueen might have become part of the Rat Pack. Ironically, after Davis was back in Sinatra's good graces, McQueen palled around even more with the multitalented black performer. (The two especially enjoyed competing at who had the fastest six-gun draw.) Regardless, McQueen and his wife Neile Adams began socializing with Sinatra, too. But the budding star later turned down a part in the Rat Pack picture *Ocean's Eleven* (1960) because he did not want to become just another Sinatra disciple, following sage advice McQueen had first received from famous film columnist Hedda Hopper.

Given McQueen's dominating nature on the set of his *Wanted* television series (sort of a small-screen Sinatra), he might have been a challenge on *Never So Few*, too. But he was cognizant of the opportunity the film afforded him. Moreover, according to Adams, McQueen followed Sturges's every direction for several additional reasons: "He was impressed with John's credits and his reputation of being a man's man . . . . [Also,] John respected and knew all about fast cars. It gave them another level of communication. Steve had just discovered auto racing and was gung-ho about the sport."[5] The relationship was further complemented by the fact that Sturges, like McQueen, had been quite the hell-raiser. Sturges also had never known his father, who died when the director was very young. Clearly, McQueen and Sturges were two men with a great deal in common.

Never So Few opened during Christmas of 1959 and was a commercial hit, though critics gave the movie mixed notices. Bosley Crowther's tongue-in-cheek *New York Times* critique caught that ambivalence in his attempt to be flippantly cool, almost as if he was trying to be a Rat Pack reviewer: "Millard Kaufman's script has the insubstantiality of Hollywood hashish. And John Sturges has directed it for kicks. Those who

Sinatra as Captain Tom Reynolds recruits McQueen as jeep driver Sergeant Bill Ringa for jungle fighting in Burma during World War II in Never So Few *(1959).*

will get . . . [the kicks] are the youngsters who can be lightly carried away by the juvenile brashness of Mr. Sinatra, by the swashbuckling antics of his pals, played . . . by Richard Johnson, Peter Lawford, and Steve McQueen, and by the flashy flamboyance of the fighting."[6] But like the *Variety* rave about McQueen that opened this chapter, critics had no reservations about the young television star. In fact, another notable Hollywood columnist, Louella Parsons, even wrote about *Never So Few*: "Steve McQueen stole the show."[7] Thus, while the film did not make this nomadic Hoosier a movie star, his winning performance as a brash con man military driver (again playing a variation of himself) positioned him on the fast track toward his dream of being a screen legend.

Sturges facilitated this ongoing McQueen ascendancy by casting him in another picture, the epic Western *The Magnificent Seven* (1960), a tale sometimes labeled "badmen-turned-benefactors." For younger viewers, this is the movie that inspired the later parody Western the *Three Amigos!* (1986). For older students of film, *The Magnificent Seven* is actually a Western remake of Akira Kurosawa's *Seven Samurai* (1954, in which a sixteenth-century Japanese village hires Samurai warriors to protect them from bandits). When Kurosawa's picture was released in the United States, it was sometimes referred to as a "far-east Western," and was retitled *The Magnificent Seven*!

Sturges's Americanization of the story transferred the action to 1880s Mexico, where villagers once again need to fend off bandits. The desperate peasants decide to hire professional gunslingers to be their protectors. Director Leo McCarey used to say 80 percent of filmmaking is in the casting, and arguably Sturges's greatest accomplishment on *The Magnificent Seven* was the troupe he put together—a group the *Los Angeles Examiner* simply called "a smash in the casting department."[8] Originally, Yul Brynner and Anthony Quinn jointly owned the American remake rights to *The Seven Samurai*. But Brynner managed to take control of the property and get it into production as the star (though Quinn fought a losing battle in the courts for years).[9] When Sturges came in as the producer/director, he orchestrated everything, including casting. But as on *Never So Few* with Sinatra, Brynner signed off on most major decisions.

Sturges's first choice for a Brynner costar in this motley cowboy crew was McQueen, who had doubly impressed the director with his ability to dominate every *Never So Few* scene in which he was featured. But Sturges quickly complemented this duo with the following future stars: James Coburn, Charles Bronson, Robert Vaughn, and Eli Wallach as the Mexican bandit leader Calvera. (The other "magnificent seven" gang members are Brad Dexter and German actor Horst Buchholz, in his film debut). Sturges's choice of McQueen was almost a mutual decision with Brynner, as the star also proved to be a fan of McQueen's *Wanted.*

Paradoxically, this central casting of McQueen (since he again steals the picture) almost did not happen. While the director and his rising star were anxious to collaborate again, McQueen's Four Star production company for *Wanted* was opposed to giving him the release time to shoot the movie. Explanations for this scheduling inflexibility vary, from fears over McQueen becoming a major player and wanting out of his series, to simply concerns about keeping enough back episodes in the can to guard against unexpected production problems/delays. (In the late 1950s, television produced more fresh material, as seasons had *thirty-nine* new episodes, as compared to today's low twenties to midtwenties range.)

Still, reading between the lines, Four Star's lack of pliability here was probably more about disciplining an unruly star. McQueen's often abrasive push for quality on *Wanted* had burned a lot of bridges with executive "suits" connected to the series. What follows is a typical "take no prisoners" McQueen tirade on his blunt formula for success on his small-screen Western: "I'm not out to win any popularity contest. I'm out to get a job done. I don't care whether Four Star burns down but as long as I'm with the show, I'll do the best I know how."[10]

Four Star's attempt to thwart McQueen backfired. The production company had not anticipated the creative con-man artistry of the actor and his agent, Hilly Elkins. McQueen had a minor traffic "accident,"

McQueen prepares to lend his gun to the fighting in the classic Western The Magnificent Seven *(1960).*

driving into the side of a bank. The incident was allegedly one of those "I hit the wrong pedal" misfortunes. Suddenly, McQueen is wearing a neck brace and Four Star can read the proverbial "writing on the wall." But despite the *Wanted* production company then having a change of heart about release time, Elkins punished the corporation by demanding a huge increase in McQueen's salary!

Cleared to appear in *The Magnificent Seven*, McQueen joined cast and crew in Cuernavaca, Mexico, then an unknown small town approximately fifty miles from Mexico City. (The former village is now a popular vacation getaway.) As is typical on any major Hollywood production, the star (Brynner) received the typical treatment, which included a private villa and pool, a large dressing room/trailer, and an army of servants and staff. The rest of the performers and production people stayed at the modest community's equally humble hotel, the Posada Jacaranda. This was probably the catalyst for a rivalry that sprung up between the supporting cast and Brynner, though McQueen literature tends to treat it as a major conflict and/or tit-for-tat upstaging between the movie star and the television hero.

Costar Robert Vaughn described a more general sophomoric uprising, noting that the rest of the cast were "trying to topple the king [Brynner] from his throne, stealing the picture in whatever way we could"—a perspective seconded by McQueen's wife. "Bobby Vaughn and Jim [Coburn], and Steve [for example] would pass by Yul, and one of them would go 'Oink, oink' [to distract Brynner in a scene]," Adams noted.[11] But McQueen seemed to be the master of one-upmanship; from fiddling with his hat to minor maintenance upon a movie weapon, the young actor had a knack for getting and holding the viewer's attention, regardless of who else was in the scene. One might describe this as a bonus component of McQueen's tendency to effectively use inanimate objects as an extension of his screen characters.

This dual-focus exploitation of props might have been a product of McQueen being a fan of James Dean, who had been equally adept at this compound use of inanimate objects. This would be most famously accomplished by Dean in *Giant* (1956), when he plays with a rope throughout a scene when he is informed of his inheritance, a scene that, at least on paper (based on scripted dialogue), should have belonged to costar Rock Hudson. A now obscure but equally effective example of Dean's theatrical larceny occurs in a television installment of NBC's *Armstrong Circle Theatre*, broadcast November 17, 1953. Titled "The Bells of Cockaigne," Dean keeps the viewers' attention during a poker game by simply being the only gambler lighting and handling a cigarette.

In Eli Wallach's memoir he recalled some of the tricky bits of business McQueen used to upstage Brynner. In the company of director Sturges, Wallach watched the shooting of a river crossing: "Brynner led the seven across . . . riding high in the saddle with a determined look on his face. McQueen took his hat off and dipped it in the water. In another scene, as they were riding on a hearse to the cemetery, Brynner was fixing his holster and lighting a cigar by striking a match on his boot

On the set of The Magnificent Seven *with cast members (from left to right) Harry Luck, McQueen, James Coburn, Horst Buchholz, and Yul Brynner.*

while McQueen pretended to test the shotgun cartridge by shaking it next to his ear before loading it into his gun. Yul's eyes darted toward McQueen with a look of 'What are you doing there?' It was a wonderful competitive moment. Sturges loved the competition."[12]

McQueen's patented outspokenness undoubtedly contributed to the idea that a serious feud existed between the two actors. "I think I represented a threat to him [Brynner]," McQueen said. "He doesn't ride very well, and he doesn't know anything about quick draws and that stuff. I know horses [from my Western series]. I know guns, I was in my element, and he wasn't."[13] Ironically, the only real conflict between the two was a product of Brynner attempting to dissipate what he felt was a press-manufactured story. This is McQueen's take on the incident, rich with the actor's combatively colloquial language: "He [Brynner] came up behind me and grabbed me by the shoulder—you know: 'I want to talk to you.' Well, I don't dig that stuff [being touched]. He said, 'There's an item going around that we're having a feud, see? And I'm an established star, and you're an up-and-coming star, and we're not having a feud, and I want you to send a letter to these people saying it isn't true.' And I said, 'Well, sure, I'll see you Friday [later], baby. Just stand back on the thirty [give me some space, a football reference to the thirty-yard line] and punt [I'll take care of it], you know.'"[14]

Sturges, with the best perspective of anyone on the subject, minimized the differences between the two actors. His final word on the subject also showcased yet another trait he shared with McQueen—a gift for colorfully casual language: "There's no feud. . . . Naturally there were some clashes. They're dissimilar characters: Yul is like a rock, Steve's volatile. Steve figured Yul was being a Big Star, that he wasn't willing for anyone else to catch flies [to upstage with small bits of 'stage business'] and Yul thought Steve was being an undisciplined smart aleck, always trying to catch a fly. He got sore because Steve was always fiddling with his hat or something. I had to [briefly] tell Steve not to busy it up all the time."[15]

As suggested by Wallach's aforementioned memories of the "competition," it was a win-win situation for Sturges. Many directors, such as Elia Kazan on *East of Eden* (1955, with James Dean and Raymond Massey), actually manufactured a conflict between performers to enhance their screen characterizations. Sturges merely fell into this creative one-upmanship, and other than some minor directorial traffic-cop action, he and film audiences were the beneficiaries. Of course, one should note again that Sturges was a master at working with mercurial movie stars.

Whatever the differences of Brynner and McQueen on *Seven*, biographical material for Brynner tends to suggest that a friendship eventually developed between the two. Jhan Robbins's book on Brynner documents a later party hosted by Jack Benny and his wife and radio sidekick Mary Livingston, where "Brynner and McQueen insisted on serenading the guests with a medley of cowboy ballads. They both had been drinking heavily, and when it came time to leave they began whistling for their horses. They were disappointed when their chauffeur-driven automobiles appeared in the driveway. 'Where's mah horse?' Yul asked drunkenly. 'Thar must be a horse thief in th' crowd,' McQueen replied."[16]

Besides Sturges's talent for navigating through the potential minefield of Hollywood egos, the director was a filmmaker capable of creating a classic. Such was the case with *Seven*. The Western is not only the most inherently American genre, it also frequently doubles as an inspired metaphorical vehicle for reinterpreting the past based upon then-current events. Released at the beginning of the iconoclastic 1960s, *Seven* was a watershed for the demythologizing of the West, movingly showcasing

Director Elia Kazan works on a script in 1954. During his career, Kazan directed twenty-one different actors in Oscar-nominated performances.

the vulnerabilities of the cowboy gunslinger. *Seven* was a harbinger of several other celebrated revisionist and/or anti-Westerns released during the decade, ranging from director John Ford's *The Man Who Shot Liberty Valance* and Sam Peckinpah's *Ride the High Country* (both 1962), to George Roy Hill's *Butch Cassidy and the Sundance Kid* and Peckinpah's *The Wild Bunch* (both 1969).

Seven is also a character-driven story where the self-referential nature of its cowboys, particularly the figures played by McQueen and Brynner, foreshadow later acclaimed 1960s Westerns in which screen gunslingers open up about their disappointments and weaknesses instead of leaving it to the audience to "read" implied meanings into their actions. Whereas the demythologizing process can lead to parody, from the underlining lampooning of Sergio Leone's "Spaghetti Western" trilogy of the mid-1960s, to the overtly broad spoofing of Mel Brooks's *Blazing Saddles* (1974), *Seven* still manages to invest its heroes/antiheroes with an inherent dignity, as they became the protectors of this terrorized Mexican village. The group's almost majestic quality is greatly enhanced by Elmer Bernstein's memorable score that later became the Marlboro cigarette theme song. (Wallach was so impressed with the music he later comically observed to Bernstein, "I wish I'd heard your music [during the production]. If I had, I would have sat upright in my saddle, ridden with [more] authority, and felt like the head of my gang."[17]) The sacrificial action of the "magnificent seven" so resonated and/or helped define the time, that film historians later labeled the 1960 picture a "Kennedy Western," à la John F. Kennedy's "New Frontier" presidency, "almost as if they [the seven] had anticipated the call of Kennedy's [compassionately helping hand] inaugural address."[18]

Seven is also an archetypal example of what Sturges did best— chronicle a band of flawed men on a dangerous mission, an apt description of all three of his movies with McQueen. And though the effective military operation-like pacing of *Seven* faltered briefly near the end, the movie also found time to celebrate certain values consistent with an earlier, more optimistic take on the Western. While a pastoral escape is not possible for the McQueen and Brynner characters, who are fated to continue wandering in the West, *Seven* closes with the only other surviving member of the group (Horst Buchholz) staying in the village to marry a Mexican girl and start over—reminiscent of John Wayne's romantic second chance at the conclusion of John Ford's *Stagecoach* (1939).

How did the multifaceted *Seven* play out for McQueen's career? One can address this question in three ways. First, unlike many great movies that are not fully recognized upon their release, *Seven* was a major critical and commercial success. An initially sluggish American reception was immediately turned around by rave reviews from Europe. The *London Times* stated, "The big screen is filled in a deeply satisfying manner. The battle is made up of the extravagant acrobatics, the leaps and dying falls which are the stuff of Western gun-battles, as stylized as the Samurai, and should be accepted with as much respect."[19]

The *Los Angeles Times* credited the movie with being "genuinely magnificent—a Western to rank with 'High Noon,' 'Stagecoach,' and the very finest of the genre ever made."[20] *Newsweek* described it as a "hard-pounding adventure movie full of exciting characters and topped off with a [moral] message that goes down as easily as nutmeg in an eggnog."[21] *Variety* called *Seven* "a rip-roaring, rootin' tootin' Western with lots of bite and tang and old-fashioned abandon."[22] As with *Never So Few*, McQueen often stole the personal notices. The *Hollywood Reporter* predicted, "McQueen, if he can get sprung from [his *Wanted* series], where he is learning nothing and only getting older, is going to be a great big star."[23] *Variety* added, "McQueen, an actor who is going places, brings an appealing ease and sense of humor to his role."[24] Indeed, the actor's gift for comedy, highlighted earlier, was often noted in the reviews, such as the *Los Angeles Mirror*'s observation, "McQueen is the only one [of the seven] to lend a touch of humor to the saga with his easy-going, laconic gunman."[25]

Though none of McQueen's lines from *Seven* have the darkly comic bite of his title cowboy character crack from *Nevada Smith* (1966)— upon first seeing a priest's crucifix, "That looks worse 'n hangin'"—the actor's *Seven* gunslinger forever keeps a casually bemused perspective on everything. This ranged from McQueen's tongue-in-cheek crack about riding shotgun on a hearse at the opening of the picture, to being the only cowboy to later wisecrack about the girls in the Mexican village. While the actor had decided to distance himself from Sinatra's Rat Pack for professionally autonomous reasons, it was like a semblance of Dean Martin's easygoing appeal had surfaced in McQueen's *Seven* performance.

The actor's off-handed comic charm might also have been fueled by simply working with friends, notwithstanding his games of one-upmanship with Brynner. McQueen confessed as much in a syndicated *Brooklyn Eagle* article upon the release of the film: "It was a ball [to make *Seven*]. We spent three months in Mexico on location during my TV break, and after 'Wanted: Dead or Alive' it all seemed like a vacation. I'd worked with a lot of the guys in the film before, so we were old friends and lived it up."[26] McQueen was particularly close to *Seven* costar Coburn, who had been a guest star on *Wanted* and later appeared with him in *Hell Is for Heroes* and *The Great Escape*. Vaughn was another *Seven* player with whom McQueen got along famously, and the actor later costarred in McQueen's favorite and definitive film, *Bullitt* (1968), as well as *The Towering Inferno* (1974).

The second way in which *Seven* impacted McQueen's career, beyond superlative reviews, was that this was the first time the actor's now famous antiheroically cool persona surfaced full blown in a feature film. Moreover, it is especially fitting this occurred in a Western because when McQueen's standard character is showcased in a contemporary story, he seems like a figure time has passed by. Pivotal examples included McQueen's maverick detective in *Bullitt*, and his equally throwback bank robber in *The Getaway* (1972). But the most interesting direct link between *Seven* and a future out-of-his-time McQueen figure occurs in Sam Peckinpah's underrated *Junior Bonner* (1972), arguably the actor's best screen performance. Like *Seven*, this contemporary Western is also an exercise in demythologizing the cowboy that eventually dovetails into an old-fashioned romantic embrace of America's quintessential roughriders.

The third manner in which *Seven* influenced McQueen's professional advancement was how his star turn almost guaranteed the actor's
involvement in Sturges's next action epic, the World War II drama *The
Great Escape*. In fact, while McQueen grabbed the lion's share of the
individual critical hosannas on *Seven*, two of his costars also resurfaced
in *Escape*—Coburn and Charles Bronson. But unlike the back-to-back
nature of *Never So Few* and *Seven*, three years elapsed between the latter
film and *Escape*, with McQueen doing three pictures in the interim.
Though these movies are examined more fully in the following chapter,
two of them have an indirect bearing on the subject at hand. That is,
like *Escape*, both *Hell Is for Heroes* and *The War Lover* (each 1962) are
World War II dramas. The late 1950s and early 1960s were the heyday
of movies about the war, including *The Bridge on the River Kwai*, *The
Young Lions* (both 1958), *The Guns of Navarone* (1961), and *The Longest Day* (1962). But whereas *Heroes* and *Lover* cast McQueen's loner
as arguably psychologically damaged military goods predisposed to be
ruthless warriors, *Escape* makes his individualistic antihero a charismatic
character the audience is only too happy to embrace.

Though *Escape* is another epic Sturges male ensemble of men on a
mission, the picture varies from *Seven* in that the genre is now the war
film, and the script is based on a true story—Paul Brickhill's nonfiction prisoner of war escape book of the same name. Sturges had been
enthralled by the text since it was first published in 1950 "and struggled
for more than a decade to find backing for the project."[27] Several factors
now made its production possible. First, Sturges had proven himself
to be a "money director," with a proven track record of box-office hits.
Second, he was not only an effective director of expensive large-scale
movies, he was also acknowledged as an early master of the challenging
technological development known as widescreen. Film historians have
described his use of the process in *Bad Day at Black Rock*, Sturges's first
signature picture, in the following manner: "Its CinemaScope frame
was brilliantly, if a bit self-consciously filled by Sturges' strategic po-
sitioning of his actors in relation to the huge, empty expanses around

them."[28] Third, as suggested earlier, World War II movies were suddenly that era's hot new genre, particularly those films epic in scope. In the motion-picture industry's then ongoing battle with television, the most effective ploy was to give viewers something they could *not* get on the small screen—widescreen spectacle.

With McQueen's past track record with Sturges, he was willing to sign onto *Escape* with a mere handshake. But here was how the director described McQueen's character to the actor: "Hilts keeps trying to break out of the POW camp, and the Germans keep dragging him back and throwing him into the cooler [solitary confinement earned him the nickname the "Cooler King"]. But they can't break his spirit. He just keeps trying."[29] Still, McQueen was not impressed with the picture's initial script, which went through enough drafts that Sturges sarcastically nicknamed it *The Great Headache.*

McQueen's simple suggestion, however, helped redefine the movie. The original story had his character trying to escape on a local German train, like most of the other POWs. But the actor, who had already generated a great deal of publicity by his real-life accomplishments as a motorcycle racer, wanted the Cooler King to attempt his getaway on a motorcycle. Sturges, like McQueen, was always receptive to embellishments and/or improvisations, so the director immediately agreed to the cycle suggestion. Indeed, the two later concocted another defining iconic component for the Cooler King. The only apparent activity of this American POW during solitary confinement was to bounce a baseball against the wall and catch it with a glove. The magic of movies is all about "doing things visually," and what more symbolic imagery of a maverick American could there be than a one-man salute to the national pastime?

Despite the ultimate inspired nature to their collaboration, early on there were rough patches between the director and his star (*The Great Escape* marked the first time McQueen received top billing in a major production). Like many performers, McQueen was always jittery at the start of a picture. Plus, he became convinced that a fellow cast member, James Garner, had become Sturges's new favorite. Like McQueen, Garner was another first-class find by Sturges from a Western television series, *Maverick*.

McQueen's mistrust, a basic component of his mean-streets youth, was completely unfounded. Garner's second-billed *Escape* character, the "Scrounger" (getting hard-to-find supplies for fellow POWs), was better defined in early script treatments. The figure also benefited from being equal parts of Garner's huckster *Maverick* gambler and a long tradition of movie POW con men, such as William Holden's Oscar turn in Billy Wilder's *Stalag 17* (1953). Consequently, with McQueen's part being more a work-in-progress, early rushes favored Garner and caused *Escape*'s star to walk off the set at least twice. Sturges was a veteran of temperamental types, however, and once McQueen's role began to be fleshed out, the director and star were back on the same page. Paradoxically, the film also marked the beginning of a long friendship between McQueen and Garner. "[They] got on quite well because they had so many common interests. Both were [especially] interested in cars and racing," Sturges noted.[30]

Though McQueen's motorcycle-riding American POW was a fictional addition to a real World War II escape story, the actor's part was still loosely based upon the British soldier George Harsh, who had been part of the attempted breakout. Also, the manner in which McQueen's Cooler King acquires his motorcycle—placing piano wire across a road in order to knock a passing German soldier off his vehicle—was a trick frequently used by the French Resistance during World War II.

Of course, there is still a certain irony to the fact that *Escape*'s defining image—McQueen's motorcycle-riding character jumping a barbed wire fence—"One of the iconic sequences of modern cinema . . . [is] the fictional highlight of an otherwise essentially true story."[31] Moreover, the irony deepens when it is further revealed that McQueen did not actually make the jump. The stunt was performed by the actor's close friend and stunt double Bud Ekins. Their longtime relationship was born through Ekin's motorcycle shop on Los Angeles's Ventura Boulevard. McQueen orchestrated bringing Ekins to Germany for the

"Cooler King" McQueen and his iconic American symbol—a baseball—in The Great Escape.

One of the pivotal images of McQueen's career—his motorcycle riding American prisoner of war from The Great Escape.

Escape shoot, reluctantly recognizing the danger to the production "if I fell on my melon [head]" attempting a dangerous stunt.

While Ekins also doubled for other *Escape* actors, too, one should quickly add that the extensive footage of McQueen's high-speed motorcycle getaway through the beautiful Bavarian countryside (with the Swiss mountains and freedom in the background) *is* the movie's star. In fact, McQueen outperformed the stuntmen hired to pursue the Cooler King and the actor came up with yet another brilliant suggestion for Sturges. Since the motorized German soldiers chasing McQueen were wearing uniforms, helmets, and goggles, the actor proposed doubling as pursuer! Audiences would not recognize him, and through the magic of editing, the fleeing American could be closely followed by multiples of himself. For a basic meat-and-potatoes man, McQueen had created the most surreal of solutions.

Another crucial invented *Escape* scene that involved McQueen is the comic Fourth of July celebration orchestrated by the American POWs in the camp. More paradox abounds here, since most of the POWs are British, and this quintessential American holiday rejoices in our revolt from Great Britain. But thanks to the drive of the Cooler King and the inventiveness of the Scrounger, a great deal of synthetic whiskey is created, and booze is a boon to "brotherhood," however nontraditional. Sturges further comically milks the event by shooting archetypal patriotic footage of McQueen marching while playing a fife, accompanied by Garner on the drums.

As was the case with *The Magnificent Seven* and the potential for friction between Brynner and McQueen, any behind-the-scenes conflict on *Escape* never got in the way of the mesmerizing movie that eventually found its way to the screen. But some participants were bothered by McQueen's demands. Experienced writer W. R. Burnett, brought in to work on the script (especially embellishing McQueen's part), was particularly virulent about the actor: "[He] was an impossible bastard. A third of the way through the picture he took charge. I had to rewrite scenes and rearrange them. Ohhh, he drove you crazy."[32] What makes this particularly sad is that McQueen's favorite movie, *High Sierra*

The Fourth of July celebration from The Great Escape *featuring McQueen and Garner (far right).*

(1941, with Humphrey Bogart), was coscripted by Burnett, as well as being based upon his novel.

Still, Burnett was the consummate professional, and he contributed to a movie-stealing part for McQueen. What gives their strained collaboration a bittersweet quality is how critics often later responded to the actor's *Escape* performance. For example, *Variety* wrote, "Probably the most provocative single impression is made by Steve McQueen as a dauntless Yank pilot whose 'pen'-manship record shows 18 blots, or escape attempts. McQueen has a style, an individuality, that is rare in the contemporary scene. He is a throwback to the personalities of earlier screen eras. He is the possessor of the kind of unique star quality with which such performers as [James] Cagney and Bogart captured the public imagination."[33] *Life* was in complete agreement: "McQueen . . . combines the cockiness of Cagney, the glower of Bogart and the rough diamond glow of [John] Garfield."[34] It was like Burnett helped segue McQueen to his twin tough-guy antiheroes of Bogart and Cagney, actors whose personae Burnett had helped shape, too.

Burnett's private take on McQueen notwithstanding, the young actor's *Escape* set behavior was praised by others. One of his strongest advocates was accomplished British actor Richard Attenborough, who played POW leader Roger "Big X" Bartlett. Attenborough later found even greater acclaim as an Oscar-winning director, taking the statuette for Best Picture with *Gandhi* (1982). Prior to that, he was second billed to McQueen in *The Sand Pebbles* (1966). Here is how Attenborough described McQueen's approach to *Escape*: "Steve was very professional. If the script was bad, which it was in the first draft . . . then yes, he put up a fuss. He was a perfectionist in every sense of the word. All those rumors about his being hard to get along with are scandalously untrue. I can remember rehearsing with him for weeks, because we had a lot of scenes together. Not one incident of ugly behavior sticks out in my mind. I admired his integrity."[35]

There was a certain irony involved in such praise, given the fact that one of McQueen's greatest anxieties going into *Escape* was working with a cast peppered with distinguished British actors. The 1960s was an era in which performers from Great Britain often dominated acting awards. When McQueen later received his first and only Academy Award nomination for Best Actor in *The Sand Pebbles, three* of his four competitors in this 1966 category were British: Richard Burton in *Who's Afraid of Virginia Woolf,* Michael Caine for *Alfie,* and Paul Scofield in *A Man for All Seasons.* The other actor in the category was fellow American Alan Arkin for *The Russians Are Coming the Russians are Coming.* Predictably, a Brit took the prize—Scofield, with some harping that Burton was more deserving. Interestingly enough, McQueen's *Escape* performance resulted in his winning the Best Actor award at the Moscow International Film Festival, a first for an American.

Buoyed by outstanding notices and business in Europe, *Escape's* domestic summer release two months later was a triumph for all concerned. The reviews read like something Sturges's mother might have

Above: Bogart makes a telephone call while Lauren Bacall looks on in another McQueen film favorite, The Big Sleep *(1946). Right: Richard Attenborough in costume for his* The Great Escape *character Squadron Leader Roger Bartlett.*

written. The *Los Angeles Times* stated, "There have, surely, been literally hundreds of prison-break movies, civilian as well as military. 'The Great Escape' digs, hammers and claws its way, if not to the top of the list, then awfully close to it."[36] The *Hollywood Reporter* said, "'The Great Escape' is a great adventure picture, tense with excitement, rich in character, leavened with humor, novel in setting and premise."[37]

Variety observed, "Mirisch Company and United Artists have hit the jackpot with 'The Great Escape,' a film of blockbuster potential in the recent screen tradition of [World War II epics] 'Kwai' and 'Navarone.'"[38] The notable *New York Herald Tribune* critic Judith Crist added, "[*Escape*] is a first-rate adventure film, fascinating in its plot, stirring in its climax, and excellent in performance."[39] Under the review title, "Stirring Epic Told Vividly," the *New York Journal American* noted, "Not since 'Bridge on the River Kwai' [1957] has there been so thrilling a film about men at war."[40] Only the *New York Times*'s Bosley Crowther had reservations about the "Rover Boyish" spirit of this POW drama.[41] But rare is the major reviewer who has so frequently *misread* the movies, or to quote Pauline Kael, the celebrated former film critic for *The New Yorker*, "Bosley Crowther . . . can always be counted on to miss the point."[42]

As McQueen had done in the first two installments of this Sturges trilogy, the actor managed to steal attention away from yet another outstanding ensemble cast. Complementing the aforementioned McQueen rave from *Variety*, *Tribune* critic Crist said, "And of course for sheer bravura, whether he's pounding a baseball in his catcher's mitt in solitary or stunting cross-country on a motorcycle with scores of Germans in pursuit, Steve McQueen takes the honors."[43] But the *Hollywood Reporter* was most sage in its harbingering of his future: "McQueen, with his unique capacity for projecting both spitting meanness and easy charm, continues his steady, unwavering climb to the highest stardom."[44] If *The Magnificent Seven* had made him a star, *Escape* added the adverb "super." Consistent with all these critical hosannas, *Escape* went on to be one of the top box-office hits of 1963, matching the grosses of Alfred Hitchcock's *The Birds* and topping the returns of McQueen's self-appointed rival Paul Newman in the latter actor's Oscar-nominated title role as *Hud*.[45]

Even today, *Escape* remains a compelling homage to what Ernest Hemingway called "grace under pressure." Almost forty years later, *Esquire* critic Tom Carson, after calling it the "greatest boys' movie of all time," credited the basic story with "such dramatic clarity that we've spared the big-picture lectures that drag down so many World War II blockbusters—the 'Dammit, man, don't you realize that Hitler has been master of Europe for four years now?' sort of thing." For all this praise of the human spirit during war, Carson goes on to state the obvious: "Steve McQueen is [still] the reason people remember *The Great Escape*."[46]

As Sturges has raised the artistic bar in each successive installment of this trilogy, McQueen has more than kept pace with his depictions of edgy antiheroic loners, gifted with a brash humor and a fierce independence. Just as McQueen's real racing exploits added a special aura to his motorcycle adventures in *Escape*, the uniqueness of the actor's persona is anchored in how much it reflects the real man. McQueen even embraced the title, "the great escape," as a metaphor for how acting saved him from a life of crime in the mean streets. But as with most memorable modern movie personalities, we often gauge greatness by how much it brings to mind past legends. McQueen manages the distinct accomplishment of being both a singular star and yet being reminiscent of his iconoclastic boyhood hero, Bogart. With Sturges's trilogy as a launching pad, McQueen was now primed to pursue a film career every bit as superb as Bogie's.

Between the Trilogy Pictures

"That's the big difference between us [Steve McQueen and first wife Neile Adams]. I mostly follow my instincts; she follows her conscience. And there's no way of compromising because we both have strong ideas about what we must or should do. She'll think of the children, and I'll think of myself."[1]

STEVE MCQUEEN (1963)

Though director John Sturges's trilogy of *Never So Few* (1959), *The Magnificent Seven* (1960), and *The Great Escape* (1963) was instrumental in making Steve McQueen an international movie star, these years were also filled with a great deal more. Just as his position in the entertainment profession had undergone great change, so had his personal life. McQueen's career had finally eclipsed that of his beautiful dancer/actress stage-star wife, Neile Adams. There would be no more mistaken references to "Mr. Adams," or the anonymity of the random show-business column blurb noting, "Neile Adams and husband" at some event. Though McQueen often paid public lip service to his wife's career in the early years, privately he would have preferred a stay-at-home spouse. This was a reflection of a childhood largely bereft of both a mother and a stable home.

While the McQueens were married in 1956, it was not until his breakout success with the television Western series, *Wanted: Dead or Alive*, that he became the primary breadwinner in the family. Consistent with McQueen's traditional ideas about the roles of men and women, it was also during this time that the couple started a family. Their first child, Terry Leslie McQueen, was born June 5, 1959. She was named after her father, who had been christened Terrence Steve. A son, Chadwick Steven McQueen, was born on December 28, 1960. While the family numbers seemed to say two children and two parents, Adams was really operating as the mother of three. As this chapter's opening quote suggests, McQueen's lack of a real childhood seemed to fuel an adult need to follow his every personal whim, acting like an overgrown adolescent. As McQueen's journalist friend Peer J. Oppenheimer wrote in 1962, "with Steve you don't allow yourself to get annoyed. You take him as he is, or you might as well not try to be friends with him in the first place."[2]

Despite this "kidult" manner, however, it bears noting that Mc-Queen was at his best with children, whether his own or those at California Junior Boys Republic in Chino, California. In addition to the time and money he contributed to Boys Republic, there were countless examples of generosity directed at youth through the years, often tied to a movie production. While shooting *The Sand Pebbles* (1966) in Taiwan, the McQueens and director Robert Wise became aware of a Catholic orphanage run by Father Edward Wajniak. Its primary mission was helping young girls who had turned to prostitution, a situation often forced upon them by their families. With most economic opportunities there available only to males, this "oldest profession" was frequently the fate awaiting the girls. McQueen found this unacceptable, and he and his wife gave the orphanage twenty-five thousand dollars, a figure matched by Wise. McQueen continued to send regular contributions until his 1980 death. These donations included cash, clothes, and even autographs—signed pictures being something he did not normally do. Thus, the resale value for the orphanage of these autographs was sizable.

Another example of McQueen's largesse toward children was his propensity to spend twenty thousand dollars at the drop of a hat when he saw a sorry excuse for a playground. Such anonymous gifts also frequently included balls and bats and other baseball equipment suddenly turning up at schools and community centers. The actor had never been much of an athlete as a youngster, but, because of his poor circumstances, he had never received any training or encouragement in that area.

McQueen's later accomplishments as a racer and a polo player revealed previously unrealized athletic skills. His many youth-directed donations promised to help children find the joy/fulfillment of tapping into these abilities when they were still youngsters. Unlike McQueen's father, the actor's relationship with children proved that the apple can fall a long way from the tree.

Even late in McQueen's life, when he was dying of cancer, the actor's connection with children surfaced in poignant ways. For example, a youngster had reportedly jumped a McQueen chain-link fence as a shortcut to his house. The reclusive territorial actor, now all but unrecognizable behind a heavy beard, eventually confronted the boy and read him the riot act. But McQueen soon felt he had overreacted and ran after the boy. A biographer of the actor's final days noted about the meeting: "It wasn't much later that the two of them returned and . . . for the next few hours . . . Steve showed off his prized possessions [which included a great array of antique toys]. The youngster may not have recognized the angry man with the beard who first chased him away but by the time he left for home that day he not only had stars in his eyes but a few mementos and an invitation to return."[3]

McQueen's love of youngsters, especially his two children, Terry and Chad, was a constant throughout his life, even when other things were unraveling. In Adams's memoir she briefly discusses this consistency, at a time when their marriage is starting to fail: "We went about our business as usual, and more and more I saw changes in his attitude towards me and toward life in general. The one thing that never wavered was his attitude toward the children. He loved them and they knew it— no matter how strange Daddy acted sometimes [such as his increased moodiness and ongoing use of marijuana and peyote]."[4] But as the chapter opening quote suggests, Adams was the day-to-day parent, with McQueen often missing in action.

Ironically, the McQueens' plans for a family, even before he professionally found himself with *Wanted* and *Never So Few*, resurrected his interest in finding his father, Bill. Though the elder McQueen had abandoned his wife, Julian, and their child when Steve was a baby, there had been some intermittent contact between the couple in later years. These clues placed Bill in the greater Los Angeles area. Since a working Adams called this same area home early in her marriage to Steve, when he had out-of-work free time to brood about his derelict dad, the troubled actor had the couple playing Nick and Nora Charles—gumshoes in search of a long missing father—during their every free moment.

This was not a happy quest, however, about a father and son perhaps reconnecting. Despite McQueen's previously established proclivity to romanticize his devil-may-care swashbuckling aviator dad, the actor had a great deal of unresolved anger about the abandonment. McQueen's obsessive compulsion to find his father was one way to work through that anger. The search continued into 1959, by which time McQueen had become a television star in *Wanted.*

McQueen discovered that his father lived only a few miles away in the Echo Park section of Los Angeles, a neighborhood prominently featured in the fictional movie mystery *Chinatown* (1974). As McQueen searched there, the area produced additional angst for the amateur sleuth, since Echo Park was where he had once briefly lived with his mother and an abusive stepfather. Ultimately the actor's persistence paid off. He received a phone call from Bill's common-law wife, who invited the actor to come and talk. This attempt at closure had a bittersweet conclusion. McQueen's father had died of heart failure three months before. In addition, the real "kick" to McQueen's detective story was that his father was a fan of *Wanted*! Each Saturday night he would religiously watch the show and ask, "I wonder if that's my boy?"

Bill's wife gave the actor his father's Zippo lighter, which had been engraved with his later nickname, "Red." She also gave McQueen a picture of Bill, which documented an uncanny resemblance between the two men. Though Steve's anger once had him claiming he could almost kill his father over the abandonment issue, a more mellow McQueen later poignantly confessed, "Did I resent him leaving us? I really don't know what to feel about him. I just wanted to stand and talk to him, no more or less. Although I never met him, I felt a real sense of loss when I found out he died."[5] When McQueen's mother died a few years later, he added these additional remarks about his dad, "I am sorry I never knew my father. I lost my mother not long ago, too, you know. I didn't realize how much it would hit me 'til it happened. [Because] we weren't all that close really. Mom always said I was [adventurous] like my dad."[6]

Interestingly, despite these heartfelt revelations, when McQueen told this story to his macho friends, such as stuntman Bud Ekins, he played the tough guy, claiming to have immediately thrown away the lighter and presumably destroyed the photograph. He seemed to be trying to embrace that emotionally detached persona he had first fashioned for himself back in his Greenwich Village days, when a former girlfriend had described this demeanor with a comic profaneness: "It was like he had put a condom over his heart." Tough guy or poser, McQueen had kept the lighter and later gave it to his daughter. The picture of his father had been saved, too. (Given that both of McQueen's parents were only in their fifties when they died, the actor had a premonition he would not live a long life. He died at fifty.)

Besides the complex mix of searching for a father and demonstrating an increased sensitivity to youngsters, the Sturges trilogy years also paralleled McQueen's immersion in automobile and motorcycle racing. Like the old axiom, "Success has many fathers," McQueen's interest in racing has numerous potential starting points. One might begin with fellow Hoosier legend James Dean, a pioneer among Hollywood stars to mix movies with racing professionally.[7] The young McQueen had aped everything about Dean, from his acting style to riding motorcycles around New York City. When a passenger once complained to Dean about his love of speed, the actor's answer now sounds like vintage McQueen: "I've got to go places in a hurry. There just isn't time."[8] In fact, here is a later similar comment by McQueen: "I want to go places and I want to go fast. I've hurried all my life. It's a way of life with me."[9] Dean's groundbreaking move to racing would undoubtedly have planted a seed in the mind of the then copycat McQueen.

Like Dean, McQueen's articulateness about racing involved the compounding mix of drama and danger. But as if to further footnote

the Dean influence, McQueen's comments sometimes mix in other
perilous passions embraced by the other actor, such as bullfighting:
"The element of danger entered into it [racing]. As in bullfighting, not
only is there danger but there's the same kind of magnificent drama,
including a matter of style."[10] In a *Saturday Evening Post* article from
1961, McQueen further embellished the idea of risking it all: "I finally
thought to myself, 'Man, you can get *killed* doing this!' But I like the
idea of having to overcome the fright, you know? It's quite a feeling,
a real pure feeling."[11] Consciously or not, McQueen's willingness to
take chances tapped into another Dean level of fascination with racing.
Death by inches was just not Dean's style. This is why he was so drawn
to both bullfighting and Ernest Hemingway's artistically concise take on
the subject in *Death in the Afternoon* (1932): "The only place where you
could see life and death, i.e., violent death now that the wars were over,
was in the bull ring."[12] While Dean had no plans to "check out" early,
he also believed, as did Hemingway, that a life without dangerous ritual
was not worth living. Obviously, this was a credo very much embraced
by McQueen. And it bears noting that both these Hollywood Hoosiers
came of age at a time when Hemingway machismo, to the point of an
elevated primitivism, set the standard for what represented a well-lived
male life.

Besides this multifaceted Dean connection, McQueen was also
drawn to racing because it avoided the collaborative nature of making movies. He was so passionate about the inherent independence of
racing that his description of the phenomenon could border on the
poetic: "An actor is a puppet, manipulated by a dozen other people.
Auto racing has [the] dignity [of being individualistic]. But you need
the same absolute concentration. You have to reach inside yourself and
bring forth a lot of broken glass [painful experiences to toughen one for
racing]."[13]

Given the fact, as previously noted, that McQueen often saw the
acting profession as less than macho, his attraction to the proverbial
"thrills and chills" of racing undoubtedly represented his connection
to that era's Hemingway/Dean mystique of manliness. For McQueen,

Above: McQueen astride one of the numerous motorcycles he owned, circa 1965. *Right:* McQueen admired actor Clark Gable (wearing helmet) and loved racing, making him a fan of the Indianapolis 500 film To Please a Lady *(1949).*

racing was that unique event in life in which there was, briefly, a real winner. But this was rarefied territory, because as he was fond of saying, "If you can't cut it, you gotta back out."[14] Though McQueen's "broken glass" monologue equated the focus needed for racing as comparable to that needed for acting, he was much more likely to comically sing the superior skills of the track: "Racing drivers are the only people I have ever really respected. . . . They are fascinating to watch. Their concentration makes an actor's concentration look like a bowl of skimmed milk."[15]

McQueen's machismo connection to racing also had another component. The actor first became seriously involved in this competition at a time when he was just emerging from a quasi-househusband role in his marriage to Adams. Whatever McQueen's reservations about the manliness of the acting profession, being in a secondary marital position in his mind was even worse. Undoubtedly, racing represented an obvious way for him to reassert his manhood. Coupled with this, of course, was a wonderfully simple bonus—McQueen was very good at racing. It is always satisfying to embrace those things at which one excels.

Ironically, the actor so triumphed as a racer that he considered leaving the entertainment industry to focus on automobile and motorcycle competition. Thus, in late 1962 he made headlines when he opted for acting over racing: "It's not that I like racing any less, or acting more but. . . . In order to be proficient in racing you must eat, sleep and think about it all the time and you must devote every minute to practicing to keep a winning edge at [a] peak. I simply don't [now] have the time, for my [acting] business interests have grown [to] considerable proportions . . . and take me all over the world."[16] Additional factors contributing to this decision were both a wife (Adams) and assorted movie producers dead set against his risky racing.

Though acting won the war, McQueen could never completely divorce himself from the racing bug. After all, it had become almost addictive. He once even claimed, "Speed rivals making love"—quite a statement from one of Hollywood's famed Lotharios. McQueen did, however, eventually focus on motorcycle competition. The actor found that, at least initially, his wife and the movie money people were less concerned about the dangers of two-wheel racing. McQueen's banner year for motorcycle competition was 1964, when he won five separate California dirt-bike races using a modified Triumph cycle prepared by Ekins. More impressively, McQueen's accomplishments accorded him the honor of representing the United States in the 1964 International Six-Day Motorcycle Trial. First run in 1913 in Great Britain, this prestigious event pitted more than two hundred entrants over a twelve-hundred-mile course that ran in daily stages of two hundred miles.

The host country for the 1964 event was East Germany—the winning team for the previous year. "I remember the night before the race they had a parade of nations in this big hall, about the size of a football stadium, and the guys from each team marched for their country," McQueen said. "I stood up there, holding the American flag, right between the Russians and the East Germans, and it was an emotional moment for me. I was really proud to be there."[17] The comic-minded McQueen also recalled the competition's opening breakfast, which included cold eel and coffee black enough "to dye your socks in." The American team won three medals, and only a spectator straying onto the course, which caused McQueen to safely crash over a ravine, kept the actor from finishing his portion of the race.

As an addendum to this accident in an international competition, as well as the belief that motorcycle racing was safer than the four-wheel variety, one should be aware of McQueen's assorted dirt-bike injuries. They included facial injuries that twice required plastic surgery, teeth knocked out, a broken shoulder bone, wrists, fingers, toes, nose, and assorted other injuries to his hands and knees. So much for "nothing to worry about." As movie productions further restricted all kinds of after-hours racing for McQueen, he became adroit at including dangerous speeding sequences in his movies, from the motorcycle scenes in *The Great Escape*, to the signature car chase in *Bullitt* (1968)—situations in which the actor could do at least some of the driving.

In 1966 McQueen even wrote an article for *Popular Science* magazine titled, "Motorcycles: What I Like in a Bike—and Why."[18] A bonus to the essay also had the actor encouraging safety for new riders: "I think you have to learn to ride away from heavy traffic. Myself, I like to ride flat out, where it's allowed."[19] But this was no random pitch for marketing purposes, because the 1960s also saw the actor invent and patent a new safety seat, the "Baja Bucket," for off-road dune buggies, which were also sometimes used in competitive racing. The Bucket has saved many lives in accidents in which the dune buggy has flipped over.

The extent to which racing defined McQueen might best be showcased in a favored prayer shared with a friend near the close of the actor's life. As implied in earlier McQueen quotes, racing had become a metaphor for life itself: "Lord, I pray as I race today, keep me safe along the way, not only me but others too as they perform the jobs they do. I know, God, that in a race, the driver sets the pace. But in this race of life I pray, help me, Lord, along the way. Although I know I am a sinner help me to believe that with God you're always a winner. Amen."[20]

In discussing McQueen and racing, or even acting in general, much has been made of Dean's influence. But there is another link from both actors' joint New York days that has often lingered in the more tabloid-orientated profiles of both men. In doing a biography on Dean it was necessary for me to address the performer's sometimes bisexual tendencies—his willingness to explore homosexuality for acting "research" (he played a gay character in the Broadway play *The Immoralist*, 1954) and simply to advance his career (Dean's live-in liaison with CBS radio director Roger Brackett).[21]

Dean strikes a contemplative pose in a scene from East of Eden. *Introduced to Dean on the set, John Steinbeck, the author of the book on which the film is based, was heard to exclaim: "Jesus Christ, he is Cal!"*

No one is making comparable claims about McQueen. But his links to the controversial fellow Hoosier, particularly an incident at Dean's frequent New York address, the Iroquois Hotel, has sometimes raised gossipy speculation about whether McQueen ever did any "experimenting" with his early idol Dean. In John Gilmore's *Laid Bare: A Memoir of Wrecked Lives and the Hollywood Death Trip*, Dean guests witnessed an intimate scene between the star and McQueen, with the latter back combing Dean's long hair.[22] Dean seemed to almost court McQueen, including inviting the worshipful actor backstage to a performance of *The Immoralist*. But as Dean was wont to do, he soon cut McQueen off completely. Speculation about any sexual "research" on McQueen's part has also been fueled by the actor's proclivity to sometimes wear attire during his Greenwich Village days linked to the gay subculture (such as short Bermuda shorts) as well as choosing to do Actors Studio sketches with a patently gay subtext.

This rather thin stack of unverified supposition represents the complete case for any questions about McQueen briefly being bisexual. Normally, this would *not* constitute enough for any further speculation. But many critics will not let the subject go. For example, Adams's memoir, easily the best of the autobiographies written by each of McQueen's three wives, was fittingly praised by *Variety*'s reviewer. Yet, the writer still takes her to task because she "never discusses rumors of her ex-husband's homosexuality."[23]

Consequently, here are some brief considerations of the subject at hand. First, there is no documented proof of anything but heterosexual activity by McQueen. Reputable McQueen biographer Penina Spiegel has explored the subject most thoroughly through various interviews with insiders and uncovered nothing.[24] Given the monetary value that this sort of story might fetch, based upon the tabloid excesses of today, the silence speaks volumes. In contrast, there has been so much chronicling of McQueen's notorious womanizing, that a precise list of his heterosexual conquests would be thicker than a New York phone book.

Second, as this book has suggested, McQueen had a mischievous sense of humor. Consistent with this, the actor might have just been posing for comic effect, or as he liked to sometimes describe his pranks, "Twisting their melons [playing with people's heads]." At least one of McQueen's Actors Studio friends, the later Tony Award-winning performer Charles Nelson Reilly, was eventually best known for how he entertainingly wore his gayness on his frequent and ubiquitous television appearances. (The actor appeared on Johnny Carson's *The Tonight Show* nearly a hundred times, and the host was fond of introducing him as, "Charles, Nelson, and Reilly . . . all three are here tonight.")[25] I would posit that any provocative McQueen action from 1950s New York, which has fueled this undercurrent of questions about his sexuality, was probably driven by a straight guy's attempts to emulate a broadly gay acquaintance, such as Reilly, for comic effect. As a footnote to the period, McQueen's New York home of Greenwich Village had a homosexual community much more open and proud of their sexual orientation than much of America's then largely "closeted" gays. Thus, McQueen's affectionate spoofing of this subculture might have been misconstrued by straights not familiar with homosexuality's high visibility in the actor's world.

While I continue to believe gay allegations about McQueen are poppycock, one could play devil's advocate and quote the line from *Hamlet*, he "doth protest too much me thinks." That is, McQueen was often overly sensitive about any implied homosexual tendencies, sometimes with unintended comic results. He once punched an English acquaintance, who asked the actor if he wanted a "fag" (McQueen was unaware that this was English slang for a cigarette). Along more understandable lines, given McQueen's youth, was the aforementioned stormy "last straw" fight he had with his mother, when the teenager learned that his new apartment roommate was gay.

Returning, however, to the "protest too much" hypothesis, one could also expand upon how McQueen's overly machismo nature (from racing to womanizing) probably bore indirect links to 1950s pop culture's love affair with the poster boy for manliness, Hemingway. Rare were the people who questioned this he-man persona during Hemingway's lifetime, though novelist and playwright Edna Ferber is alleged to have once kidded him, "Why don't you take that false hair off your chest and let us see what's really behind it." Only later, in Hemingway's posthumous publications, such as the 1970 novel *Islands in the Stream*, does it become possible to believe his overly macho persona was a smokescreen for more ambiguous feelings about his sexuality. Might this same scenario have also applied to McQueen? Although it is possible, all this speculation seems like "much ado about nothing."

In addition to the aforementioned personal history that transpired during the Sturges trilogy years, McQueen actually made three other movies: *The Honeymoon Machine* (1961) and *Hell Is for Heroes* and *The War Lover* (both 1962). Though they had neither the critical nor the commercial success of the Sturges films, this second trilogy, by default, was also important in the ascendancy of McQueen's career.

The first of the trio, *The Honeymoon Machine*, now plays as atypical McQueen fare, given one's action adventure expectations for the actor's filmography. *Honeymoon* is a serviceman farce about two sailors (McQueen and Jack Mullaney) and a civilian (Jim Hutton) who use a navy computer to try to beat a Venice casino roulette wheel. Couple these con artists with two pretty girls (Paula Prentiss and Brigid Bazlen), and mix in a loud-mouthed admiral (former Oscar-winner Dean Jagger), and one has the ingredients for huckster high jinks and romance. Though not in a class with the then recent naval farce, *Operation Petticoat* (1959, with Cary Grant and Tony Curtis), *Honeymoon* is a still entertaining outing in this serviceman comedy subgenre. (Interestingly, *Honeymoon*'s home studio, Metro-Goldwyn-Mayer, originally wanted to cast Grant in what became the McQueen part. But the Hollywood icon was unavailable. Still, in fairness to McQueen, Grant had then been at the top of Hollywood's farcical film player's list for years.)

Honeymoon's reviews were mixed, which is possibly fitting, given that it was based upon only a modestly successful Broadway play, *The Golden Fleecing* (eighty-four performances in 1959). Consequently, while the *New York Times* complained, "It is a wild and labored operation, and when it finally comes to an end, one wonders whether it has even been bona fide farce," the *New York Daily News* called it "a delightful old-fashioned slapstick comedy."[26] As if to average things out, the *Hollywood Citizen News* assumed a modestly positive middle ground: "It's a far-fetched tale, but nicely and briskly directed for laughs, and there's sufficient romancing to keep the ladies happy, too."[27]

Honeymoon did better with movie industry insider publications, from the *Motion Picture Exhibitor* calling the picture a "very funny comedy" to the *Independent Film Journal* describing it thus: "A side-splitting color and CinemaScope comedy, *Honeymoon* hilariously expands on the plot and personalities of the stage play."[28] Given Mc-Queen's often mediocre notices in later comedies, such as *Soldier in the Rain* (1963), the biggest eye-opener about the *Honeymoon* reviews was the superlatives for his performance. Both *Variety* and the *New York Journal American* said essentially the same thing: "[McQueen] reveals a promising flair for romantic comedy."[29] And the *Los Angeles Examiner* praised his acting as "brisk, sure, cocky, [and] his comedy timing as Lt. Fergie Howard sets the pace of the plot."[30]

Ironically, McQueen author Casey St. Charnez later revealed that the actor was never pleased with his *Honeymoon* performance: "He hates himself in it. He can't believe he's made a movie he hates more than *The Blob* [1958]."[31] McQueen is too hard on himself. While his comedy acting might now seem a bit forced, with a "smart-ass delivery" (to borrow a phrase from St. Charnez), this downgrading of McQueen's performance here is more a product of how it currently clashes with the action-hero minimalism that became his persona. Though this is still early in his career, McQueen had already successfully tapped into this less-is-better characterization, from his television bounty hunter on *Wanted: Dead or Alive* to the previous year's loner gunslinger in the epic Western *The Magnificent Seven* (1960). While McQueen did not fully articulate it at the time, *any* broad comedy would have clashed with the maverick misfit screen persona he was intuitively constructing even then.

Paradoxically, his minimalist acting precluded much of McQueen's natural wit from being showcased in his movies. Of course, his propensity to play the quiet loner did up the ante when he said something with comic efficiency, such as telling Eli Wallach's bandit in *Seven*, "We deal in lead, friend." All in all McQueen was right to embrace this pared-down personality. The way it complements a movie reminds me of a Leonard Michaels short story: "All the ornament seems burned off, purified; the narratives distilled and gorgeously plain, as only a great stylist's can become."[32]

This more "purified" McQueen was certainly on exhibit in the picture that immediately followed *Honeymoon*, director Don Siegel's *Hell Is for Heroes* (with working titles *Separation Hill* and *The War Story*). Siegel's long screen career is now most famous for its many collaborations with Clint Eastwood, including *Coogan's Bluff* (1968), *Two Mules for Sister Sara* (1970), *The Beguiled* (1971), and *Dirty Harry* (1972). But like Robert Wise, McQueen's later director on *The Sand Pebbles* (1966), Siegel was first well known in the 1940s as a film editor. In the 1950s he was hailed as a directing "auteur" of note by the influential publication *Cahiers du Cinema*, with two provocative B pictures putting him on the movie map, *Riot in Cell Block 11* (1954) and the original *Invasion of the Body Snatchers* (1956). Transcending their separate genres, the films became pop-culture phenomena that still resonate with audiences.

Siegel was a late addition to *Heroes*, which had a script by Oscar-winning writer Robert Pirosh. The screenplay was based upon Pirosh's World War II experiences, a subject area that he had already mined for an Academy Award on *Battleground* (1949). Plus, his war experiences later were the basis for the long-running television series *Combat* (1962–67). The well-qualified Pirosh was set to direct *Heroes*. But in an early show of star power, McQueen had him bounced from the production over creative differences on the script. The actor wanted more focus on his character.

Siegel came in as both script doctor and director, giving the picture a greater antiwar emphasis that met with McQueen's approval. But this did not mean there was any kind of lovefest between the two. Indeed, their differences almost led to physical confrontations. "On several occasions . . . [we] were close, very close, to fighting," said Siegel. "He [McQueen] walked around with the attitude that the burden of preserving the integrity of the picture was on his shoulders and all the rest of us were company men ready to sell out, grind out an inferior picture for a few bucks and the bosses. One day I told him that his attitude bored me, that I was as interested in the picture being good as he was, and that when this fact sunk through his thick head we would get along. I could see he was angry. I knew he was capable of violence and I knew he could whip me. So I decided that if he got up and came toward me I would hit him first as hard as I could and hope for the best. Fortunately, for me, he didn't get up. Eventually, we grew to like each other."[33]

Like *The Magnificent Seven*, *Heroes* is about seven men asked to do a dangerous task. *Heroes* also anticipates *The Great Escape*, in that both films are ensemble pieces based on true World War II stories. More specifically, there are also certain parallels between McQueen's character from *Heroes* and the war figures he soon played—the prisoner-of-war flyer in *Escape* and the bomber pilot in *The War Lover*. *Heroes*' screenwriter Pirosh later provided this description of McQueen's character in the film: "[Reese] was just a guy who probably couldn't make it on the outside and away from the army and who had terrible feelings about going back to civilian life. He was an off-center guy, a misfit, a killer but not a psychopath."[34] This is a description that perfectly matched his title character in the fittingly named *The War Lover* and is a first cousin to his Cooler King in *Escape*. In fact, many critics, Pirosh's claim notwithstanding, would be comfortable with labeling the trio psychopathic. For example, of these three McQueen characters, his *Escape* flyer is the most normal. Yet, the *Los Angeles Times*'s review still described him as "psychopathically intense."[35]

Given these parallels, one could posit that McQueen's much-praised work in *Escape* was built upon a two-picture warm-up. But in *Escape* some McQueen humor and humanity (such as that ball and glove in solitary confinement) is allowed into his characterization. Both *Heroes* and *War Lover* lay bare a rather frightening figure—the *Hollywood Citizen News* even called his *Heroes* soldier "stone-faced and unpleasant."[36] McQueen's soldier is part of a small American unit forced to hold off a German attack, with part of their defense being the ruse that their numbers are much larger. The unit's tricks range from McQueen's costar and real-life friend James Coburn making a jeep sound like a tank, to a miscast Bob Newhart recycling a signature element of his stand-up routine (the telephone monologues) as a way to fool the Germans (the comedian uses a bugged phone to make the enemy think the ridge is crawling with Americans). Although Newhart is funny in a supporting role, his part is at cross-purposes with the picture's overall somber tone.

Late in the film, with their officers dead or missing, Coburn's character finds himself in charge, and he asks McQueen's Reese for advice. Predictably, the killing-machine star suggests attacking the German pillbox that controls the area. The attempt proves futile and McQueen's character is criticized. But ironically, new orders and new troops are soon brought in, with the pillbox again the target. Siegel later said of this finale: "I am particularly pleased with . . . the entire ending in which McQueen is killed and the battle goes on while the picture ends. That wasn't the end of the picture as we had written it. The [original] ending was more affirmative and we had shot it but when I edited the picture I realized that at the peak of the battle I had nothing else I wanted to say, no feelings of possible affirmation. I wanted to show that my hero was blown up, which was horrifying, and that the rest were still going forward, that he would be forgotten, that the action of war is futile."[37] Consistent with these comments, film historian Jean-Pierre Coursodon later wrote, "All of Siegel's best films focus on conflicts between the individual and the hostile society around him, ending, quite often, with that individual's defeat."[38] This is certainly true of *Heroes* and Siegel's late masterpiece, *The Shootist* (1976, with John Wayne).

Heroes was a major critical hit, with McQueen pulling in outstanding notices. Yet, later biographies of the actor often gave his acting here short shrift. Malachy McCoy's McQueen book said, "The critics also found nothing particularly stimulating in his [*Heroes*] performance."[39] What follows are some of those "nothing" notices. The *New York Times* opened its *Heroes* review with this statement: "An arresting performance by Steve McQueen, a young actor with presence and a keen sense of timing, is the outstanding feature of . . . 'Heroes.'"[40] The *Hollywood Re-*

porter raved, "Steve McQueen, a young actor who has yet to give a mediocre performance, is arresting as a single-minded killing machine."[41] The *Los Angeles Examiner* credited him with giving a "grippingly real performance," while *Variety* waxed poetic at length: "McQueen plays the central role with hard-bitten businesslike reserve and an almost animal intensity, permitting just the right degree of humanity to project through a war-weary-and-wise veneer."[42]

Despite this high-profile praise, much remains underreported about the picture. Despite its anticipation of the later big-budget war ensemble film *Escape*, *Heroes* was a small movie monetarily. Things became so bad at one point that tough guy McQueen even had to turn his combativeness to physically defending the production from foreclosure on the cameras. Taking a stick, McQueen drew a circle in the sand around them and defiantly said, "Anyone who steps over that line gets the shit knocked out of him."[43] (For a more complete picture of McQueen at such an angry but defining positive moment, imagine his words spoken through the teeth of a chomping jaw, fortified with his standard two pieces of Juicy Fruit gum.) Another largely unknown *Heroes* factor is that it included a prologue during its theatrical run from President John F. Kennedy, a World War II veteran. This prologue was usually dropped in later television screenings, at least prior to the cable era. (The year after *Heroes* appeared, Hollywood produced a screen version of Kennedy's war heroics titled *PT 109*, with Cliff Robertson as the future president.)

Heroes was immediately followed by *The War Lover*, which also played very much like a Siegel picture. McQueen's bomber pilot faces another "hostile society," and he, too, dies during a final mission. Though *Lover* is flawed by having neither *Heroes'* quality script, nor a director of Siegel's abilities, *Lover* does recommend itself by simply granting McQueen more screen time. No ensemble cinema here, the film equally showcases McQueen's flyer with costar Robert Wagner, who together create sort of a contrasting bad "lover"/good "lover" competition over English beauty Shirley Ann Field.

McQueen's pilot also apes another pivotal Siegel element—his warrior mentality seems from an earlier time and place. (This might best be demonstrated in Siegel's movie milieu with Clint Eastwood's title character in *Dirty Harry*. His "modern" cop is really a throwback to the vigilante justice of the loner Western sheriff.) Having said this, however, *Lover* is McQueen's first film to also tap into the sexual charisma the actor evidently oozed in private. Thus, while his *Lover* character, to quote Hazel Flynn's *Hollywood Citizen News* review, describes his "cruel, almost hateful . . . dirty tricks," she still calls him a "very attractive man."[44] And there is certainly more chemistry between bad boy McQueen and the lovely Field, as compared to her scenes with the conscientious, wholesome-playing Wagner.

Variety's review addressed the picture's primary weakness: "The scenario seems reluctant to come to grips with the issue of this character's unique personality—a 'war lover' whose exaggerated shell of heroic masculinity covers up a psychopathic inability to love or enjoy normal relationships with women."[45] (Paradoxically, this clinical-sounding critique might also double as an insight into McQueen's ongoing problem with male-female relationships—life imitating art.) While John Hersey's novel, from which *Lover* is adapted, manages to make this correlation between the warrior mentality negating the traditional use of the term "lover," the movie struggles with the concept.

Though critics invariably noted this flaw, their praise of McQueen did not fault him. The *Los Angeles Times* said, "One may quarrel with the fact that those in charge . . . haven't developed motivation for McQueen's role sufficiently . . . [but] the actor gives a stout, vigorous performance."[46] *Variety* added, "That the central character emerges more of an unappealing symbol than a sympathetic flesh-and-blood portrait is no fault of McQueen, who plays with vigor and authority."[47] Many other reviews, such as the aforementioned *Hollywood Citizen News*, minimized the qualifiers, noting, "Performances are . . . of high caliber, with McQueen impressive as the man in love with fighting."[48]

McQueen later told syndicated Hollywood columnist Hedda Hopper that playing the almost psychopathic B-17 bomber pilot had been exhausting, resulting in the actor taking several months off: "It really twisted me up, so I decided to knock off for a time. But I think it'll be a magnificent picture. It's the best work Bob Wagner has ever done. . . . I'm trying to regain some of the weight I lost before I go back to Eu-

rope [*Lover* was shot in England] for 'The Great Escape.' I'm not an
actor who can go on the set and just turn it on when the cameras start
to roll; I have to live with it and it's very uncomfortable."⁴⁹

Of course, part of the exhaustion from the time spent in England
for the production of *Lover* had nothing to do with filmmaking. The
major attraction of going to Great Britain was to take in the country's rich racing tradition, particularly the Brands Hatch Circuit. Not
surprisingly, McQueen's competitive instincts kicked in, and despite
warnings about being sued by *Lover*'s home studio (Columbia) if the
production had to shut down due to an accident, McQueen did some

Above: *McQueen as Captain Buzz
Rickson and Robert Wagner as First
Lieutenant Ed Bolland at the controls of
a bomber in* The War Lover *(1962). His
role in the movie as a pilot was a partial
catalyst for McQueen's later real-life flying.* **Right:** *McQueen, Shirley Ann Field,
and Wagner stride together in front of a
B-17 bomber for the World War II film*
The War Lover.

minor racing during weekend club events. The actor's new best friend was British racing legend Stirling Moss, who tutored the American on the fastest route around several circuits. Fittingly, McQueen's two primary purchases in England were a four-wheel-drive Land Rover and a 1,100cc Formula Junior Cooper racing car.

The actor's joy in all things mechanical once prompted him to observe, "I love machinery. I'd walk a hundred miles to see a piece of good machinery. Why I even love washing machines!" This attitude also had ties to the *Lover* production.[50] McQueen was fascinated with the three restored B-17 Flying Fortresses used in the shoot. Though the actor did not obtain his pilot's license until the late 1970s, this picture was a factor in that development. But beyond simply flying, McQueen the mechanic was drawn to the bombers' massive engines.

McQueen's time in England for the production of *Lover* even involved some unintended slapstick. That is, with a new picture payday high of seventy-five thousand dollars—almost a year's salary for his recently completed television series—the actor decided to embrace the on location good life by staying at London's tony Savoy Hotel. But McQueen's casual entertaining habits turned into a Mack Sennett-type incident that resulted in the Savoy kicking him out. While fixing cheese toast in his underwear for some late-hour guests, the star's hot plate caused the curtains to catch on fire. In search of a fire extinguisher, the boxer shorts-attired McQueen skidded into the hotel corridor like Wile E. Coyote pursing the Road Runner. Snobbish guests were not amused by this misadventure, despite seeing a movie star in his underwear, and an ultimate happy, water-soaked conclusion (a wet film "finis" often being favored by Sennett, too). Regardless of what the Savoy management thought, McQueen was on the verge of never again having to be concerned about what anyone else ever thought.

1960s Stardom, Despite Some Under-the-Radar Movies

"Right now I've got a real chance to grab that big brass ring, and, man, you better believe I'm ready to do some grabbin.' I got me a house on a hill, an ol' lady who digs me, two healthy kids, and plenty of fruit and nuts on the table. The lean days are over—and the ride from here on leads straight to Candyland!"[1]

STEVE MCQUEEN

The seventy-five thousand dollar salary Steve McQueen made for *The War Lover* (1962) had jumped to three-quarter of a million dollars for *The Sand Pebbles* (1966). Fueled in large part by the monster success of the John Sturges-directed *The Great Escape* (1963), McQueen was one of the seminal screen stars of the 1960s and 1970s, a regular fixture among the annual top-ten box-office stars from 1967 to 1975.[2] In 1963 the McQueens had moved from a relatively modest home in Los Angeles's Nichols Canyon to an eighteen-room mansion overlooking the Pacific Ocean. The title of a later *Architectural Digest* article summarized the setting: "A Brentwood [Los Angeles] Retreat Suited to the Dynamic Star." The same piece recorded McQueen's first view of the house: "We drove through this big electric gate and started around a mountain with a rock wall on one side and all these trees. Finally we came to the top and drove under a stone archway into this medieval Spanish courtyard—and my eyes were popping."[3] According to McQueen's first wife, Neile Adams, the couple felt "love at first sight" for the estate, immediately nicknaming what would soon become their new home "the castle."

Major selling points for the actor were the walled privacy and the isolation, and a large stone courtyard with which to show off his growing collection of sports cars and motorcycles. Given Adams's Latin background, she was especially attracted to the mansion's Mediterranean style, sort of a French château in southern California. The furnishings were casually elegant, mixing McQueen's rustic tastes with Adams's art-conscious decorations. The living room featured original paintings and antiques, with bull horns over the fireplace and a slate pool table—a special favorite with friend Peter Sellers. Accenting "the castle" nickname, and giving the home a masculine tone, were interior walls often composed of textured stone, with complementary flagstone floors. Although the three-acre estate also featured both a large swimming pool and an ocean-side terrace, McQueen spent most of his time in the multiple attached stone garages that the then health-conscious actor/mechanic had converted into a combination gym and automobile shop. Maybe McQueen's favorite aspect of the estate, however, was that "top of the mountain" location—such a fitting metaphor for the actor's new standing in the Hollywood pecking order.

Unfortunately, the "straight to Candyland" quote that opens the chapter, with its thankful references to wife and family, point a misleadingly positive profile of the actor. "That big brass ring" he speaks of grabbing included an endless stream of women and drugs. If being a brand-new movie star was not enough license to taste every temptation, suddenly having this power in the "free love" and drug experimenting 1960s broke down any final barriers.

In addition to Adams's frequent memoir references to her husband's sexual indiscretions, she is even more thorough about McQueen's drug abuse, noting that "it was a source of irritation throughout our marriage, this trying anything and everything new—whether it be peyote or LSD—but I learned to live with it to keep him happy. Having 'grass' [marijuana] in the house was by this time a given . . . Steve had several hiding places built especially for his stash. To please him I became adept at drying and separating the seeds from the grass itself . . . Steve was [also] adamant they [the help] not know about his drug use for fear they might sell this juicy bit of information."[4]

The memoir of B movie actress Mamie Van Doren provides another slant on this subject, mixing McQueen drug use with infidelity. Orchestrating a romantic tryst at the home of his friend Jay Sebring, the famous Hollywood hairdresser later murdered by the Charles Manson family, McQueen encouraged a reluctant Van Doren to take a form of LSD before sex: "Mamie, I've got some of the finest Sandex Sunshine Acid here. Let's drop a tab or two. . . . No bad trips on this shit. It's made by a pharmaceutical company. It's the best. It makes sex a totally new experience."[5]

McQueen's infidelities were not only hard on Adams, who often tried to look the other way, they also frequently made his wife see the potential for an affair in seemingly innocent situations. Well before the Van Doren escapade, Adams believed that Natalie Wood "was making a play" for McQueen during the production of *Love with the Proper Stranger* (1963).[6] While both Adams, and Wood's definitive biographer Suzanne Finstad, later indicated nothing had occurred, the actor's affairs undoubtedly added a great deal of stress to being Mrs. McQueen.[7] An

McQueen and Natalie Wood in a scene from Love with the Proper Stranger *(1963).*

Adams quote used as the title of a 1966 article about the couple perfectly captures the watchdog nature of being McQueen's wife: "'A Married Man Should Never Be Left Alone.'"[8]

Whether one reads hypocrisy into the aforementioned "Candyland" quote or not (with its references to home and hearth), that term would be applicable to some other McQueen public pronouncements during the 1960s. For example, when asked about that era's rebellious young, he replied, "I'm objective not emotional about the young people. I'm against LSD and I don't believe in student agitation for the sake of agitation."[9] While McQueen is obviously caught here in a "Do as I say not as I do" scenario with regard to drug use, this quote is also telling for missing a key point about "student agitation"—it seldom was just for the "sake of agitation." The 1960s rebelliousness was generally inspired by one or more of three very passionate causes: the anti-Vietnam War movement, civil rights, and equal rights for women.

Maybe McQueen misread the nature of this agitation because he was in opposite camps on two of the causes, Vietnam and feminism. As previously noted, the actor's blue-collar marine background had him strongly in favor of the war. And while he paid lip service to women's rights, such as being supportive of a working wife when Adams's career overshadowed his, McQueen's actions in private were anything but prowomen. The irony is that the two movies that anchored his international stardom, *The Magnificent Seven* (1960) and *The Great Escape*, helped fuel the 1960s youth movement against injustice. The first film was about helping persecuted people of color; the latter was a show of defiance against history's most infamously intolerant regime (Nazi Germany).

French film director Jean Renoir, one of cinema's greatest humanists, was fond of saying, "Everyone has his reasons." One might soften and/or at least better understand McQueen's sometime hypocritical comments by the fact that he wanted to believe in midwestern middle-class values. As a child he had never known a traditional, supportive home life, and that fueled his previously noted children-orientated charities. When the actor's widow, third wife Barbara, was doing the 2007 television talk-show circuit promoting her coffee table tribute book to the actor, *Steve McQueen: The Last Mile*, her most poignant revelation involved a sad pastime he enjoyed.[10] The couple engaged in an ongoing game of spying on seemingly normal families hoping for a voyeuristic look through a random window at something McQueen had not known as a child. Worse than the tragedy of Orson Welles's title character in *Citizen Kane* (1941, a movie McQueen admired), where an innocent childhood symbolized by a sled (Rosebud) is taken away when Kane the boy inherits a fortune, McQueen's wealthy adulthood never compensated for a black hole of a youth. At least the fictional Kane had memories; the aging McQueen, with Barbara as an accomplice, had to resort to "stealing" other people's memories by being peeping Toms.

This later moving tale notwithstanding, the 1960s McQueen, like many men, often had feet of clay and a short fuse if things did not go his way. As critic and historian David Thomson later wrote of the actor, "It isn't a pretty story but you feel its emotional authenticity. A lot of male movie stars live on the aura of toughness while hardly being on nodding terms with it in real life. By nature or early upbringing, McQueen was a hard, ungenerous spirit, a man who trusted no one and used anyone. From the beginning of his movie career, some of this hardness glared through the glamorized light and could not be explained away. In his early work [especially the focus films of this and the previous chapter], the business seemed uncertain whether to cast McQueen as a possible hero, or as a loner, psychotic or villainous."[11]

Ironically, Thomson's comments bring one back full circle to the 1960s; despite all these McQueen contradictions, he was the personification of the decade's coolest component, individualism. To borrow a lyric from a 1968 Frank Sinatra hit, McQueen always "did it my way." Here is a mid-1960s quote from McQueen that captures both that sense of independence and his ear for pop-culture language: "Racing is my sport, that's all. Sure I bust my melon [head] now and then, but I dig it a lot more than some of these hippy-dippy, finger-poppin' [formal Hollywood] parties they got going around town."[12]

McQueen biographer Christopher Sandford compared the actor to another musical icon more firmly anchored to the 1960s: "No one could be more fun than McQueen, no one more alive, with those bursts of joy, gloom, grit, aggression and vulnerability oddly intermingled in his vivid personality. He was the perfect Beatles-era film star, like the Fabs themselves, matching doses of irony and sincerity, frequently both flaunted at once. No wonder the studios freaked out."[13] (Paradoxically, like the Beatle to whom McQueen was closest, John Lennon, both men's treatment of women would be called into question by first-wife memoirs.[14])

Star status or not, not every 1960s McQueen movie was a major hit. After the career-making *Great Escape*, he would go three years before his next blockbuster success, *The Sand Pebbles*. Between those two epics he starred in five films: *Soldier in the Rain* (1963), *Love with the Proper Stranger* (1963), *Baby, the Rain Must Fall* (1965), *The Cincinnati Kid* (1965), and *Nevada Smith* (1966). Only *Stranger* scored at both the box office and with critics, though it was perceived as more of a vehicle for Wood. And while *Smith* received only mixed reviews, it was one of the "sleeper" commercial hits of a year in which ticket sales were dominated by James Bond and his parody knockoffs: *Thunderball*, *The Silencers*, and *Our Man Flint* (all 1966).[15] Still, all these McQueen movies are of interest, and not just for aficionados of the actor. In fact, with the passage of time, I would now argue that *Cincinnati* is not only the best of the bunch, it also merits inclusion on any list of McQueen's pantheon pictures.

The weakest picture in the group of five is *Soldier in the Rain*. The follow-up to *Great Escape* was a try for something entirely different. *Soldier* is a broad comedy peppered with sentimental drama, as Jackie Gleason plays an army sergeant swinger, with McQueen as his dumb fellow sergeant and protégé. While the Allied Artists production company ludicrously pitched the teaming in press releases as a variation of MGM's earlier pairing of opposites Clark Gable and Spencer Tracy, *Soldier*'s Gleason and McQueen are more reminiscent of a poor man's Stan Laurel and Oliver Hardy. Indeed, the movie's coscripter, Blake Edwards, the later director of Pink Panther fame, was a great fan of the duo. Moreover, Edwards's movie mentor, the great comedy director Leo McCarey, had teamed and molded Laurel and Hardy.[16]

McQueen was a Gleason fan and undoubtedly enjoyed the rotund comedian's beating of Paul Newman at pool in the much heralded *The Hustler* (1961, for which Gleason was Oscar-nominated). Newman, as noted previously, was the performer McQueen had long ago targeted as the star to beat on the road to the top of the Hollywood mountain. With James Dean's death, Newman had become a new McQueen role model, too. Biographer Penina Spiegel drew the following analogy: "[Newman] was everything Steve wanted to be: Newman raced, he acted, he was an intellectual, and he conducted a private life and a private love affair with the same woman. He had a reputation for sensitivity and good breeding, yet he was indisputably masculine. Newman was verbal, he was bright, and he was seemingly comfortable in his skin—all the things McQueen felt he wasn't."[17]

Ironically, for all this arbitrary competition and envy toward Newman as a paper lion, McQueen's attraction to no-account screen characters often seems Newman-like. Prime Newman examples from this

Jackie Gleason warily listens to a suggestion from McQueen in the military comedy Soldier in the Rain *(1963).*

period would be his high-profile Academy Award-nominated title characters in *The Hustler* and *Hud* (1963, when the actor seemed attracted
to several titles with the letter *H*). Even if McQueen's antiheroic outsider types do not remind one of Newman, McQueen's roles from this
time frequently have Newman's fingerprints on them. For example, Mc-
Queen's part in *Love with the Proper Stranger* was originally earmarked
for Newman. And *The Cincinnati Kid* is very much like *The Hustler*, in
which another young hotshot is pitted against a wily veteran—only the
game has changed, from pool to poker.

For all the promise of a McQueen teaming with Gleason in *Soldier in the Rain*, the picture ends up being a misfire. Plus, the fault lies
with McQueen. Gleason's performance is entertaining and borrows
nuances from the 1950s golden age of television, including Phil Silver's celebrated Sergeant Bilko (*Phil Silvers Show*), as well as Gleason's
own debonair comic character Reggie Van Gleason III (*Jackie Gleason
Show*). In contrast, McQueen's title character, from this William Goldman novel, is played as such a stereotypically stupid southern character
that one almost questions the wit of his *Great Escape* performance. *New
York Daily News* critic Wanda Hale, normally one of McQueen's biggest
fans, addressed that very subject in her *Soldier* review: "McQueen, with
phony accent, jumps around as if he had ants in his pants, overdoing it
so much that I could hardly recognize the fine comedian of 'The Great
Escape' and 'The Honeymoon Machine.'"[18]

Hale's *Honeymoon Machine* reference is yet more evidence on why
McQueen later disowned the part, though as I will note shortly, some
period critics enjoyed his performance. The actor even seems to borrow the broadness of his cartoonlike *Soldier* character from the, at
times, overplayed *Honeymoon* figure—yet another comic member of
the military. Though McQueen's *Honeymoon* con artist is far from the
backwoods simpleton of *Soldier*, the actor does seem to dumb down his
comedy characters. Even in the later underrated *The Reivers* (1969, from
William Faulkner's autobiographical novel), McQueen "essays" yet another down-home type, Boon Hogganbeck. All these figures are in stark
contrast from the dry wit that characterized McQueen's quasi-serious

parts, starting with his Josh Randall bounty hunter from *Wanted: Dead or Alive.*

McQueen's need to slip into "Ham City" when playing broad comedy is hard to explain, since he was also naturally funny in real life and had a flair for contributing understated humor to serious parts.[19] One could blame lack of direction, since all his marquee directors were bunched among the dramas. But maybe the secret lies in a more poignant explanation. Faulkner describes Boon in the novel as having the "mentality of a child."[20] As suggested earlier in the book, McQueen lived much of his adult life as if he was making up for the childhood he never had. While the public clearly preferred his maverick minimalist action persona, maybe the actor felt closer to his broadly comic characters because they tapped into the arrested-development adolescent who was the real McQueen.

Regardless, period critics were less than taken with the actor's *Soldier* characterization. *Variety's* panning review even negatively compared it to a misuse of a fellow Hollywood Hoosier's signature comic figure: "McQueen will not please fans with the characterization he has created—a kind of Southern-fried boob who reminds one of [Red Skelton's] Clem Kadiddlehopper. The style of portrayal is exaggerated and unnatural, and seems unnecessary."[21] The *New York Times* said, "There's nothing very funny about a halfwit, no matter how hard he may try to project himself as a comedian."[22] The *New York Post* stated, "[This] should set back his [McQueen's] blossoming career one full season to mid-winter. You will search a long time before you find a performer, riding as high as he did in 'The Great Escape,' falling as low as this."[23]

In fairness to both McQueen and the picture itself, some publications found positive things to say about *Soldier*. *Newsweek* believed Gleason was masterful in a three-dimensional characterization that avoided being a Sergeant Bilko caricature. Although it noted *Soldier* was clearly Gleason's film, the publication credited McQueen with being "a perfect ballet of the loose-limbed and loose-minded noncom, [who] even embodies the physical characteristics novelist Goldman described."[24] *Film Daily* observed, "McQueen is effective as an Army sergeant whose enlistment has one week to go," and the *Motion Picture Herald* added, "Curiously, while it is Gleason who is more usually associated with the humorous, it is McQueen who comes off better at that difficult art here."[25]

The disappointing response to *Soldier*, undoubtedly further fueled by a release less than a week after President John F. Kennedy's assassination, was a double frustration for McQueen. Besides his generally negative acting reviews, the Allied Artists production had been produced in conjunction with McQueen's own company, Solar, named for the Nichols Canyon Los Angeles street on which the McQueens lived when McQueen's two children were born. Thus, the first Solar outing, despite the actor's insightful casting of Gleason (for whom he generously gave top billing), ended up laying an egg. As a closing comic footnote to the film, McQueen's dangerous love of speed resulted in his receiving a fitting end-of-production gift from Gleason—Saint Christopher medals in the form of cuff links.

After being savaged by most reviewers on *Soldier*, McQueen did a quick critical turnaround in his next movie outing, *Love with the Proper Stranger*. The film was part romantic comedy, part melodrama, and McQueen played an antiheroic musician whose one-night stand with Wood resulted in an unwanted pregnancy. McQueen's notices were the sort that encourage the purchase of a scrapbook. "The performances of both Natalie Wood and Steve McQueen are brilliant indeed," gushed *Newsweek*, "and it would be only reasonable to expect Academy Award nominations for both of them. [Wood did receive an Oscar nod, losing to Patricia Neal for her performance in *Hud*]."[26] The *Saturday Review* waxed even more poetically, "Mr. McQueen . . . has developed, lately, into just about the best actor Hollywood has on hand. He always seems to believe in what he's doing and saying, manages humor and emotion without evidence of perceptible strain, and for modesty, offhandedness, and all-around ability could probably offer Marlon Brando a few lessons."[27] The *Hollywood Reporter* added, "McQueen slips into his role with deceptive facility. His bewilderment is keen, his disinclination to pay the piper heartfelt, but his strength of character is dominant and triumphs. McQueen does a fine job all around, a puppet in others' hands, and a live person taking the reins in his own hands."[28]

Twenty years after its Christmas 1963 release, the program notes for a special *Stranger* screening at the Los Angeles County Museum of Art linked the film with *Hud* as the surprise cinema hits of 1963.[29] After the broad comic overplaying of McQueen's *Soldier* performance that same calendar year, the actor's minimalist, but moving, acting in *Stranger* is a revelation. *Time* magazine's review even innocently tapped into an explanation on just why he was so natural in the part—a compliment that could double as a description of the real McQueen: "he makes a [romantic] pass in the offhand manner of a man who takes his love the way most people take after-dinner mints."[30]

Wood, who received a Best Actress nomination for her role as Angie Rossini, the pregnant salesgirl from Macy's department store, faces off with McQueen in Love with the Proper Stranger.

The Method-trained McQueen might also have borrowed from his sudden and unlikely marriage to Adams as a life lesson for the ultimately improbable union of his and Wood's characters in *Stranger*. Flaws noted at the time, such as the overly creepy setting for an illegal abortion (which is then canceled), or McQueen and Wood not really passing as Italian Americans, remain problematic. Still, the picture is an entertaining outing in a genre, romantic comedy, seldom associated with McQueen. The picture's unexpected hit status makes one ponder "What if?" questions about the action star's filmography—other directions in which McQueen might have taken his career.

In hindsight, *Stranger*'s success should not have been such a surprise. The picture's production team of director Robert Mulligan and his producer partner Alan Pakula had just orchestrated several Oscar wins for the previous year's instant classic, *To Kill a Mockingbird*. *Stranger*'s scriptwriter was the hot Broadway playwright Arnold Schulman, whose credits included *A Hole in the Head*, which he had adapted to the screen as director Frank Capra's last hit film in 1959. And Wood and McQueen, *Soldier* notwithstanding, were two of 1960s cinema's most promising young stars. Moreover, with this black-and-white picture often shooting on the streets of New York, the production felt like a slice-of-life homecoming for McQueen, who came of age in the city.

With regard to this New York realism, Mulligan and McQueen were on the same page. The director confessed, "[The movie] has lots of humor but it is not a comedy in the sense that a Stanley Shapiro movie [such as *Pillow Talk* or *Operation Petticoat*, both 1959] is a comedy. We are trying for [comic] realism. Under such conditions humor can come even from misfortune [an unwanted pregnancy, considering an abortion]. It all depends on how well we capture the authenticity of the people."[31] This sort of edginess is what drew McQueen to the movie, and a role he had to campaign for, since Newman was first on Mulligan's list. McQueen's passion for the part undoubtedly contributed to his performance.

The fact that McQueen did not receive an Academy Award nomination for *Stranger* might simply be explained by the randomness associated with awards. Plus, as with most years, there were several strong performances. The Oscar-nominated actors for 1963 were: Albert Finney for *Tom Jones*, Richard Harris for *This Sporting Life*, Rex Harrison for *Cleopatra*, Paul Newman for *Hud*, and winner Sidney Pointier for *Lilies of the Fields*. But just to play devil's advocate, one should add that actors are sometimes punished at awards time for being difficult. The most famous such example is the general belief that Judy Garland, though nominated, lost a near sure-thing Oscar for *A Star Is Born* (1954) for her detrimental behavior during that movie's production. Grace Kelly's win for *The Country Girl* (1954) seems today even weaker by comparison.

Flash forward a few years, and McQueen was the Hollywood poster child for being difficult, a trait first associated with his perfectionist tendencies during the run of his television series, *Wanted: Dead or Alive*. When asked by *Newsweek* about this subject, upon the release of *Stranger*, the actor bluntly replied: "Difficult. I'm difficult. That's the word around this town [Hollywood], is that McQueen's difficult. I am difficult, and that's because I always think I'm right. Guys who have been through a lotta hassles themselves are going to hold out for what's right, for the truth." During the same interview, McQueen went on to further embellish his provocative take on difficult: "[It] means to buck the system. The system is these old bastards with 30-year-old outlooks whose main concern is how much money they can scam out of a picture. Money is compromise and they seek compromise. It's their compromise that's killing the industry."[32] Did these kinds of comments, and a history of being a challenge cost McQueen an Oscar nomination for *Stranger*? One will never know. But I would bet it did.

With *Stranger* opening in late 1963, there is a mistaken belief that McQueen *immediately* took much of 1964 off to race motorcycles. The fact is McQueen went from *Stranger* to work on *Baby, the Rain Must Fall* (1965), whose working title was *The Traveling Lady*, the name of the 1954 Horton Foote play from which it was drawn. After production ceased on *Baby*, McQueen focused on racing, partly out of passion and partly to get over the disappointment of not scoring an Oscar nomination for *Stranger*. The motorcycle competition culminated with his selection to the United States team for the international Six-Day Motorcycle Trial, to be held in East Germany in September 1964.

McQueen's attraction to *Baby* was obvious—he would again be working with the *Mockingbird/Stranger* team of Mulligan (director) and Pakula (producer). In addition, they were bringing in their Oscar-winning screenwriter from *Mockingbird*, Foote, who had adapted Harper Lee's inspired novel to the screen. Not surprisingly, given this preestablished team, there are certain parallels between *Stranger* and *Baby*. McQueen again plays a self-centered, loner musician. Indeed, a comment by *Films and Filming* critic Ian Johnson, in his review of Mc-

McQueen and Lee Remick at the haunted house-like residence of his scary guardian in the bleak drama Baby, the Rain Must Fall *(1965).*

Queen's *Stranger* performance, applies equally well to the actor's *Baby* role: "Why are most antiheroes musicians?"[33] Another key link between the two properties is that both are essentially women's pictures. *Stranger* was a then-daring example of a woman embracing sexuality much as the stereotypical man would—a casual one-night stand. She then remains independent enough to refuse any and all marriage proposals of convenience when it turns out she is pregnant. McQueen's *Baby* costar, Lee Remick, must embrace the more traditional components of an old-fashioned women's film—the ever-faithful wife dealing with a problematic husband while trying to raise a child.

There is a final bittersweet link between the two pictures, if they are considered jointly. While *Stranger* ends with romantic hope, as McQueen's character literally pickets for consideration as a husband (outside pregnant Wood's workplace, New York's Macy's), *Baby* sadly documents what will probably become of that union, an unhappy marriage caused by a music-focused absentee husband/father. But while McQueen more than holds his own with Wood in *Stranger*, Remick and her six-year-old screen daughter (Kimberly Block) steal *Baby* from him. The reason is all in the story, or the lack thereof. That is, one readily sees what drives Remick's pain (a less than sympathetic husband). But McQueen's angst is not fleshed out. He wants to be a rockabilly singer but is handicapped by psychological problems seemingly tied to a frightful spinster guardian (Georgia Simmons) who reared him and still exerts a sinister control over the young man from her spooky old house. In fact, the first time one screens the movie the possibility of a horror genre subplot, especially as tied to the gothic atmosphere of the residence, seems a distinct possibility. But sadly, neither McQueen, nor this promising backstory, is realized. *New York World Telegram and Sun* critic William Peper perfectly captured this viewer frustration when he wrote, "Anticipation is high until it is realized that the mood is an end in itself, that the characters are not going to develop and that with the inevitability of a ballad, McQueen will turn violent again and go back to jail. [The film had opened with his character just getting out of prison after serving a sentence for a stabbing conviction.]"[34]

McQueen's wannabe Elvis Presley is such an unrealized boor that some critics even qualified their praise of Remick by questioning her figure's stoical acceptance of him. While the *New York Times*'s Bosley Crowther politely asked "why . . . [this] woman, who seems a sensible person, doesn't make a single move to straighten him out," the *New York Herald Tribune*'s Judith Crist simply became belligerent: "For her continuing acceptance of McQueen we must term her either masochist or moron."[35] McQueen's under-written role is also hurt by his musical numbers, with a lip-syncing job that falsely seems to suggest that the actor is *not* doing the singing. With uncredited studio coaching from Glen Campbell, McQueen actually handled the vocals himself. Take away the poor staging of the music, and the actor has an effective singing voice.

As with many McQueen movies, the actor ended up bedding his *Baby* costar, Remick, a fact also later documented in Adams's memoir (at this point in their marriage he still sometimes felt a compulsion to

McQueen and Remick's on-screen roles as lovers in Baby, the Rain Must Fall *briefly came true in real life.*

confess his indiscretions).[36] I bring this up only to give added credibility to Remick's comments on McQueen, which confirm previously noted facts about him: "He was friendly and nice and funny and odd. He wasn't just your ordinary run-of-the-mill actor. I don't think he liked acting very much, that's the feeling I got. I didn't feel his heart was in this movie. He liked action movies better. This was a little too delicate and soft and tender for his taste. He did it very well, however."[37]

Ironically, Remick's comment about McQueen having done the part "very well" possibly contributed to critical indifference, since his musician character is so unlikable. The *Los Angeles Times* reviewer fully articulated this perspective: "McQueen plays him for what he is, which is nothing. It is an almost totally unsympathetic role and no one feels sorry for him."[38] All these negatives notwithstanding, an occasional art-house critic found positives in McQueen's performance. *Films and Filming*'s Allen Eyles went so far as to claim, "It is a study in boyish confusion, a mixture of defiant courage and inner fear, that is put across without tricks and is perhaps the best study of this kind of character that Hollywood has yet given us."[39] Eyles also suggests that *Baby* might be compared to the film *Fear Strikes Out* (1957), in which baseball star Jimmy Piersall is driven to mental illness by a domineering father (the implication being that the problems of McQueen's musician have been caused by the controlling guardian). This is an interestingly provocative suggestion. But the flaw inherent to this proposal has already been addressed by other reviewers—Simmons's scary spinster is underdeveloped. There is nothing comparable to the frighteningly three-dimensional dictatorial father played by Karl Malden in *Fear Strikes Out*. One can only have wished that Eyles might have sat in on *Baby*'s preproduction script readings.

Like the critical yo-yo effect exhibited by bad notices for *Soldier in the Rain* and raves for the follow-up *Love with the Proper Stranger*, McQueen came back from *Baby*'s generally disappointing reviews to earn kudos for *The Cincinnati Kid*. Nevertheless, while he and costar Edward G. Robinson received much praise, the film was often called to task for its parallels to *The Hustler*. The *New York Times* said, "even in excel-

lent Technicolor, the film pales beside 'The Hustler,' to which it bears
a striking similarity of theme and characterization."[40] The *New York
Herald Tribune*'s Crist found much to celebrate, but still felt compelled
to open her critique with its ties to Newman's picture: "'The Cincinnati
Kid' is quite literally 'The Hustler' in spades—a melodrama about gambling and gamblers that climaxes with one of the more exciting—and
most beautifully filmed—stud poker marathons on record."[41]

Hustler's unique hold on viewers went beyond just coming out
several years before *Cincinnati*. *Newsweek*'s review of the latter picture
effectively summarized *Hustler*'s more cinematic nature: "A pool game,
with its Newtonian neatness of colliding balls, is intrinsically more pho-
togenic and dramatizable than a poker game . . . [and] poker faces."[42]
Conversely, while the *Hollywood Citizen News* also noted the obvious
link to *Hustler*, this publication creatively credited *Cincinnati* with
indirect ties to a genre then still in ascendancy, as well as having close
ties to McQueen: "[*Cincinnati* is] an authentic Western-styled plot if
there ever was one. The showdown poker hand substitutes cards for six-
shooters."[43]

Just as Newman's title character challenges "the man" (Jackie Gleason as Minnesota Fats) and loses in *Hustler*, McQueen's title figure also
succumbs to the wily veteran (Robinson) in *Cincinnati*. Very few critics
asked the most basic of questions concerning these two—why did they
fail? But the *Saturday Review*'s Hollis Alpert posited two explanations
for McQueen's gambler: "On the one hand, he's met a man bigger than
himself [Robinson] . . . on the other hand it's a flaw of character [the
Kid is not yet ready]."[44] One is also tempted to state the obvious—Mc-
Queen's antiheroic loner is predicated upon his *Cincinnati* character
remaining an outsider. If he had won and become "the man," he would
cease to be that edgy underdog to which modern cinema is drawn.

So how is McQueen's acclaimed gambler different from the generally panned musician from *Baby*, another antiheroic loner? His *Cincinnati* character is more fleshed out, not so much in language as in action.
The movie introduces him in a low-life poker game in a setting just

McQueen makes his escape from a railroad yard in The Cincinnati Kid *(1965) on his way to achieve his goal of being the king of stud poker players.*

The Cincinnati Kid spars with his nemesis, Lancey Howard, played by Edward G. Robinson. Spencer Tracy was originally cast in the Howard role, but dropped out.

waiting for a murder. In fact, the Kid's winning of a final small pot has a disgruntled fellow player/thug going after him with a knife. McQueen dramatically escapes by making a glass-smashing dive through a window and dodging his way around an always cinematic railroad yard. This misadventure speaks volumes about our antihero—a figure either so desperate to get by he puts himself at risk for a cheap nothing pot, or simply a player desperate to hone his skills regardless of the poker game's dangers. Granted, McQueen's gambler is no better with women than in *Baby*, from his scene-stealing naïve girlfriend (Tuesday Weld) to Ann-Margret's sexpot. But at least Cincinnati's disinterest is not at the expense of a loyal wife and a vulnerable child. Plus, his edginess is a threat to only himself, not to society in general, which was the case with McQueen's *Baby* musician.

McQueen, a real-life cardsharp as a New York youngster trying to get by, is an underplaying revelation as the pretender to Robinson's "man." But despite the minimalist acting of both men, playing it "close to the vest," to punningly borrow an actual poker phrase, McQueen and Robinson deliver performances that quietly overwhelm you, like smoke under the door. Fittingly, they received superior, often tandem, notices. *Variety* said, "In McQueen . . . [the picture] has the near-perfect delineator of the title role. Robinson is at his best in some years as the aging, ruthless Lancey."[45] The *New York Journal American*, under the punning review title, "'Cincinnati Kid: A Sharp Card," added, "The story accent . . . is entirely on McQueen and Robinson, and both handle their roles convincingly."[46] Robinson's presence seemed to elevate McQueen's performance, a common occurrence when conflicting characters are played by iconic actors. Paradoxically, Robinson's role was originally set to star Spencer Tracy, one of McQueen's idols. The young actor had even written to Tracy, promising him top billing. But the veteran did not relate to the part and passed on it. In hindsight, Robinson now seems a better fit given his long history of playing tough guys, as well as being a movie gangster colleague of *the* McQueen hero, Humphrey Bogart.

Speaking of near misses, *Cincinnati* was originally to have been directed by Sam Peckinpah, who had first made his name known in cinema with the elegiac instant classic Western, *Ride the High Country* (1962). But just as Peckinpah's later career was equally famous for his ongoing creative differences with the Hollywood powers that be, he was bounced from *Cincinnati* over being adamant about both shooting the production in black and white and including a brief nude scene in European prints of the film. While Peckinpah later successfully collaborated with McQueen on the movies *Junior Bonner* and *The Getaway* (both 1972), his *Cincinnati* replacement, Norman Jewison, was a good choice.

Like Peckinpah, Jewison was one of those rare directors who managed to work with the volatile actor on more than one project, also directing him on *The Thomas Crown Affair* (1968). Jewison creatively managed to control his set by dealing directly with McQueen's many

For an action hero, McQueen also had a large number of bedroom scenes, including one with Tuesday Weld in The Cincinnati Kid.

insecurities. Setting down a star who was only five years younger than the thirty-nine-year-old director, Jewison said, "Steve, I don't know what you want from me. Maybe you're looking for a father figure. God knows I can't be that. But I'll tell you what I can be. How about we think of me as your older brother, the one who went to college? I will always look out for you. You and I are totally different. You work with your hands. You can take engines apart, and you're fascinated with speed, you're great with a motorcycle. I can't do any of the things you do. But I'm the older brother, and I'm the guy who's always around taking care of your best interests."[47]

In addition to Jewison, *Cincinnati* was blessed with a number of other creative people behind the scenes, starting with the dark comedy-orientated scriptwriters Ring Lardner Jr. and Terry Southern, who adapted the Richard Jessup novel. A pointed example of that wit comes in the portrayal of Ann-Margret's character; her cheating sex-kitten tendencies are inspiringly crystallized in one of her jigsaw puzzle habits—using a pair of scissors on parts that do not fit! The editing from Hal Ashby, particularly late in the movie, is outstanding. Ashby would go on to collect an Oscar for *In the Heat of the Night* (1967), before moving on to direct such dark-comedy favorites as *Harold and Maude* (1971) and *Being There* (1979).

The always insightful Eyles of *Films and Filming* was most taken with the look of *Cincinnati*: "It's most striking achievement is an impeccable sense of period atmosphere seeping from a mellowed brown-yellow image (a subdued yet still rich Metro-color) representing the New Orleans area in the 'thirties. This feeling for a time is somehow stamped on all the performances in the film."[48] Those superb performances were drawn from an all-star cast that included, in addition to McQueen and Robinson: Ann-Margret, Weld, Karl Malden, Joan Blondell, Rip Torn, and Cab Calloway. *Cincinnati* is a picture whose stature has continued to grow through the years.

McQueen went from a young director and a quasi-Western scenario on *Cincinnati*, to a seasoned megaphoner of the genre, Henry Hathaway. Hathaway's filmography stretched back to the 1930s and such memorable movies as *The Lives of a Bengal Lancer* (1935, which starred yet another McQueen favorite, Gary Cooper). Hathaway's then most recent picture was the previous year's hit Western, *The Sons of Katie Elder* (1965, with John Wayne and Dean Martin). He would now direct McQueen in yet another horse opera, the epic *Nevada Smith.* While Jewison used psychology on McQueen, Hathaway got by on reputation—"probably the toughest son-of-a-bitch in Hollywood." But to underline just who the boss was, Hathaway sat McQueen down for a talk/lecture and warned the young actor that he would not tolerate any "star complex bullshit." The two got along just fine after this one-way "discussion."[49]

Nevada Smith is an early example of what has now become known as the prequel. McQueen's title character is drawn from Harold Robbins's best-selling novel *The Carpetbaggers*, which was made into the hit 1964 movie of the same name. Set during the 1920s and 1930s, the film is a sexploitational rip-off of a Howard Hughes-like (George Peppard) Hollywood producer. One of the more interesting *Carpetbaggers* supporting players is an aging Western screen star (Alan Ladd), who was once a real cowboy. McQueen's "Nevada Smith" is Ladd's character as a young man, with a Native American mother.

In John G. Cawelti's watershed genre study, *The Six-Gun Mystique*, he counts the revenge story as one of the most pivotal of Western narratives.[50] *Nevada Smith* could easily serve as the ultimate poster child for this sagebrush subgenre. The parents of McQueen's title character are brutally murdered at the movie's opening by three cowboys (Karl Malden, Arthur Kennedy, and Martin Landau). In this prologue of sorts, McQueen effectively passes as a half-Indian teenager determined to track down these killers. But he is unprepared for his task until he meets gunsmith Jonas Cord (Brian Keith), who mentors him like a father. Cord represents another direct link back to *The Carpetbaggers*, since Peppard's studio head is the son of Cord. The older Smith (Ladd) of this picture looked out for Cord Jr. (Peppard) because of his debt to Cord Sr. (Keith).

McQueen in a scene from Nevada Smith *(1966) with the mountain backdrop communi-*
cating a Western view of life—a hostile environment and a character made psychologically
jagged by a need for revenge.

McQueen's odyssey of revenge takes him all over the country, driven in part by a sense of guilt, too. As one reviewer noted, "A clever [script] touch gives . . . [him] a feeling of accidental complicity in the murders, for he had informed the trio of friendly-seeming strangers of the where-abouts of his parents' home."[51] The most elaborate of the film's revenge chapters involves McQueen's pursuit of Kennedy's character, who becomes a prisoner on a Louisiana chain gang. The avenging son gets himself sent up the river and before enacting his payback meets a young woman (Suzanne Pleshette) who begins to soften his attitude about revenge. This lengthy Louisiana segment also predates McQueen rival Newman's Southern chain-gang film *Cool Hand Luke* (1967) by a year. Visually, this forty-one minute portion of *Nevada Smith* also, at times, anticipates McQueen's later epic prison picture *Papillon* (1973).

Pleshette, now best known as the first television wife of Bob Newhart (*The Bob Newhart Show*), was a close McQueen friend—without any sexual baggage. The star had met Pleshette when she was a teenager and had acted like a protective older brother since, despite his tendency, to borrow a comic line from Red Skelton, "To be a hard dog to keep on the porch." Pleshette had been kiddingly frustrated about this "sibling" relationship for years! Regardless, she was also an adoptive "aunt" to McQueen's two children, and a frequent prankster in his life. For ex-ample, during the *Nevada Smith* production she comically cooked up a plan to get back at McQueen's notorious tightness. Pleshette arranged a restaurant dinner party that included both the star and director Ha-thaway. But her secret to McQueen was that no one was to pick up the check—they would wait out the cheap star. Finally, after it had gotten exceedingly late, Hathaway took care of the bill. When Pleshette later got tough with this Hollywood tough guy for wrecking her fun, Hatha-way revealed a mischievous side of his own. The filmmaker had signed McQueen's name to the bill—with a hefty tip, too!

Although reviews would sometimes be mixed for *Nevada Smith*, this same comically manipulative Hathaway often garnered movie starlike critiques for his direction of this picture. The *Motion Picture Herald* stated, "The great Henry Hathaway, whose distinguished half-century in show business has embraced production and direction of about all the kinds of motion pictures there are, reached far back in his memory to the bold, free-ranging era of primitive Western melodrama for this swift, emotion-charged story of vengeance." The same review also likened the trio of killers to a classic silent screen heavy—"Villains as dark as Ernest Torrence in [Henry King's] *Tol'able David* [1921, a movie which also featured three heinous criminals]."[52] The frequently hard-to-please *New York Times* described McQueen's *Nevada Smith* evolution from "naïve cowpoke to furious gunslinger" as a thing of "humor and poignancy."[53] *Films and Filming* added, "Steve McQueen is [especially] excellent in the early stages of the film as the callow youth who sets out with rifle, a horse, eight dollars, and a great deal to learn about life."[54]

McQueen shares a kiss with close friend Suzanne Pleshette in Nevada Smith. *Pleshette went on to win fame as the wife of Chicago psychologist Bob Hartley in the classic television sitcom* The Bob Newhart Show.

The focus films of this chapter proved several things to what was still essentially a "factory" town. First, despite McQueen's reputation for being difficult, this minifilmography demonstrated a willingness and an ability to work, and to work often. Second, though these movies were not all critical and/or commercial hits, they remained films worth watching—no small accomplishment in Hollywood. Third, McQueen showed a gameness and ingenuity in a varied assortment of genres, with the biggest box-office numbers during this stretch occurring in two radically diverse types, the romantic comedy of *Stranger* versus the epic Western *Nevada Smith*. Fourth, even with McQueen's moniker for being difficult, especially for executive "suits," the actor was popular with Hollywood's blue-collar rank and file. During a movie production he routinely ate with the grips, the electricians, the stuntmen, and the generally dirty-nails set. More impressively, he knew these folks by name. This earned a lot of support with the real men and women behind the movies. And while McQueen might have continued to have some reservations about the manliness of performing, he probably would have accepted this paraphrasing of his craft: "Acting is not a life but I think that sometimes it can be a way back to life."

McQueen had now fully arrived as a 1960s filmmaker, but three of his most memorable movies of the decade, and his career, were on the immediate horizon, and they would happen back to back to back.

7

Another Pivotal Trilogy:
"What the hell happened?"[1]

Like Steve McQueen, his Sand Pebbles *character, Jake Holman, is obsessed with all things mechanical. When someone denigrates serving on a gunboat, Jake defensively responds, "They've got engines, ain't they!"*

Unlike the John Sturges trilogy addressed earlier in the book, the following late 1960s trio of pictures—*The Sand Pebbles* (1966), *The Thomas Crown Affair*, and *Bullitt* (both 1968)—feature different directors and more varied story lines. But the first film, Robert Wise's *The Sand Pebbles*, did have ties with one frequent Sturges component, a predisposition toward the epic. Wise spent well over two years in preproduction. The story was based upon writer Richard McKenna's 1962 best-selling novel of the same name. The author drew upon his American navy experiences in 1926 China, when Chiang Kai-shek's Nationalists were trying to unify a war-torn country and drive out various imperialist interests, including the United States. Many later reviews of the picture were fascinated by the parallels with America's then involvement in Southeast Asia. For example, the *New York Times* said, "it is not an historical romance that . . . [the movie] is likely to grab the audience but is a weird sort of hint of what has happened and is happening in Vietnam."[2] (The film also speaks to the racial tolerance of 1960s by showcasing both a friendship between McQueen and his Chinese machinist assistant, and the marriage of Richard Attenborough to a Chinese girl.)

As had happened so often in McQueen's career, his *Sand Pebbles* part had originally been offered to Paul Newman. But with Newman's refusal and the release of McQueen's blockbuster success in Sturges's *The Great Escape* (1963), McQueen had moved to the top of the casting heap. Still, when McQueen signed on for the project he had no idea of the time commitment the film would entail. Shot on location in Taiwan and Hong Kong (because Red China was still not recognized by the United States), bad weather and an epic production (almost fifty speaking parts) lengthened the shoot from two to seven months. But with Wise's aforementioned Academy Award wins on *West Side Story* (1961) and *The Sound of Music* (1965, which was then on the verge of eclipsing 1939's *Gone with the Wind* as the biggest box-office hit in cinema history), Twentieth Century Fox continued to give the director carte blanche on the picture.

Ironically, the delays were most problematic to McQueen. But it went beyond the frustrations of keeping him and his family abroad for more than half a year. The actor was anxious to move on to his next film, a large-scale European road-racing collaboration with Sturges tentatively called *Day of the Champion*. But Warner Brothers, the studio making *Champion*, would only follow through on the movie if the company could start shooting prior to Metro-Goldwyn-Mayer's similar production, *Grand Prix* (1967). Sadly, *Sand Pebbles'* problems sabotaged the Warner arrangement, and a flawed *Champion* only appeared years later as McQueen's *Le Mans* (1971, with creative differences forcing Sturges out of the picture). Paradoxically, by the time *Le Mans* finally appeared, even McQueen's self-appointed rival, Newman, had released a well-received racing film, *Winning* (1969).

Going back to 1965–66 production of *Sand Pebbles*, an on-location McQueen had to suffer through a double-whammy disappointment when he heard that *Grand Prix's* starting date had moved ahead of *Champion*. Not only was his own picture knocked out of the box, *Prix* starred his friend and next-door neighbor James Garner, who only recently had started racing professionally himself. Sensing that McQueen would "read" this as a form of disloyalty, Garner called McQueen in

Taiwan to discuss the project. Garner knew his friend. While McQueen was civil on the phone, he was decidedly cool toward Garner for some time after the call.

This constitutes another possible slant on why McQueen had few real celebrity friends—what the actor might see as disloyalty could be all encompassing. But in fairness to McQueen, he was essentially a blue-collar guy who had many reservations about the very craft/art of acting. It makes perfect sense that he gravitated toward working-class friendships. Consistent with this "everyman" perspective, McQueen's famous friends, such as Garner and James Coburn, were stars who prided themselves for being regular guys. Here is Coburn's 1966 take on trying to remain the same person he had always been: "To me the ideal is to be an egoless actor—to become so lost in . . . [film] that you become self-less. . . . The important thing is to find out what kind of a human being you are, and whether you are growing—and if not, why not."[3]

Interestingly, McQueen, Garner, and Coburn all came out of late-1950s and early-1960s television Westerns, with the first two men starring in their own small-screen programs, *Wanted: Dead or Alive* and *Maverick*. Coburn's early work involved guest spots on such celebrated sagebrush shows as *Gunsmoke, Bonanza,* and *Wanted,* where his friendship with McQueen first developed. Coburn's early films were also Westerns, such as the classic Randolph Scott picture *Ride Lonesome* (1959) and Sturges's *Magnificent Seven* (1960, again with McQueen). Coburn's long career, culminating in a Best Supporting Actor Oscar for *Affliction* (1998), also suggests the rich character-actor parts McQueen might have later undertaken had he not died at the age of fifty in 1980. McQueen's last movie, the underrated *Hunter* (1980), with its affectionate spoofing of his aging action-hero persona, even seems to be working in that character-actor direction.

Regardless, the long shoot on *Sand Pebbles* reveals some basic insights into just who McQueen was, given that he was forced to transfer a lifestyle abroad. First, despite his weakness for brief sexual affairs, part of him very much needed a family base. Thus, his wife, Neile Adams, and their children, six-and-one-half-year-old Terry and five-year-old

Chad, were with McQueen throughout the production. During the family's stay in Taiwan, former stage star Adams also entertained American troops stationed there, as well as organizing and teaching exercise classes for military wives at the local army club.

In a telling 1966 McQueen article filtered through the making of *Sand Pebbles*, one receives a telling insight into Adams's life. Writer Arthur Marcede turns to literature when he observes, "Steve McQueen's wife is a wise woman indeed. She has learned well the lines of the famed nineteenth century poetess Mrs. Aphra Behn, who wrote: 'I hold my love lightly, for things with wings held tightly, want to fly.'"[4] Fittingly, the piece uses a defining McQueen quote for its title: "I Must Be Free to Live in My Own Way." As suggested earlier, despite many good times, Adams's relationship with her husband was based on an ongoing compromise, a loophole to lewdness. But I should hasten to add, that the full implications of this essentially one-way open marriage were not addressed in the article. Only later revelations, such as Adams's balanced biography/memoir, *My Husband, My Friend*, helps fill in the blanks.[5]

Second, McQueen enjoyed the company of tough-guy buddies, sort of his own blue-collar "Rat Pack." *Sand Pebbles* costar Candice Bergen later had the following take on McQueen's entourage, noting that McQueen had "arrived in Taiwan with a commando unit of six stunt men, none under six feet and all ex-Marines. [Ex-marine McQueen was always generously listed as five feet, ten inches tall.] They were like his personal honor guard, and when he moved, they jumped. Hard-drinking, hard-fighting—as time on the island ticked by McQueen and his gang grew increasingly restless and often spent nights on the prowl, roaming the little city [Taipei, Taiwan]."[6]

Third, for much of McQueen's life he was very much into physical fitness. This was never so true as during the production of *The Sand Pebbles*, when he had a special gym set up in the floating focus of the shoot, the U.S. gunboat the *San Pablo*. (The picture's title came from the crew's nickname for themselves.) McQueen's elaborate shipboard workout facility was a far cry from his Greenwich Village days with Adams on the lower west side of 1950s Manhattan. At that time his only exercise "equipment" was a stolen street sign with a still-attached cement base—a poor man's lopsided dumbbell. For someone who lived life at a fast pace, he felt his coordination-directed exercise would help him maintain all those proverbial "balls in the air." With his comic hipster sense of language, he capsulated this in the following manner: "Keep your body cool, and you're on a natural high all the time."[7]

McQueen's embrace of working out, however, went beyond just staying in shape. His acting had a physicality that bordered upon the athletic, a component inherent to the performance style known as the Method. This was especially true of Method guru/director Elia Kazan,

McQueen as Jake Holman witnesses the marriage of his shipmate Frenchy (Attenborough) to Maily (Emmanuelle Arsan) as Holman's love interest, Shirley Eckert (Candice Bergen), an American teacher at the China Light Mission, looks on.

who forever mixed sports and art. Kazan, noted a biographer of Marlon Brando, "had a thing about his body. He kept in tip-top shape by a lot of tennis and walking tirelessly."[8] Appropriately, Kazan's first pep talk to new Actors Studio members keyed upon a sports metaphor: "This is not a club, this is a gym for actors to work out in. Everybody is expected to work hard."[9]

In addition to McQueen being exposed to this philosophy through years at New York's Method "Studio," he also naturally gravitated toward a minimalist physicality in his acting—getting his perspective across by saying little but implying much through his actions. On *Sand Pebbles*, as on most of McQueen's movies, he worked with the director to *cut* his lines, getting his mood/attitude across through a look, a gesture, and/or using a prop as an extension of his character. This is best demonstrated in *Sand Pebbles* by the scene in which McQueen's character, navy machinist Jake Holman, first examines the ship's extensive engine. While Holman's nominal love interest is supposed to be Candice Bergen's teacher/missionary, *Sand Pebbles* real romance is between McQueen and the ship's power source. Not since Buster Keaton's inspired movie *The General* (1927), has there been such an organic connection between a star and a giant mechanical prop. But be that as it may, Jake's initial visit to the engine room is reverential, like a baseball fan visiting Cooperstown. The scene is about serenity, the knowing touch, and

Like McQueen in The Sand Pebbles, *Buster Keaton is driven by his character's love of machines in his greatest movie,* The General *(1927).*

an oddly moving moment when McQueen's sailor actually introduces himself to the huge machine. Like the neglected paintings of Gerald Murphy, in which mechanical-related subjects suggest a sanctuary from some human hurt, McQueen's engine room escape in *Sand Pebbles* belies an individual damaged from failed personal relationships—a scenario that could also be used to explain the actor's real-life interest in engines.

Unfortunately, for all of McQueen's fixation on athleticism, the actor's physical fitness tendencies were frequently challenged by his weakness for junk food. These calorie-laden tendencies were no doubt driven by a deprived childhood, when sweets, not to mention food in general, were often in short supply. Consequently, while McQueen made sure his favorite health foods (such as apple-and-nut salad, vegetables, yogurt, and wheat germ) were available during the *Sand Pebbles* shoot, he also relished such rich items as multiple portions of chocolate cake, sugary coffee, and breakfast items such as French toast heavily doctored with sweet toppings. Just as McQueen's personality was mercurial, so were his eating habits. Plus, to pun his large "appetite" for life (acting, racing, collecting, countless sexual conquests, etc.), he continued to put away gargantuan amounts of food. Comically, this sometimes even played out in his movies. For example, there is a perfunctory luncheon scene early in *Sand Pebbles*. While the other actors are merely playing at a meal, McQueen is very much chowing down.

Richard Crenna, who played the *San Pablo* captain in *Sand Pebbles*, later said, "[McQueen] was born to play this role."[10] This was the feeling in the McQueen household, too. Adams had read the novel upon its publication and alerted her husband to the lead role's appropriateness for him. Throughout their marriage, she was his best career adviser—someone on whom he came to depend, a rarity for the actor. Beyond the shared interest in machines, McQueen and Holman were also similar in their Hemingwayesque self-containedness. Indeed, the conclusion of *Sand Pebbles* brings to mind two signature novels by Hemingway, *A Farewell to Arms* (1929) and *For Whom the Bell Tolls* (1940). That is, late in *Sand Pebbles*, Holman performs a personal "farewell to arms" by

McQueen as Holman tinkers with the engines of the gunboat USS San Pablo. *In a memorable line from* The Sand Pebbles, *McQueen's character says: "Hello, Engine; I'm Jake Holman."*

telling his patriotically imperialistic commanding officer, "I ain't got no more enemies; shove off, Captain." Yet, like *Bell's* Robert Jordan, McQueen's Holman finds he must sacrifice his life in a delaying action against the enemy so that his love interest and others can escape.

Despite these natural McQueen-Hemingway links to the Holman figure, and how they tie into the novelist's basic goal of "grace under pressure," the actor's dying words in *Sand Pebbles* seem more darkly comic modern in their absurdist anger: "I was home. What happened? What the hell happened?" In Jordan's case, there is no eleventh-hour questioning, and Hemingway's novel ends with him still alive but waiting on death: "He could feel his heart beating against the pine needle floor of the forest."[11] In contrast, Holman's dying frustration is made all the more poignant by the fact the viewer witnesses a second bullet taking his life as soon as he utters those words.

The actor later added controversy to the close by questioning whether, in real life, he would have been so self-sacrificial.[12] Yet, with Holman's last words being ever so ambiguous, McQueen playing devil's advocate only seems to make him as much of an enigma as Holman. Regardless, McQueen and the picture were roundly praised by critics and embraced at the box office. The *New York Times* said of McQueen's performance: "the most restrained, honest, heartfelt acting he has ever done."[13] The *Los Angeles Herald Examiner* observed, "He gives a truly fine performance, provides a key for the action and also . . . [creates] the basic conflict when his integrity forces him to balk against the status quo."[14] The *Hollywood Reporter*, praising his minimalism, added: "McQueen is a unique actor, one of remarkable conviction, and one who can project subtleties of character and development with a flick of his eyes or a slight shift of body English."[15] Film historian/critic Arthur Knight was summarily succinct for the *Saturday Review*, "[McQueen] is nothing short of wonderful in the pivotal role of Holman."[16]

As this kudos consensus might suggest, McQueen's *Sand Pebbles* role led to an Academy Award nomination as Best Actor, his first and only time to be up for an Oscar. The film received eight nominations, including Best Picture, but took home no statuettes. (The Academy Award-winning film that year was *A Man for All Seasons*, with the star of that movie, Paul Scofield, also beating McQueen in the Best Actor category.) McQueen's consolation prize, of sorts, that year was being honored with the male "World Film Favorite" award at the Golden Globes. (Julie Andrews was given the award as favorite female.)

Interestingly, McQueen had witnessed some of that "world film favorite" hysteria while filming *The Sand Pebbles* in Asia. His action-film work, starting with *The Magnificent Seven*, had made him especially popular in Japan. The Japanese also relished McQueen's real-life sense of humor. During the *Sand Pebbles* shoot the McQueens took a side trip to Tokyo. But the family became hung up at the city's Haneda Airport, when customs found a .38-calibre revolver in the actor's bags. When McQueen was asked to explain why he had the registered gun with him, the performer observed with tongue firmly-in-cheek, "It's for bear hunting." The media soon reported, "The Japanese [public] loved that [response]."[17]

While American theater owners did not officially recognize McQueen's box-office clout until *The Sand Pebbles* was released, the rest of the world had been in on the secret for years.[18] During McQueen's September 1964 visit to Europe for the Six-Day Motorcycle Trials in East Germany, he was first made aware of the adoration of the French populace. Soon after that visit the country named McQueen their most popular foreign actor. But his popularity there even preceded the actor's early action films. The French had been gaga over him since his Western television series had gone into French syndication.

To paraphrase an old movie line, if history teaches us anything, it teaches us some days are best spent in bed. Despite the critical praise McQueen received for his *Sand Pebbles* performance, he would have preferred to have missed the experience. It had been a grueling shoot, he fretted that his character was ultimately too idealistic, and the picture had cost him, at least for the time being, his coveted racing film. (Ironically, *Grand Prix* opened simultaneously with *Sand Pebbles*.[19]) McQueen's negative feelings about his *Sand Pebbles* part only increased at 1967 Oscar time, when his loss brought back bitter memories of the "sure thing" nomination that was not to be for *Love with the Proper Stranger* (1963). Paradoxically, Adams expressed relief about her husband losing: "If he'd won, he'd have been impossible to live with, not because of a big head but because he'd be worrying how to top himself next. I prayed he wouldn't win it. To be nominated was marvelous. It was just great to get near the [Oscar] target; this way he still had something to aim at."[20] The fear of following up an Academy Award-winning film with a worthy project was common in show business and it was sometimes referred to as "Oscar-itis."

Given McQueen's litany of *Sand Pebbles*-related complaints, including the extended period abroad, the star accented his homecoming by dropping to his hands and knees when his flight touched down and kissing the American soil. He then took a year off, but this alleged sabbatical is misleading. Both he and Adams pored over possible scripts— scripts that would *not* involve a weapon-toting McQueen. Some publications have since made much of the fact that the star achieved top ten box-office status that "vacation" year (1967), despite no new McQueen movies opening.[21] Yet, the easy answer is that *Sand Pebbles* premiered at Christmas of 1966 and played prestigious, lucrative road-show engagements well into 1967.

Though seldom remembered today, part of this McQueen holiday was also spent flirting with the perfect business opportunity for someone who loved eating—opening a restaurant. The proposed establishment was to be on Los Angeles's Sunset Strip and would serve only Mexican food, McQueen's favorite. The star even had a provocative name picked out, La Rebellion de Adolescentes. Had McQueen gone through with it, his partner in crime would have been the actor's longtime friend, Elmer Valentine, who operated the popular Los Angeles nightclub and frequent McQueen haunt, the Whiskey A Go-Go.

Though nothing came of the restaurant venture, the McQueens had better luck finding a film project that would feature a potentially softer side of the star. But now the trick would be for McQueen to convince Hollywood power brokers that he could play an atypical part—a sophisticated millionaire who orchestrates the perfect bank heist. Initially called *The Crown Caper*, the picture was to be directed by

Norman Jewison, who had worked with McQueen on *The Cincinnati Kid* (1965). McQueen was not even close to the tailored-suit elegance that Jewison, and first-time screenplay writer Alan Trustman, had in mind for the title character of what became *The Thomas Crown Affair* (1968). The figure of Crown had been patterned upon the super cool Sean Connery, then in the midst of his James Bond fame. Jewison concurred on this casting choice, but when Connery begged off from overwork, other British actors such as Richard Burton were considered for the role. (Interestingly, when the film was remade in 1999, the lead was played by the then reigning James Bond actor, Pierce Brosnan.)

When McQueen came to Jewison to plead his case, the director affectionately kidded him about how inappropriate he was for the part. Jewison's manner was consistent with his promise during the production of *Cincinnati* that he would look out for the actor like an older brother: "The [Crown] character wears suits, Steve. You've never worn a suit in a movie. Or in real life for that matter . . . Thomas Crown is a Dartmouth graduate. You didn't get out of high school. You're wonderful on a movie screen but this part doesn't seem like a natural fit at all."[22]

McQueen, however, could be most convincing when he wanted something. Plus, Jewison was impressed that the actor was personally pitching his position, something the director had seldom experienced in what he liked to comically refer to as "this terrible [Hollywood] business." Factor in McQueen's new *Sand Pebbles* clout as major box office, or his approaching pop-culture validation as a superstar (handprints and footprints immortalized in the forecourt of Grauman's Chinese Theatre on March 21, 1967) and the actor soon had the role.

Though McQueen was fascinated by the challenge of the part, he felt real fear for his future if he failed: "I got to do it. But if people laugh at me, my ass is gone . . . if I fuck up now, it's over."[23] Not surprisingly, he did not "fuck up," and *Crown* went on to be a major critical and commercial hit. Screenwriter Trustman's pep-talk description of the part to McQueen, whose casting he had initially fought, helps explain why the movie worked. Using the actor's film hero as a model,

As his wife Neile Adams smiles proudly, McQueen's handprints and footprints are commit-ted to history at Grauman's Chinese Theatre on March 21, 1967.

he coached: "You could be the new Humphrey Bogart. You are shy, you don't talk too much. You are a loner but a person with integrity. You're quiet, you're gutsy as hell. You like girls but are basically shy with women. You have a tight smile; you don't show your teeth, but it's a small smile around your mouth, and you never deliver a sentence with more than five or ten words long, because paragraphs make you lose interest or something goes wrong with your delivery. As long as you can stay with that, you can be number one."[24]

Though Crown was from a privileged, sophisticated background, Trustman recognized that his character possessed a maverick minimalism that was synonymous with McQueen's persona, as well as his screen hero, Bogie. As the *Hollywood Reporter*'s review later suggested, "For McQueen [as Crown], it is less a change of image than of costume, the glove fit of an expensive Ron Postal [designer] wardrobe."[25] In addition, McQueen and Crown had another pivotal point in common—they both hated the Establishment. Crown's bank heist threatened to bankrupt the largest insurance company in America (insurance companies cover the loss in robberies, not banks). McQueen had also used this Crown connection when lobbying for the part with Jewison. But he had translated it into his own jazz musician-like lingo, "It's about juice [power]. Who's got the juice."[26]

Jewison's formalistic approach to filmmaking also eased McQueen's assimilation into this unusual for him part. Formalism is the self-conscious use of technique to tell the story, which takes the accent off acting. Indeed, actors can become like pawns in this system, manipulated by the director. For instance, one of Jewison's heroes was Alfred Hitchcock, whose shower sequence in *Psycho* (1960) remains a seminal example of film formalism—viewer angst about the murder of Janet Leigh is entirely created by the rapid editing.

The major formalistic device Jewison brought to *Crown* was the multiplescreen technique—several varied images of related, simultaneous action showcased in the same film frame. But this was not merely art for art's sake. McQueen's character was masterminding a robbery from afar with gang members unknown to each other, meeting for the

McQueen as the sophisticated title character of The Thomas Crown Affair *(1968).*

first time during the heist. Crown had also managed to keep his identity anonymous to them. The use of multiple screens as a storytelling device simplified a tale that might have been bogged down with laborious traditional editing to maintain all these story trends.

Having justified this use of formalism, however, Jewison was fascinated with simply the look of the film. Because the brilliant but brief script by first-time screenwriter Trustman was short on dialogue, Jewison was encouraged/forced into "sort of making it up as we went along," frequently referring to the film as "an exercise in style over content."[27] Formalism, or not, there are several scenes that play on McQueen strengths. For example, upper-class Crown was a polo player, and while the actor had never played the sport and he had comic issues with horses going back to his Western television series, McQueen was an excellent rider. Using that skill and his athletic ability, he convincingly mastered polo for the in-film sequences of the sport.

Playing upon the actor's interest in cars and machines in general,

The Bogart character closest to the Thomas Crown role played by McQueen would be Rick Blaine from Casablanca *(1943).*

the director added a dune-buggy scene. The story explanation has Crown building a beach house, which allows McQueen to show off his sand-dune driving skills to the story's love interest, Faye Dunaway, an insurance agent also investigating the movie's heist. But even when a *Crown* sequence is not in McQueen's normal wheelhouse, such as a chess match with Dunaway, it soon segues into more familiar territory, a love scene. (The original screenwriter called the whole sequence "chess with sex." And the dialogue during the chess match has the same sexual suggestiveness of the race horse discussion—being in the "saddle"—between Humphrey Bogart and Lauren Bacall in *The Big Sleep*, 1946.) *New Yorker* critic Penelope Gilliatt comically felt, however, that the couple's prolonged kiss (Jewison was attempting the longest in screen history) seemed more like "two goldfish going after the same crumb," causing "hard-stomached men around me . . . [to go] 'Ech!'"[28]

As if anticipating such criticism, Jewison bails out of this romantic sequence with more formalism, a technique much to the liking of the *Motion Picture Exhibitor* reviewer: "[The] love scene between Dunaway and McQueen dissolves into a riot of color that, through its restraint and subtlety, is more meaningful and aesthetic than an explicit sex scene would have been."[29] Jewison might also have been influenced by the cutaway to fireworks just as things get romantically hot and heavy between Cary Grant and Grace Kelly in Hitchcock's *To Catch a Thief* (1955). The director frequently used Grant as a model for Crown when discussing the part with McQueen. Interestingly, Jewison's fondness for all things Hitchcock might have contributed to the fact that Dunaway is very much in the tradition of the celebrated director's icy blondes such as Kelly, with a suggestion of a sexy potential.

A bemused McQueen later described the kissing sequence to the *New York Times*: "It took seven or eight hours to shoot—with a break for lunch, Norman Jewison, the director, didn't tell me to do anything special. I just grabbed her and kissed her. It just kind of happened. My lips were pretty sore afterward."[30] To add humor to the stressful situation of trying to be passionately romantic with a production crew looking on, McQueen persisted in yelling for "Chapstick!" between takes.

A signature scene for a Jewison film is either a funeral and/or a cemetery sequence. Consequently, he has the *Crown* heist money drop take place in an old Boston cemetery. One of the bonuses of location shooting is to discover special embellishments. The "found" item here (not in the original script) was a cemetery bell that was wrung whenever a funeral was taking place. Jewison then uses it for some added drama—the bell rings just as McQueen's character picks up the money. But neither Crown nor the viewer initially knows what the ringing signifies, briefly suggesting he is about to be caught. Given Jewison's macabre fascination with death, explaining his trademark use of cemeteries, one might also think having a money drop in that setting might foreshadow being apprehended there. But like the often manipulative use of formalism, the director is only playing with the audience, and McQueen gets away.

This slick box-office hit received generally positive notices. *Variety* said, "*The Thomas Crown Affair* is a refreshingly different film which concerns a Boston bank robbery . . . [orchestrated by] McQueen . . . neatly cast as the likeable but lonely heavy."[31] The *Hollywood Citizen News* noted, "McQueen brings off an excellent and understated performance unlike anything he's done. He seems as much at home in these high fashions and penthouse life as he was in [the Western] 'Nevada Smith.'"[32] The *Films and Filming* critic added, "I have rarely seen such a sophisticated and diverting account of an affair between two people."[33]

Although those who praised the film were impressed with the director's formalism, such as the *Motion Picture Herald*'s comment, "Jewison has given it a visual elegance that is dazzling," critics also focused on that area.[34] *Time* magazine found *Crown* a "glimmering, empty film," while the *New York Post* complained, "By the time the picture ends you're ready to concede that it's all style and manner. The substance is cream-puffery."[35] Such criticism seems overly harsh, though the razzle-dazzle technique does often distance one from the characters. The viewer roots for McQueen's Crown, but there is not the angst-ridden connection one experiences from the realistic long take, long shot technique used by director Sam Peckinpah to sell/make sympathetic the title figure played by McQueen in *Junior Bonner* (1972). That link

"*The Kiss*" *from* The Thomas Crown Affair *involving McQueen and Faye Dunaway reportedly took eight hours to film over a period of days.*

between character and viewer also gives a figure such as Bonner an added slice-of-life resonance that lingers longer with an audience than the pleasantly diverting mind candy of *Crown*. A more balanced look at *Crown* comes from the *Los Angeles Times*'s review: "It is . . . escape, a romance, an exercise in beguilement, glamour and sophistication, a show of directorial high style, a nifty never-never tale set in a splendidly accoutered right now. It is as enjoyable and as conscientiously unimportant and relaxing a movie as I have seen in some little time."[36]

Keeping *Crown* a lone wolf at the end was an artistically brave thing to do, as well as being consistent with McQueen's screen persona. However, if one had wanted to give the story more warmth, without sacrificing the formalistic elements, the love story played out between the two romantic adversaries might have been given the promise of a future, as was the case with the *Crown* remake released in 1999, starring Brosnan and Rene Russo. A more romantic scenario would also have been consistent with one of Jewison's models for his film, the Hitchcock-like romantic thriller *Charade* (1963, with Cary Grant and Audrey Hepburn). Though Hepburn has reservations about Grant throughout *Charade*, this adds to the film's amusing sexual tension, as well as making their ultimate coupling all the more satisfying.

Unlike the extended holiday McQueen took after *Sand Pebbles*, the actor had finished shooting the police thriller *Bullitt* even before the release of *Crown*. Thus, while McQueen was involved in press junket activity on *Crown*, journalists also peppered him with questions about *Bullitt*. Given that the era's filmmakers had a proclivity for the stylistic (formalism again) showcasing of violent death, such as the famous rapid editing sequence that closes *Bonnie and Clyde* (1967, with Dunaway as Bonnie), McQueen was frequently asked his thoughts on cinema mayhem: "There is violence in the streets and I don't think we should hide it [from films]. I just finished a police movie called 'Bullitt' in San Francisco, and there were five homicides there in one weekend, and we did go . . . there [included such graphic acts in *Bullitt*]. It isn't gratuitous violence. I did it the way I thought it should be. You couldn't soft pedal it. I don't think hiding it is any good."[37] (After the release of *Bullitt*, new promotions for the still-in-release *Crown* sometimes used the marketing tag line, "Bonnie vs. Bullitt.")

While *Sand Pebbles* gave McQueen acting credibility with an Oscar nomination, and *Crown* added the sophistication of a Boston blueblood, *Bullitt* gave him the status of a legend, an icon for the ages. That fact remains obvious today to even the casual surveyor of pop culture. *Bullitt* images of the actor dominate a sea of McQueen memorabilia, starting with a cottage industry in revisionist books and articles about an actor recently described in a documentary title as "The Essence of Cool."[38] Or, check out the resurgence of interest in McQueen as a marketing force, starting with the Ford Motor Company's periodic use of the long-dead actor as a symbol synonymous with the Mustang, the car McQueen drove in *Bullitt*'s famous eleven-minute chase scene.

So what makes *Bullitt* a McQueen touchstone? Is it the story? Yes and no. The scenario, cowritten by *Crown* author Trustman (from the Robert L. Pike novel *Mute Witness*), is as obtuse as a film-noir classic starring McQueen's favorite actor, Humphrey Bogart. That is, *Bullitt* has police detective title character McQueen assigned to oversee the protection of a surprise star witness in a San Francisco mob trial. But the witness is gunned down in a police custody hideaway before McQueen's shift begins. Surprisingly, the victim had let his assassins in. Bullitt's subsequent investigation reveals that the real witness had merely used the murdered man as a pawn to cover his attempted escape with a fortune in mob money. Yet, none of this is clear to the viewer throughout the movie. The *Los Angeles Times*'s positive review even offered the following challenge: "I defy anyone . . . to decipher the shadowy sequence of events before and during the main titles. As a matter of fact, you may have trouble deciphering the events *after* the titles. It doesn't matter a damn."[39]

Consequently, why would such a convoluted story contribute to the McQueen legend? Well, like a film-noir detective, Bullitt perseveres in a seemingly nihilistic, existential world where nothing makes sense. Unlike McQueen's *Sand Pebbles* character, who is destroyed by the absurdity of a military action in which he should not have been involved—whose dying words poignantly tell the tale, "What the hell happened?"—Bullitt survives the chaos and ultimately makes sense of it. His loner man-in-the-middle dilemma is further accented by the fact he must battle both traditional forces of evil (a duplicitous witness and a murderous mob) *and* an Establishment politician, played with villainous slickness by McQueen's *Magnificent Seven* friend Robert Vaughn.

If this charismatic aura of an outsider were not enough to attract one to McQueen's Bullitt, the mesmerizingly simple, yet cinematic, ways he responds to evil—shooting people and engaging in arguably film history's greatest car chase—would totally win the viewer over. But this is not a new McQueen. His title character is built upon a litany of previous minimalist antiheroes, all fiercely independent, though not always endowed with such payback powers. Ultimately, one embraces his vigilante violence because he comes across like Gary Cooper's embattled Western marshal in *High Noon* (1952). One half expects McQueen to ape Cooper's movie-ending display of disgust—throwing his badge to the ground. Indeed, Clint Eastwood does borrow the gesture in *Dirty Harry* (1972), a picture that owes a great deal to *Bullitt*. In fact, McQueen was the first one offered the title role in *Dirty Harry*, but turned it down because it seemed too similar to *Bullitt*. In either case, both Harry and Bullitt seem like men out of their time—throwbacks to a time when a hero simply did what he had to do.

The *Bullitt* reviews were outstanding and often followed a familiar pattern, as best exemplified by this *Hollywood Reporter* notice: "It is simply one of the most exciting and intelligent action films in years, probably the best good-cop film we can expect to encounter . . . [And] one gasping 11-minute chase sequence packs more excitement than anything since the second 'Ben-Hur' [1959] chariot race."[40] The picture's celebrated chase sequence was inspired by McQueen, who liked to include driving scenes in his movies as comic revenge against studios that tried to prohibit his real-life racing because of safety concerns. This usually ended up being a win-win situation for the actor, since he seldom let anyone restrict his dangerous personal habits. McQueen first became aware of how a speeding vehicle in hilly San Francisco could sometimes become airborne when he drove around the city late at night on his motorcycle. The actor decided right then that this hill-jumping, or "flying," phenomenon should be incorporated into *Bullitt*'s car chase.

Ironically, as with the motorcycle jump sequence in *The Great Escape*, McQueen would *not* do most of the driving in the *Bullitt* chase. Reports have varied through the years. Yes, he did; no, he did not. One story even had his wife Adams putting her foot down over safety fears, which resulted in a suddenly rearranged shooting schedule that, unknown to McQueen, kept him out of harm's way for the better part of a day. This spousal intervention actually did occur, but it only involved the most dangerous day of a lengthy car-chase shoot. While McQueen

Lieutenant Frank Bullitt, the title character of McQueen's 1968 smash hit Bullitt, *anticipates Clint Eastwood's gun-toting cop in* Dirty Harry *(1972).*

did do some of the driving, most of the dangerous sequences were left to the actor's stuntman friend, Bud Ekins.

One nerve-racking experience McQueen had during the chase experience occurred while *Bullitt* director Peter Yates was in the car to see how the actor/driver handled one of those airborne hill-jumping stunts. McQueen not only demonstrated "grace under pressure," he threw in some of his patented humor, too. Yates told him, "Okay, Steve, you can slow down now. We're out of film." Steve replied, "That's nothing. We're out of brakes."[41] McQueen saved a dangerous situation by both downshifting through the gears and suddenly turning into a street that ran uphill.

The actor also put himself in harm's way during the airport shootout at the film's conclusion. The chase is now on foot, and McQueen ends up on the runway dodging the wheels of a moving Boeing 707 jet preparing for takeoff. Eventually he has to hit the tarmac and let the plane pass over him. Again, the actor used a comic touch to defuse a scary stunt: "It's all a matter of timing, of knowing when to get my butt down."[42]

For all the thrills and chills inherent to *Bullitt*, I am equally drawn to the quietly amusing scenes of McQueen minimalism, when his detective is not yet on the work clock. This is most entertainingly demonstrated by the sequence in which his police partner (real-life friend Don Gordon) comes to his apartment. Bullitt has overslept, and Gordon is reduced to a monologue as McQueen's character tries to wake up. This is yet another example of the star giving up lines in order to play a scene through expressions and body language. It is charmingly simple and realistically funny, yet one rarely sees it portrayed in a serious film, let alone an action adventure. Slice-of-life scenes such as this one help an audience relate to a character, as opposed to the slickly formal disconnect of a formalistic picture like *Crown*. Quite simply, realism plays out humanistically.

McQueen's leading lady in *Bullitt* is the stunningly beautiful British actress Jacqueline Bisset. But she largely serves as lovely window dressing, with director Yates serving up more amusingly insightful looks at being a detective by focusing on a solo McQueen in some brief throwaway sequences about the downside of this loner life. The viewer sees McQueen's *Bullitt* character buying a stack of TV dinners at the grocery, or stealing a newspaper from one of those coin-operated boxes by smacking it (he does not have correct change). Again, these scenes humanize his figure, who is decidedly *not* a James Bond type, the original model for McQueen's *Crown* character. Thus, when Yates has Bullitt do uncommonly common things, the director records on film pieces of time that define us, too. This encourages the viewer's "Walter Mitty" moments, when he imagines being the macho McQueen of *Bullitt*.

The humanist slant is also naturally coupled to McQueen playing a blue-collar cop, a profession the actor was originally reluctant to embrace. As a tough kid from the streets, the police were often the enemy. During *Bullitt*'s production this turnabout merited headlines, such as the title of a *Los Angeles Times* interview: "Bad Boy McQueen Does Switch to Play Cop Role." In this same article, McQueen acknowledged

McQueen and real-life friend Don Gordon in a scene from Bullitt. *Gordon went on to appear with McQueen in the films* Papillon *(1973) and* The Towering Inferno *(1974).*

the paradox and confessed, "Yeah, I know. My head's right on the block [cops were not then popular to the political left]. I never liked cops in my whole life. . . . We're trying to show [in *Bullitt*] what a cop could be like. Everybody dislikes cops till they need one."[43]

McQueen also used this interview to soften his sometimes conservative slant toward the 1960s counterculture, as well as documenting the actor's ongoing proclivity for current slang: "Cops shouldn't make trouble for the hippies. They've contributed so much that's groovy. It takes a brave man to walk down Sunset in his bare feet and long hair. They need people like that in the police department." McQueen was probably recognizing what a later biographer summarized, "In the sixties . . . the world had finally caught up with . . . [him]. The blue jeans that had been his uniform for years became the fashion of a generation, as did his hipster speech, the smoking of marijuana, and the rebelliousness of his youth."[44]

Further into the *Bullitt* shoot, McQueen's admiration for the difficulty of being a cop had increased greatly. Again, this transition is mirrored in the title of a period McQueen interview from another Los Angeles newspaper, the *Herald Examiner*: "The Movies . . . Steve McQueen Cutting the Mustard, Learning to Like Cops." A tired McQueen said in the article, "I'm getting a [law enforcement] education. I never liked cops before in my whole life. . . . But I've learned what cops have to go through, that they deserve a fairer shake."[45]

Given this sympathetic police slant from a performer normally playing antiheroic outsiders, *Bullitt* had an opportunity for a very broad audience—if McQueen and company could deliver a strong picture. As the reviews document in detail, they more than delivered. Frequently, the reader did not even have to go beyond the critique title. For example, *Life* magazine labeled its *Bullitt* review, "Crime Flick with a Taste of Genius," while *Time*'s title was more succinct, "Cop Art."[46] Both *Cue* and the *Hollywood Citizen News* credited the picture with "edge-of-the seat" tension, and *Variety* added: "[*Bullitt* is] an extremely well-made crime melodrama . . . [and] Steve McQueen delivers a very strong performance."[47]

As with *Sand Pebbles* and *Crown*, McQueen was able to mine his minimalism into a winning performance—short on words, big on action. *Crown* costar Dunaway later praised the actor's work ethic and attempted to define his persona, taking a perspective that sounds like Adams, McQueen's first wife: "I can't say enough good about Steve. I've seen him help young actors to an extreme degree, and he works very hard. There's a feeling of control in him that a woman always responds to. It's difficult to try to analyze his appeal. It stimulates that cuddly feeling. He's the misunderstood bad boy you're sure you can cure with a little warmth and some home cooking. There was a time when I couldn't take my eyes off him when he was on the screen. But later [after working with him] I was able to know him. I'm sure that must

In Bullitt, *McQueen's character is involved once again in a bedroom scene, this time with English actress Jacqueline Bisset.*

be one thing that attracts most women to him, because there's a feeling that everything's OK, you can relax."[48]

One might have coupled these components with the added praise that McQueen *never* played it safe. To paraphrase an axiom from one of his heroes, Marlon Brando, "Steve McQueen liked to jiggle the molecules [keep it lively and unexpected]." Otherwise, one was taking away the creative mystery, such as adding electricity to a haunted house. As a product of the streets, McQueen was without tradition. Unlike a methodical academic, his regular guy was a pluralist, a creative magpie. Thus, the actor's first film after his late 1960s trilogy was *not* what his public expected, and the box office suffered. But today the comedy merits a reappraisal.

A Neglected Comedy, Hollywood Murders, and Vanity Racing

"If you ever want to reach your manhood, sometimes you've got to say 'Goodbye' to the things you know and 'Hello' to the things you don't!"
BOON'S (STEVE MCQUEEN'S) ADVICE ON GROWING UP IN *THE REIVERS* (1969)

After the "essence of cool" action-hero adventures of Steve Mc-Queen's signature film *Bullitt* (1968), the public was not prepared to see him as a buffoonish country boy in a turn-of-the-century comedy, a screen adaptation of William Faulkner's Pulitzer Prize–winning last novel, *The Reivers* (1962). As *Entertainment World*'s otherwise positive review stated, "McQueen's choice of 'The Reivers' as a vehicle is hard to understand."[1] However, if one can get past the always independent-minded McQueen's choice of material, *The Reivers* is an inspiringly warm, winning picture.

Though set in Faulkner's standard southern setting, the mythical Mississippi town of Jefferson in Yoknapatawpha County, this tale avoids the often comic/tragic tone of a more typical work by the novelist, such as *As I Lay Dying* (1930). *The Reivers*, which Faulkner subtitled "A Reminiscence," is a populist feel-good coming-of-age comedy about the novelist at age eleven. If not exactly true, it is how Faulkner entertainingly chooses to remember things. The humorous settings and situations are Mark Twain-like. Indeed, *Time* magazine's positive review of the film adaptation described it as "a kind of motorized *Huckleberry Finn*."[2]

For The Reivers *(1969), McQueen played the flamboyantly comical Boon Hogganbeck.*

Faulkner's late-in-life departure from his normal artistry might be likened to fellow tragedian Eugene O'Neill's *Ah! Wilderness* (1933), an uncharacteristically upbeat comic play, though O'Neill then returned to darker theater themes. Faulkner, who died only two months after the publication of *The Reivers*, enjoyed creating the comic novel more than any of his other books, adding: "It was fun to write because it's a happy story. My only regret at completing this book is that I can't have the fun of writing it another time."[3]

Faulkner's "happy story" very much comes across in the film adaptation, which *Boston after Dark* credited with being "very welcome proof that great literature really can be translated effectively to the screen . . . the film captures the feeling of the Nobel Prize winner's wandering, memory-laden prose, rich with the vernacular and the atmosphere of the deep South, and embellishes it with effective cinematic touches."[4] The title for this critique also generously linked the star's talents to the success of the adaptation, "'The Reivers': Faulknerian and McQueenian Charm."[4]

This exercise in Americana keys upon a four-day trip to Memphis with McQueen, black actor Rupert Crosse, and freckle-faced youngster Mitch Vogal—the "reivers," an antiquated term for thieves or rascals. Both McQueen and Crosse are grown wards of Boss McCaslin's (Will Geer) county-dominating family. McQueen's character was unofficially adopted as a child and stays on as a handyman and, most recently, chauffeur for the family's shiny new yellow Winston Flyer, the area's first automobile. Crosse's connection to the family was a blood kin going back to slavery days, a fact he comically uses whenever his "reiver" ways got him into trouble.

With most of the McCaslin clan leaving Jefferson for a funeral in Saint Louis, McQueen's Boon sees a window of opportunity for a road trip visit to his special girl, Carrie, a young Marilyn Monroe-like Sharon Farrell, who can be anybody's "special girl" since she works in a Memphis brothel. But between the writing and Farrell's performance, the part is imbued, as were most Monroe roles, with a natural innocence that belies her profession. She keeps a hope chest!

Like the real McQueen, the Boon character is fascinated by automobiles, most especially the Winston Flyer owned by Geer. Thus, Boon hatches a plot to involve young Vogel's character, Lucius McCaslin, in his rascally/reiver adventure. Despite the affectionate warning about Boon from Lucius's grandfather (Geer)—"[He] knows no obstacles, fears no dangers, knows no castes [restrictions]"—the boy is easily persuaded by McQueen's character to tell a series of whoppers to babysitting distant relatives, and the motorized mischievous mission begins. As the voice-over narration by Burgess Meredith, Lucius's character as an elderly gentleman, amusingly summarizes, "The rewards of virtue are colorless, odorless, and tasteless—not to be compared with the rewards of sin."

The road trip's first surprise occurs when Crosse's figure, McCaslin, pops up as a stowaway. This is the catalyst for yet another scene of comic frustration from Boon, first showcased early in the picture when Ned had taken the Flyer for a joyride that nearly wrecked the prized car. On that occasion McQueen had wildly chased Ned through the streets of Jefferson (shot on location in Carrollton, Mississippi), and then nearly killed his ongoing comic nemesis. As previously noted, McQueen's choice of humor roles usually had the actor playing them broadly, which is in direct contrast to his minimalist action heroes. While this had often proved unsuccessful in previous parts, McQueen's Boon is genuinely entertaining, a winning combination of writing and acting.

One should add that while the story's humor, southern milieu, and maverick white man teamed with rebellious black man rightfully conjure up images of *Huckleberry Finn*, there are some distinct differences in the Boon-Ned relationship. The actions of the Huck and Jim duo were largely orchestrated by the former figure, with runaway slave Jim more often the comic victim, especially when Tom Sawyer makes a late appearance in the novel. But the Boon-Ned teaming is a veritable Laurel and Hardy movie, with McQueen playing the Hardy part; he thinks he is in charge, but Laurel's actions/mistakes gum up the works. Like Laurel, the equally thin and gangly Crosse as Ned drives the comic action, though he is more calculatingly aware of his actions than Hardy's companion. (As a further corollary to the differences between Twain's work and *The Reivers*, there is also the sexual card played by Faulkner's use of a brothel.)

Ultimately, this film adaptation of *The Reivers* works on several levels. Most obviously, as the *Saturday Review* suggests, the movie is a charming exercise in depicting an earlier "picture-postcard America, where the sky is always clear and the paint always fresh, where grandfathers are wise and whores demure. . . . Let's not be curmudgeonly and wonder whether life in Mississippi could really have been this seraphic. It's pleasant to find yourself in never-never land once in a while."[5] One might add that when the present seems iffy and the future appears dark, the past represents promise and/or forgotten hope. For someone like McQueen, who idolized an old-fashioned family life he never knew as a child, it is easy to see the attraction of *The Reivers*. In fact, in the years immediately after making this picture, the actor began collecting all matter of Americana, from antique toys to vintage motorcycles. For him this portal to the past was probably not so much about promise but rather the unrealized hopes of a neglected little boy—positive pieces of time on which he had missed out.

Second, despite these flirtations with an idealized earlier America, a trip down a memory lane that never was, *The Reivers* also exists as a morality play. Like any good fantasy, the story is populated with poles of good and evil—from the kindly sensitive grandfather figures (Geer and Juana Hernandez's Uncle Possum), to the racist slovenly sheriff played by Clifton James. For all the "fresh" paint and "clear" skies, bad things happen here, too. Boon and Ned find themselves unfairly placed in jail, and Carrie is forced to use her "craft" with the sheriff to free them. Even this sacrifice produces dissent among our reiver trio, with lover Boon blackening Carrie's eye (though thankfully, that scene is not played for the camera).

Third, this morality play dovetails into a coming-of-age story for young Lucius. While the tale's roller-coaster ride of events movingly impacts all the characters, Vogel's character is experiencing them for the first time. These memorable moments, a kaleidoscope of growing up,

McQueen and the young Mitch Vogel enjoy traveling in their Winston Flyer in The Reivers.

ranged from a minor knife cut suffered defending Carrie's honor to a poignant bedtime in Uncle Possum's modest sharecropper's cabin. Ultimately, the key life lesson learned by Lucius comes from the cracker-barrel philosopher Geer, who saves his grandson from a beating for his lies by telling the boy that his punishment will simply be that suffered by all transgressors, learning to live with their errors, because "A man accepts the responsibility of his actions." But having said this, Geer's character kindly offers Lucius a comic axiom with which to soldier through his discomfort, "Trust in the Lord. He's up all night."

Fourth, casting McQueen in what was originally a supporting role necessitated expanding the part and embellishing the slapstick and farcical components already inherent to *The Reivers*. A prime example of this included the Laurel and Hardy-like dilemma of Boon and Ned getting that clean new car stuck in the mud, triggering yet another installment of comedy anticipation. Or, put another way—how long before everyone and everything is covered in mud? Of course, the catalyst for much of the humor is tied to Ned's outrageous trading of the yellow Flyer for a horse that he plans to race in order to win back the automobile! But unlike the car, this animal is anything but a "flyer," so that happy ending is in jeopardy until near the picture's close. Suffice to say, Ned's every action causes Boon's comic blood pressure to go up. *Films and Filming* went so far as to compare *The Reivers'* comic mood to "the determinedly good humored *Butch Cassidy* [*and the Sundance Kid*, also 1969] and [it] moves at a rollicking pace."[6]

Fifth, for the real student of McQueen, his *Reivers* past is a poignant window into the man. As noted earlier in the text, Faulkner described Boon as having the "mentality of a child"—a description of the arrested-development adolescent McQueen in a nutshell. Now, while I am not suggesting the actor was quite the overgrown dopey child that was Boon, there were more than a few parallels, from a naturally comic nature to a violent mercurial moodiness triggered by not getting his way. Factor in a fascination with automobiles, a natural affinity for children, a preference for unplanned adventures over the status quo, and an active sex drive, and one could just as easily be talking about

McQueen. Plus, *The Reivers* was the closest the actor would come to playing a film father figure. This was a role he relished in real life, always trying to make up for a father who abandoned him as a baby. But again like Boon, McQueen's parenting skills frequently played out more like a fun-loving mischievous older brother, or one's favorite kidder of an uncle—just the sort of person who would "borrow" the family car for an impromptu trip to a Memphis brothel. At the time, McQueen said of the Boon part, "I act only in films where I'm satisfied I can work without hypocrisy. Everything I do is really a little piece of me."[7] Naturally, *The Reivers*'s use of a brothel was another realistic footnote to the real McQueen, given that he had worked in a bordello during his early vagabond days. But maybe the actor's closest link to Boon was the common philosophy of life he shared with Faulkner's figure—the axiom that opens this chapter: "If you ever want to reach your manhood, sometimes you've got to say 'Goodbye' to the things you know and 'Hello' to the things you don't!"

Sixth, McQueen's winning performance as Boon documents a greater acting range than is normally suggested by his standard stoic persona. Moreover, several reviewers, such as the *Variety* critic, believed this newfound depth boded well for his future: "McQueen gives a lively ribald characterization that suggests he will have a long career as a character actor after his sexy allure thing."[8] The *Hollywood Reporter* added that McQueen was "the perfect casting for the ingratiating reiver, in a performance that allows the greatest opportunity for his comic gifts." The *Reporter* review also wins the cigar as the most affectionately positive critique title of any McQueen picture: "How Long Since You've Seen a Movie for Fun? Here's One."[9]

For all the populist spirit inherent in the finished film, the on-location shoot was often rife with stress, brought about by McQueen attempting to assert his authority on the production. Though the actor had authorized the hiring of friend Mark Rydell as director, McQueen seemed jealous of him throughout the filmmaking process. Why? There is a litany of potential reasons. The handsome former actor Rydell had once dated McQueen's wife, Neile Adams. Indeed, McQueen had es-

McQueen receives an angry reception from Diane Shalet's prostitute character after a quarrel with his brothel girlfriend in The Reivers.

sentially taken Adams away from Rydell. *Reivers'* director of photography, Richard Moore, later suggested McQueen was jealous of Rydell's ongoing romantic charms. Noting the director's stardom on the popular television soap opera *As the World Turns,* Moore remembered Mississippi autograph seekers "falling over themselves to get to Mark Rydell and when McQueen arrived, they didn't seem to care much. Steve was a competitor, especially around women; he was the center of attraction. It might have tweaked him a bit that Mark was getting all this attention."[10]

Another friction factor was that Rydell was fairly new to directing, with only one feature film under his belt, the acclaimed art-house movie *The Fox* (1968, from a D. H. Lawrence novella). But it was not as if Rydell could not handle more macho themes. Like McQueen, he had cut his teeth on small-screen Westerns, including directing several episodes of the *Gunsmoke* series. But compared to McQueen's previous experiences with veteran directors such as Henry Hathaway and Robert Wise, Rydell was essentially a novice—ripe for bullying by the picture's star. To Rydell's credit, he stood up to McQueen, and the crisis might have passed had not a production accident shut down the film for a month. Vogel had a riding accident and broke his arm.

With time on his hands, McQueen took the opportunity to focus on past dailies—footage shot but not yet assembled in finished story form. This is often a traumatic experience for actors, because they are not cognizant of the director's overall vision for a film. All the performer sees is an apparent jumble of disjointed scenes with little or no apparent narrative flow. When McQueen made *The Cincinnati Kid* (1965), director Norman Jewison sat his star down and firmly explained, along lines similar to those just noted, why he was not going to show dailies to him. McQueen had complied. But by the time the actor made *Reivers,* he had forgotten this lesson. Thus, McQueen was very disappointed with the rough film footage, and he attempted to have Rydell sacked. The star was unsuccessful, but it hardly made for a happy working relationship.

To McQueen's credit, he later admitted to Rydell that the finished film was excellent. But the damage was done. Rydell, who would go on to direct many star-laden diverse hits in multiple genres, ranging from the Western *The Cowboys* (1972, with John Wayne), to the family melodrama *On Golden Pond* (1981, with Katharine Hepburn, Henry Fonda, and Jane Fonda), decided there would be no more collaborations with McQueen. While he did remain friendly with the star, over a decade later, after McQueen's death, Rydell confessed, "[On the set] he was hard and he could be mean and he had me with my back to the wall. [But] I knew why Steve was the way he was. After all, when I was in summer camp, he was in reform school."[11]

A final friction component for McQueen's bad-boy behavior toward Rydell might simply have been fear. While most performers are predisposed toward this tendency anyway, McQueen had it in spades. Moreover, his anxiety was working overtime on *Reivers*. For all McQueen's joy in taking creative risks and not playing it easy, like turning down what became the "Dirty Harry" franchise because he had already done that story with *Bullitt*, he also agonized over taking chances. Consequently, he confided to several people during *Reivers* production that the movie was going to be a "disaster," and his career would be over.

Paradoxically, given all these negatives, McQueen's interaction with fellow *Reivers* cast members was often entertainingly positive, possibly fueled by a Method-trained actor playing Boon, an inherently comic character. One amusing element of these production relationships involved Crosse, who played Ned. At six feet, five inches tall, he was a skinny giant compared to the generously listed five-foot-ten McQueen. The star had wanted someone shorter. But in preproduction, when Rydell still had more clout on the project, he convinced McQueen that the two actors had great chemistry together. All this lobbying for Crosse, however, was put in jeopardy by an incident at a McQueen-sponsored welcoming party for the black actor. McQueen was a major student of martial arts, with none other than Bruce Lee, prefilm fame, as his personal instructor. When the party conversation turned to this subject and McQueen demonstrated a move, Crosse corrected him, telling the star he was "off balance." McQueen's Missouri "show me" background surfaced. When Crosse then flattened McQueen, Rydell saw all his salesmanship for the gangly actor going out the proverbial window. But McQueen came up laughing, and there was an instant bond with Crosse, who, it turned out, had a black belt in karate. Comically combative, as the two men shook hands after the takedown, they almost segued into an affectionate arm wrestling bout. The incident struck an entertainment chord with Rydell, and he used a variation of this incident in *Reivers* whenever Boon and Ned had to make up after a fight.

As a footnote on Lee, though he had many high-profile Hollywood martial-arts clients in the late 1960s, he spent a great deal of time on location with McQueen during the making of *Reivers*. While this predated Lee's film work, he had experienced some action acting success as Kato in the *Green Hornet* television series. Lee's character was the manservant/partner to the crusading newspaper editor/publisher Britt Reid (Van Williams), who secretly doubled as the Green Hornet. The series was a quick follow-up to the phenomenal success of television's *Batman*, which had premiered in midseason, 1965–66. As much as McQueen, the former street kid, relished any defense skills he could learn from Lee, the martial-arts master was even more anxious to become an action star. Fittingly, when that fame came, Lee enjoyed calling himself the "Oriental Steve McQueen."

As the previous pages suggest, the unconventional casting of McQueen in an equally unconventional Faulkner screen adaptation was a major critical success. The across-the-boards raves included one from *Newsweek* that called *Reivers* a "wonderful, unabashedly schmaltzy movie of a young boy's initiation into the adult world."[12] Even the normally hard-to-please *The New Yorker* confessed the picture "does make one feel good . . . [because] the filmmakers just naturally remembered that the young [viewers] are *people* and will enjoy a good tall tale."[13] And review after review seconded that praise about McQueen, from the *Motion Picture Exhibitor* crediting him with giving "a virtuoso performance as

Boon, a role that represents a decided change of pace from his tough detective parts," to *Cue* calling him and Crosse "highly amusing as the unlikely pair of adventurers."[14] (Crosse received an Oscar nomination for Supporting Actor, but lost to Gig Young for *They Shoot Horses, Don't They.*)

Sadly, while critics fully embraced McQueen as Boon, the actor ultimately had problems with his part: "After *Soldier in the Rain* [1963] I promised myself I'd never tackle another comic role. Yet here I was, hamming and grinning and strutting away down there in Mississippi. It seemed the right thing to do at the time, after *Crown* and *Bullitt*, but I ended up not liking it very damn much."[15] As with many actors, Mc-Queen often filtered his likes and dislikes through box-office returns. Though *Reivers'* domestic numbers were respectable, the revenue was only a fraction of McQueen's *Bullitt*. Worse yet, unlike *Bullitt's* equally impressive box-office figures abroad, *Reivers* laid an egg in foreign markets. Audiences outside the United States related neither to a broadly comic McQueen, nor to a picture steeped in Americana. Apparently, due to this less-than-stellar outing, some later McQueen authors, like the actor himself, have been unfortunately lukewarm toward the film.[16] Regardless, *Reivers* is an excellent *comic* McQueen movie that deserves a rediscovery.

After the completion of the picture but months prior to its Christmas 1969 release, a bizarre multiple murder case unfolded that almost included McQueen. Charles Manson, a failed singer-songwriter/film-maker, took his revenge on Hollywood by orchestrating, through his Manson Family cult, the killing of four people at the rented home of actress Sharon Tate, the pregnant wife of director Roman Polanski. In addition to Tate, the other victims included her friends Abigail Folger, Voytek Frykowski, and famous hair stylist to the stars Jay Sebring.

McQueen had been especially close to both the beautiful Tate and Sebring, with the latter figure also helping to facilitate McQueen's womanizing ways (such as the previously noted rendezvous with Mamie Van Doren) and the star's increasing drug use. Ironically, while McQueen had been invited to Tate's home the night of the murders, another one-night stand presented itself and the actor skipped the party. Of course, while most McQueen biographies now key on the randomness of his missing a date with death, one could argue that the tough former street kid and martial arts-trained Marine veteran might have *saved* some lives that fateful night.

The aftermath of the murders sent Hollywood into shock mode, with many in the community arming themselves. For the already gun-collecting McQueen, carrying a pistol was now part of his wardrobe. Adams later described a potentially frightening situation at Sebring's funeral. Before the service a "strange man" went to the altar and began to chant. Warren Beatty was sitting next to Adams and "was ready to throw me onto the floor, fearful that some sort of altercation was about to occur. He was aware Steve had a gun and was concerned what might happen if anybody opened fire. But somebody removed the man who was chanting in front of Jay's body and order resumed."[17]

After the eventual capture of Manson and his clan, some measure of order returned to the film capital. But a more old-fashioned problem was now threatening the McQueens' marriage. The star's approaching fortieth birthday (March 24, 1970) had sent him into a midlife crisis. McQueen's womanizing had always tested his marriage, with ever-increasing temptations fueled by his growing fame and the "free love" ways of the 1960s, but turning forty sent him into a panic. McQueen, the man certain he would die young, exhibited less and less discretion with his many conquests—Adams's major requirement for looking the other way.

The paradox for the star, as is often the case in a dissolving marriage, is that the union seemingly had everything going for it. McQueen had a beautiful, supportive, *forgiving* wife, two young children who idolized him (and were already into their father's dirt bike obsession), and a film career at its apex (McQueen won the National Association of Theatre Owners Male Star of the Year Award for 1969). Indeed, the latter point might have been part of the problem. The push to pass his self-appointed target, Paul Newman, had occurred. Thus, the often self-centered star felt even more justified in being Mr. Indulgent.

A family friend and young employee of McQueen's Solar Productions, Mario Iscovich, later described the star's nonworking days during
the late 1960s: "Steve was stoned all the time. That [quasi-bachelor pad]
house on [Palm Springs'] Southridge was a veritable whorehouse. He
picked these girls up from anywhere. He even picked up hitchhikers! I
used to ask him, 'Why do you do this? You're gonna blow it all, Steve.'
His answer was, 'Hey, look at me. I'm the leading sex symbol in the
whole world, man. I want it all.' I didn't know what to tell him. I just
knew he was crazy!"[18] Things became so bad for Adams that she had a
1969 revenge affair with Academy Award-winning actor Maximilian
Schell (*Judgment at Nuremberg*, 1961). When McQueen later found
out, there would be the proverbial hell to pay, but that is getting ahead
of the story.

One might call the actor's next movie, the long-delayed *Le Mans*
(1971), a documentary-like look at France's famed twenty-four-hour
automobile race. *Le Mans* was essentially McQueen revisiting his dream
to make the ultimate racing picture, a project originally titled *Day of
the Champion* that was to have followed *The Sand Pebbles* (1966). But
production delays on the latter picture sandbagged *Champion*, and
McQueen had remained obsessed with doing a racing film. Plus, an
added catalyst for *Le Mans* was McQueen achieving his greatest real-life
triumph as an automobile racer the previous year—finishing second
to only the great Mario Andretti in the celebrated twelve-hour Sebring
race. In fact, there was even talk of him racing competitively at Le
Mans.

Sometimes when one wants things in the worst way, that is the way
they turn out. While *Le Mans* is an often fascinating look at a grueling
endurance test of a competition, McQueen's stonewalling approach to
making a pure racing picture contributed to a huge financial fiasco. On
paper, the actor's simple salute to the dignity of racing sounds amusingly moving: "I'm making . . . [*Le Mans*] so that my grandmother in
Montana [McQueen had no grandmother in Montana—he meant the
average individual] who knows nothing about cars will understand."[19]
Unfortunately, most potential viewers did not have McQueen's un-

adorned bare-to-the-bone passion for racing. Or, as *Playboy*'s review noted, "Long before the end of the first hour . . . the less dedicated will find themselves restive, for the story, if it can be so called, is thin to the point of invisibility."[20]

Worse yet, while a star vehicle can skimp on story, there is no surviving a lack of characters to identify with. The *Hollywood Reporter* addressed this hole in the picture: "[*Le Mans*] is an unsatisfying film because we know no more about the people at the end than we did at the beginning."[21] Though no more viewers would have been added by immediately embracing this stark documentary-like style, enormous production costs would have been saved, because McQueen fought everyone, including initial director John Sturges, over attempts to embellish both the story and the characters.

The clash with Sturges, however, was not over just a question of minimizing the story. McQueen's ego and passion for the subject matter had made him a victim of what is sometimes called the "Chaplin disease."[22] Charlie Chaplin was that rare film artist who successfully wrote, directed, produced, composed music, and starred in his pictures. The "Chaplin disease" refers to filmmakers who stumble when attempting to wear multiple production hats, as was the case with McQueen on *Le Mans*. With National General (a coproducer with the actor's own Solar company) complaining that "[The story-less footage was all] cars, cars, cars, who gives a fuck?" and McQueen becoming ever more difficult, Sturges entertainingly exited the *Le Mans* morass with the following comment, "I'm too old and too rich to put up with this shit."[23]

Yet McQueen was even more controlling to Sturges's replacement, television director Lee H. Katzin. Eventually, after cost overruns totaling millions of dollars, Cinema Center Pictures pulled the plug on the actor's de-facto generalizing. Ironically, the finished film still reflects essentially what McQueen was after—a documentary-like look at racing. With hundreds of thousands of film footage exposed, grafting a story onto the proceedings proved impossible. The closest thing to the love story with which Sturges wanted to anchor the picture is a friendship with a fellow driver's widow, played by Elga Anderson. They have only one significant scene together. Yet, it is a pivotal one, as it is the only important dialogue-driven sequence in the movie. Anderson's figure is attempting to make sense of her husband's death, asking McQueen, "When people risk their lives, shouldn't it be for something very important. What is so important about driving faster than anyone else?" McQueen's racing reply brings to mind James Dean's fascination with bull fighting, and Ernest Hemingway's book on the subject, *Death in the Afternoon*. Calling racing a "professional blood sport," McQueen's character states in a Hemingwayesque manner: "A lot of people go through life doing things badly. Racing is important to men who do it well. When you're racing—that's life, anything that happens before or after is just waiting." It is an eloquent statement that spoke for the real McQueen, too. Had there been a few more scenes of this mettle,

McQueen as race-car driver Michael Delaney in the long delayed Le Mans *(1971).*

Le Mans might have been elevated to greatness. The final paradox, of course, is that today's standard movie reference book often gives the picture high marks as a racing spectacle.[24]

Much of McQueen's life might be defined by a line borrowed from Lady Bird Johnson, upon the November 22, 1963, assassination of President John F. Kennedy. With the elevation of her husband, Lyndon Johnson, to the White House, Lady Bird spoke these elegiac words, "I have moved on stage to a part I never rehearsed."[25] Though applicable to so much of McQueen's proverbial rags-to-riches story, the First Lady's comments were even more pertinent to the making of *Le Mans*. Like the high-profile crash McQueen's character survives in the movie, his behind-the-scenes actions on the production were a metaphorical wreck.

I am reminded of another now-notorious later cinema spectacle failure, Michael Cimino's *Heaven's Gate* (1980). McQueen's *Le Mans* damaged his reputation as a filmmaker, while boosting his image as a racer to the general viewer. A critical and commercial failure in the United States, this flop reduced McQueen's production company, Solar, to simply a tax shelter. Like another much lambasted epic picture, *Cleopatra* (1963, which eventually showed a profit), *Le Mans* did make money abroad. But the star never saw a dime. When Cinema Center elbowed him and Solar out of control, McQueen had to forfeit his salary and any profit sharing just to keep the picture in production.

McQueen's marriage to Adams is often also listed as a casualty of *Le Mans*. But this gives too much credit to the idea that they still had a marriage. Adams and the children, Terry and Chad, visited McQueen on location in France, but just as the production was out of control, so was his personal life. There was no attempt to hide the other women, and Adams ultimately left McQueen, but not before experiencing physical violence and a gun to her head. McQueen had found out about Adams's affair with Schell.[26] Paradoxically, McQueen's *Le Mans* nemesis was also a German (played by Siegfried Rauch), and a darkly comic (or was that revengeful) McQueen later kidded about getting Schell cast in the movie, given that "accidents" often happen in racing. At the time, the couple's separation was blamed on McQueen's continued obsession with the dangerous sport of racing, something the actor had frequently promised Adams he would quit. But while his wife's concerns on the subject were real, and McQueen's broken promises about racing were legion, the separation and eventual divorce were all about his cavalier, and now frightening, personal behavior.

After months of editing to find a semblance of a picture in all that raw racing footage, the movie opened in late June of 1971. The advertising campaign was fairly simple: "Steve McQueen takes you for a drive in the country. The country is France. The drive is at 200 MPH!"[27] The premiere was in America's racing capital, Indianapolis, but the Hoosier-born star was a no-show. National reviews were respectfully adamant that the picture was not a commercial property. A certain critical pattern, best demonstrated by the *New York Times*'s review, was typical. The notice started with qualified praise, "Racing-car buffs will probably flip over 'Le Mans' . . . [and the technical work] is dazzling." But then came the damning qualifier: "[The] star's exchange of monosyllabic utterances and long, meaningful stares with other drivers . . . add up to tepid, monotonous drama during the . . . [lengthy] race intervals. Dramatically, the picture is a bore."[28] Here is a similar take from the *Los Angeles Herald Examiner*: "'Le Mans' is remarkable as a photographic record of racing and race cars, even to those of us who are enamored of neither. . . . But Steve McQueen and his Solar Productions . . . constructed a story as phony as the handshake of a used car salesman, and added some embarrassingly superficial dialogue and profound looks that pass as psychological probings."[29]

There were some positive reviews. *Variety* waxed poetic throughout its critique: "'Le Mans' is a successful attempt to escape the potboiler of prior films on [the] same subject. . . . Steve McQueen stars (and races), looking better than he ever has before. . . . [The] film establishes its mood through some outstanding use of slow motion, multiple-frame printing, freezes [freeze frames], and a most artful use of sound."[30] *Box-office* even chronicled how *Le Mans* was a natural progression for a star who had always tried to mix a love of racing with the filmmaking craft, from *The Great Escape*'s motorcycle riding prisoner of war to *Bullitt*'s detective with the souped-up Mustang.[31]

Such praise, however, was in the minority. Plus, unlike the mind-candy summer releases of today, *Le Mans*'s immediate cinema competition was often moody textured, thought-provoking entertainment. To illustrate, *Le Mans* opened simultaneously with such classics as Robert Altman's anti-Western/dark parody *McCabe & Mrs. Miller* (1971, with Warren Beatty and Julie Christie), and Alan J. Pakula's thriller/character study *Klute* (1971, featuring an Oscar-winning performance by Jane Fonda).[32] More potentially disturbing to McQueen was the rash of prerelease material starting to appear about the Don Siegel/Clint Eastwood collaboration *Dirty Harry* (1972). The early buzz on this *Bullitt* copycat was strong. Thus, whether or not McQueen second-guessed the decision to turn down the part at this point (given the *Le Mans* failure), he must have gnashed his teeth over Eastwood's period comments: "[*Dirty Harry* will] probably be compared to 'Bullitt.' But it's not at all similar. Let's face it: without the chase scene, 'Bullitt' would have been a bomb."[33] (As a footnote to *McCabe & Mrs. Miller*, Western fan McQueen had been impressed with the script and would have liked to have starred in the offbeat picture himself.)

While the general public continued to be impressed with Mc-Queen's apparent racing moxie, there was a sense among many of *Le Mans*'s credited fifty-six "top race drivers" that the star was simply creating a vanity piece.[34] Certainly the movie's pictorial presentation of Mc-Queen between driving sequences suggests a broodingly self-conscious track god from some racing Valhalla. Along related negative insider lines, even McQueen's friend/hero and racing legend, Sterling Moss, was appalled by the picture: "I thought it was a ghastly film. . . . I was surprised it got past him. Absolutely abortive. It had neither passion nor emotion. . . . A very bad film in my opinion. One takes part in the sport because of the passion and humor. Racing drivers are a special lot—great fun. But none of this comes across in the film at all."[35]

Paradoxically, a modest documentary, *On Any Sunday* (1971), which should have been the production model for *Le Mans*, almost immediately erased any questions about McQueen's real passion and talent for racing. *Sunday* was a motorcycle film written, directed, and produced by Bruce Brown, a filmmaker whose interest in the sport dated from McQueen's character jumping the barbed wire fence by motorcycle in *The Great Escape!* Brown, already famous in nonfiction film circles for his documentary on surfing (*The Endless Summer*, 1966), now wanted to do the definitive picture on motorcycle racing. Budgeted by McQueen's Solar production company for a mere three hundred thousand dollars, before it went belly up with *Le Mans*, the little documentary grossed an amazing twenty-four million dollars worldwide. Moreover, this box-office number topped the revenue for *Le Mans* by five million dollars, with a production cost of only one-tenth the other film. Sadly, McQueen did not see any profit from this movie, either. By the time of *Sunday*'s release, less than a month after *Le Mans*, any Solar profits were being funneled to creditors.

Still, McQueen got the satisfaction of knowing a realistic look at motorcycle racing was a hit with the public. While Brown was the total artistic auteur on the project, McQueen had been the one to first suggest doing the movie to the filmmaker after the two men kept meeting at motorcycle races. Despite McQueen being a big Marlon Brando fan, he believed that the king of Method actors' motorcycle movie, *The Wild One* (1954), had set the sport back "about 200 years." McQueen hated that most films portrayed motorcycle types as outlaws, à la the Hells Angels. Even the star's one extended line in the documentary underlines the "bikers as nice guys" perspective: "Every time I start thinking of the world as all bad, then I start seeing some people out here having a good time on motorcycles—it makes me take another look." Otherwise, McQueen is just one of the racers highlighted in *Sunday* (he did use a comic pseudonym, Harvey Mushman, in the film).

As *Sunday*'s box-office numbers suggest, critical praise was equally strong for the documentary. The *New York Times* said, "On the basis of his new film . . . [Brown is] becoming the unofficial poet of the sports world."[36] *Variety* added, "'On Any Sunday' may do for motorcycle racing what 'The Endless Summer' did for surfing. . . . 'Sunday' is an exciting documentary of one of the most dangerous of all sports." These and other reviews also praised McQueen's motorcycle skills. The aforementioned *Variety* critique said of the star, "McQueen's prowess as a racer is demonstrated time and again and his name should spark interest in a film that alone stands as a spectacular piece of filmmaking."[37]

As McQueen's racing movies take him into the last decade of his life, a passing reference in one of the reviews seems prophetic. *Cue* noted, "[There is] visual poetry in the 24-hour grind at Le Mans, even in the disasters he slow motions, with cars coming apart like the bodies in [director Sam Peckinpah's] 'The Wild Bunch.'"[38] The last great cinema artist with whom McQueen collaborates will be Peckinpah, who would direct the star in *Junior Bonner* and *The Getaway* (both 1972). There is also a certain metaphorical appropriateness for the maverick McQueen hooking up with Peckinpah at this time, as the star's life was unraveling, and this director was synonymous with lives (his own included) in crisis and chaos. Indeed, examining the worlds of McQueen and Peckinpah brings to mind the artistic focus of author Arthur Miller: "Dramatizing men and women like [*Death of a Salesman*'s] Willy [Lohman] as they're broken by society."[39] But even then, one wants to qualify the verdict to something Hemingwayesque, i.e., broken but not defeated. Regardless, McQueen and Peckinpah made a good artistic pairing.

From Peckinpah to *Papillon*, Plus a Real "Love Story"

When the always independent Steve McQueen signed to make the film
Junior Bonner (1972) with the controversial director Sam Peckinpah,
the actor comically observed, "The studio is buying a lot of aspirins."[1]

In many ways Steve McQueen and Sam Peckinpah were cut from
the same cloth—hard-living, womanizing U.S. Marine Corps veterans
who were uncompromising in their movie work ethics. Both moved
from 1950s television Western successes to film greatness in the 1960s.
Each man was also famous for his violent action-adventure pictures,
from Peckinpah classics such as *Ride the High Country* (1962) and *The
Wild Bunch* (1969), to the seminal McQueen movie sandwiched in
between, *Bullitt* (1968). In fact, Peckinpah edited one of his most provocative examinations of violence, *Straw Dogs* (1971), during the making of *Junior Bonner*. These were clearly not men remotely connected to
some stereotypically soft image of polite artists one lemonade short of
a good Sunday. Yet ironically, both individuals were attracted to *Bonner* because the story was *not* violent. Though McQueen's title character
is an aging rodeo star who has returned home (Prescott, Arizona) to a
celebrated local contest, the movie is essentially a comedy/drama about
a dysfunctional family. Still, the Western setting gives an added resonance to this bittersweet study that showcases "how people can care for
one another despite deep-seated differences and the inability to live up
to each other's expectations."[2]

Though both McQueen and Peckinpah had careers intertwined
with the Western, McQueen remained a reluctant cowboy, a love-hate

relationship which went back to his comic misfortunes with a horse on the series *Wanted: Dead or Alive*. Of course, McQueen's fellow motorcy-cle-and-racecar-loving friends preferred to kid that the star's real problem with horses was that they never went, "Va-room!"

Regardless, McQueen's reservations about the Western were not assisted by the injuries he suffered doing many of his own stunts on *Bonner*—a sprained finger, a deep cut to his nose, and a possible fracture of his left wrist. At the end of shooting, McQueen was asked if he would be interested in doing a documentary on the modern rodeo, à la the star's involvement in the nonfiction film on motorcycle racing, *On Any Sunday* (1971). The actor comically replied, "That I'll leave to John Wayne. The great thing about bikes and cars, however dangerous they may be, is that they don't kick and they never bite."[3]

McQueen had also been drawn to *Bonner* because he related to the estrangement between his character and Junior's father, Ace Bonner (Robert Preston). Indeed, it was McQueen's decision to accent this fact by calling Preston's figure "Ace," instead of "Dad" or "Father." While their screen relationship was always closer than anything McQueen had experienced in real life, with a father who had abandoned the family when he was a baby, the actor enjoyed "essaying" a cinematic reconcilia-tion, of sorts, since it was a "part" he never got to play in reality.

Reading between the lines, *Bonner*'s father-son dynamics offer some additional connections with McQueen and Peckinpah. Preston's char-acter, like the actor's real father, is a vagabond, with one of *Bonner*'s key plot points involving Ace's attempts to get a grubstake to go gold prospecting in Australia. And just as McQueen was very much like the father he never knew, Junior and Ace Bonner are ever so similar, too—both have longtime ties to the nomadic rodeo circuit.

Peckinpah was also drawn to this father-son story, with the direc-tor's favorite scene being a railroad station sequence between the two Bonners. Ace first talks about the old days, trying to soften up his son for a grubstake request. But when it comes out that Junior is also broke, Preston's character takes a half swing at Junior and knocks his son's hat off—something the senior Peckinpah would do to the director whenever he was disappointed with him. Then, in a visual touch reminiscent of the cinematic use of trains in *The Cincinnati Kid* (1965, a film from which Peckinpah was fired as director), just as Preston's figure attempts to retrieve the hat, a passing locomotive and several railroad cars poignantly accent the separateness of the two Bonners by physically coming between them. Despite this inspired use of legendary director Leo McCarey's most basic filmmaking precept, "Do it visually," this sequence has an upbeat comic conclusion, as McQueen's character tells Ace he has entered them as a duo in the Prescott Rodeo's "Wild Cow Milking Contest."

If there is fence-mending to be done between Ace and Junior, McQueen's former rodeo champion is on much better ground with his screen mother, Elvira Bonner (Ida Lupino). Elvira has managed to weather several independent men: a wayward husband and two sons, Junior's clone of his father and Curly (Joe Don Baker), a crass video cowboy real-estate broker. McQueen was equally fond of Lupino, the costar of the actor's favorite film, *High Sierra* (1941, with McQueen's hero, Humphrey Bogart). Lupino had also "been one of the Four Star[s]

Bogart and Ida Lupino in a scene from High Sierra.

who gave McQueen his break in *Wanted . . .* [and] the actor returned the favor by hiring her in *Bonner's* supporting cast."[4]

On the set McQueen frequently talked to Lupino, whom he respectfully referred to as "Miss Ida," about old Hollywood, from Bogie stories connected to *High Sierra* to the *Wanted* series. But it was not all fun and games between them. McQueen had a habit of shortening and/or changing his lines, which created an ongoing conflict with the more traditionally trained Lupino: "The moment when Junior and his mother meet in the picture, when they're outside, Sam [Peckinpah] had us ad-lib that, and it went very well. But when it came time to do the inside portion of that same scene, Steve had rewritten it. I had already learned what I was supposed to say, and I said that I needed more time to learn these new lines. I had loved the original but wasn't as fond of

(Left to right) McQueen, Lupino, Joe Don Baker, and Robert Preston (back to camera) in Junior Bonner *(1972).*

what Steve had changed it to. But I went ahead and tried to be [as] cooperative as possible because I felt that it was necessary for a mother and a son to be motivated by a common background for the scene to work."[5]

Despite the tough-guy image of both McQueen and Peckinpah, the *Bonner* shoot was something of a father-orientated production. The director cast his young son, Matthew, as one of Baker's children in the movie, and Peckinpah's adult daughter, Sharon, was signed on as a continuity person. She described a tough-love philosophy about her father, which would also be true of McQueen once his children were older: "He'd help . . . [anyone] if you paid your dues. But his own children had to pay twice. It wasn't just working. You were his daughter and he expected a certain decorum. You were supposed to act a certain way because it was a reflection on him. It was like that line William Holden said in *The Wild Bunch*: 'Either you learn to live with it or we'll leave you.'" Just how much Peckinpah and McQueen were on the same parenting page is best demonstrated by another *Bonner* scene. Matthew recalled that he was not paying attention to his father's direction, and all of a sudden, "McQueen poked me in the chest and said, 'Listen to what your dad is telling you.'"[6]

Along related lines, both of McQueen's children spent a great deal of time on the *Bonner* shoot. Twelve-year-old Terry and the eleven-year-old Chad idolized their dad, with McQueen's son's desire to be an actor, and his daughter's goal to be a pioneering woman's motorcycle racing champion. Both children were proficient dirt bike riders; Chad also drove miniature racing cars and aped his dad's interest in martial arts. After the McQueens' divorce became final (1972), Chad eventually lived with his father, and Terry remained with Neile Adams. Ironically, given this arrangement, each child resembled the opposite gender parent: "[Terry] had . . . [Steve's] fair hair, blue eyes, and lean body, while Chad took after his mother, shorter, [by then] chunkier, with her heavy eyebrows and dark coloring."[7] McQueen, the less-than-ideal husband, remained a caring dad. For the student of Sidney Poitier's "spiritual autobiography," *The Measure of a Man* (2000), which defines its title as the way a man treats his children, McQueen's love for Terry and Chad could be called his greatest legacy.[8]

The presence of the actor's children and Lupino helped make *Bonner* a pleasant shoot for McQueen. All this is not to say the shoot was without anger, a commodity McQueen always had in abundance. But such incidents were modest in number and resolved in the actor and Peckinpah immediately working together again on *The Getaway* (1972).

One initial difference McQueen and the director had on *Bonner*, however, offers a window into the star's sense of machismo. McQueen was opposed to having his hat knocked off in the aforementioned scene between himself and his screen father. At first, McQueen believed that no response from his character lessened Junior's manhood. But he was made to understand that letting Preston's patriarch vent his disappointment, followed by Ace retrieving the hat, made McQueen's Junior a bigger character. Ultimately, such scenes give the methodical *Bonner* a casual drive-by brilliance.

Along similarly significant lines, a sequence from Peckinpah's opening for *Bonner* is a metaphorical microcosm of the story that is about to unfold. The first Prescott stop for McQueen's prodigal son is the family's modest old home, now an abandoned building about to be flattened by a bulldozer. After a brief trip inside, which reveals a newspaper clipping documenting Ace's past glories with the rodeo (and thus suggesting special links with his rodeo son Junior), this same son attempts to stop time—the destruction of his past—by briefly blocking the bulldozer's path with his car. But it is a confrontation he cannot win, and he makes way for the destruction of the old neighborhood. The scene is played for comic poignancy, as McQueen's character has about as much chance to win against this piece of giant machinery as Don Quixote battling windmills.

Consistent with this retreat, the *Bonner* tale that unwinds does not fix a dysfunctional family. Indeed, by Junior's movie-closing act of benevolence (spending hard-earned rodeo prize money on a first-class ticket to Australia for his father), he further hastens the disintegration of the Bonner clan. Yet, it is the thing to do. Junior's parents have long been separated, and the proud Ace had become an unofficial ward of his disappointing son, Curly, who is an affront to the family's Western legacy. The freeing of Ace to look for a new West "down under" is a vote for the rebirth of that heritage. Moreover, McQueen's Junior goes on to the rodeo circuit's next stop, continuing that American mystique of the cowboy loner wandering the West.

While Frederick Jackson Turner is famous for his thesis that America was shaped by the Western experience, with *Bonner* both Peckinpah and McQueen seemed to be revisionists who embraced the idea that it is now a *romantic image* of the West that continued to redefine America. And if one applies the academic Peckinpah overview to *Bonner*— "the story of a loser who doesn't know when to quit"—the addendum requires a *romantic* asterisk.[9] Junior and Ace might be "losers" to the extent that their immediate futures are long shots (panning for Australian gold, or an aging cowboy staying on the rodeo circuit), but their ongoing passion for pursuing an illusive goal is at the romantic core of that thing called the American dream. Plus, *Bonner*'s modern setting makes it yet another movie by Peckinpah and/or McQueen in which characters are out of sync with their times. Consequently, as *American Classic Screen* analyzed Junior's confrontation with the earthmover, "It is pointless to confront modern society on its own terms . . . one must back off and find other ways to preserve one's uncompromising life style."[10]

Given all the superlatives noted in the previous pages, it should be no surprise that the reviews were often stellar. The *New York Post* said, "McQueen has a chance to do a lot of what he does so well: nothing much while he thinks about some action that has happened or will. . . . McQueen keeps it all in focus with those steady blue eyes of his. A hero from the past. . . . You stay with it, past or present, and it makes a good movie to watch."[11] The *New York Daily News*'s Kathleen Carroll observed, "A nice, loose, easy-going rodeo picture. McQueen has met with a role that fits him like a glove."[12] The *London Times* stated, "For those of us who have come to expect (or fear) that each new Sam Peckinpah film will be a new bloodbath, this comes as a pleasant surprise, a reminder of milder, gentler films."[13] The *New York Times* added, "'Motel cowboys' is the way someone describes them [modern rodeo competitors] in Peckinpah's funny and elegiac new film . . . [continuing his] preoccupation with what might be called reluctant post-primeness, that quality of being about to find oneself over-the-hill (and not liking it a bit)."[14]

If the positive notices were to be expected, the poor box office was not. McQueen blamed poor distribution: "I liked *Junior Bonner* very much. It was the first time I'd worked with Sam, and we got it together. I thought the script was tremendous—one of the best properties I've come across. But I think the film is a failure . . . financially. . . . In distributing the picture, I was dealing with a man named Joe Sugar [of ABC Pictures], who wanted to release it big—Grauman's Chinese and the whole bit. I told him that it should be released [modestly] as an art picture starting in more select, smaller theaters and letting the picture catch on. He continued to disagree, and, of course, the picture was released his way and it fell flat. But I think that it's a picture that'll do very well over the long haul. Not today, not tomorrow. But give it time, and people will recognize it for what it's worth."[15]

McQueen was on target with his long-term assessment. In fact, the *Bonner* role is now often considered his best performance, a conclusion seconded by Peckinpah at the time. In the following quote from a 1972 *Playboy* interview, the director also placed *Bonner* at the top of his own filmography: "I think *Junior Bonner* . . . may possibly be my best picture. I'm truly delighted with it. And I don't think McQueen has ever been better, which is saying a lot."[16]

For all this praise, however, Hollywood is driven by box-office numbers. Beyond McQueen's hypothesis about faulty distribution, *Bonner* was undoubtedly hurt by not meeting the violent expectations of a collaboration between Peckinpah and the actor. Though the *London Times* was pleased this was not a "new bloodbath," rank-and-file viewers probably would have lined up for fresh carnage if it had been orchestrated with Peckinpah's patented montage magic, as best demonstrated by the "Bloody Porch" conclusion to *The Wild Bunch*.

Bonner's box office was undoubtedly also hurt by there having been a rash of similar movies coming out at the same time. These pictures included Cliff Robertson's tour-de-force efforts as director/cowriter/star of *J. W. Coop* (1972) and *The Honkers* (1972, which starred McQueen friend James Coburn). *Bonner* reviews that noted this three-picture pile-up, such as *Variety* and the *Village Voice*, invariably designated the McQueen movie as the best of the bunch, with the former publication christening the phenomenon a minigenre of the "misunderstood-rodeo-drifter."[17] Still, any time multiple variations of the same story open almost simultaneously, revenue will suffer. One could also add that the early 1970s were the last hurrah of the Western, a genre that had dominated the American film market for three decades. Thus, *Bonner* had to compete with period cowboy pictures, too, including, paradoxically, a sequel of the Western that had established McQueen as a star, *The Magnificent Seven Ride!* (1972, which was even reviewed in the same *New York Times* issue as *Bonner*).[18]

Like this roller-coaster ride for the picture (good notices, poor business), McQueen's love life was equally confusing. Though a womanizer, he was also a man forever in need of a companion. This role was filled during the *Bonner* production by actress Barbara Leigh, who also played his girlfriend in the film. Sources differ as to whether Leigh got the part because she was already involved with McQueen or if life simply copied art once the shoot began. Leigh, a twenty-four-year-old, beautiful, long-legged starlet, later said the couple enjoyed a "wonderful, intense relationship."[19] Yet, McQueen still had hopes of reconciling with his wife Adams, and Leigh turned out to be pregnant—with someone else's baby! This romantic melodrama was at its worst during this 1971 period when the separated McQueen and Adams attempted the occasional "date," with the approval of her psychiatrist. Sadly, McQueen again turned abusive, and it became inevitable they would divorce. Still, given their fifteen-year marriage, two children, and a persistently abiding friendship, they remained close until McQueen's death in 1980.

The parade of women in McQueen's life during the late 1960s and early 1970s was not limited to the passing pretty groupie, or the conveniently available actress on a shoot. For example, he was romantically linked at different times to model Lauren Hutton and Supremes singer Mary Wilson. The latter relationship is especially interesting, given a 1977 Lawrence Kasdan script written with McQueen in mind. The screenplay has him playing an ex-Secret Service agent acting as head of security for a pop-star singer, before the story inevitably dovetails into romance. Eventually filmed as *The Bodyguard* (1992, with McQueen fan Kevin Costner and Whitney Huston), the original production would "have co-starred McQueen with [the Supreme's lead singer] Diana Ross, but the interracial romance was considered too controversial during his [McQueen's] lifetime."[20] (In the later film, Costner plays nonstop homage to McQueen, from his minimalist cold-as-steel mannerisms, to a closely cropped hairstyle reminiscent of the late actor.)

A love story/scandal on McQueen's next picture, the Peckinpah-directed *Getaway* (1972), dwarfed any previous tabloid fare with Hutton

After working with McQueen in Junior Bonner, *actress Barbara Leigh went on to do two pictorials for* Playboy *magazine.*

or Wilson. His *Getaway* costar and newest romantic interest was former model Ali MacGraw, who had catapulted to film fame as the "Jewish-American Princess" of *Goodbye, Columbus* (1969, from novelist Philip Roth's stinging examination of a suburban Jewish family). MacGraw further cemented that overnight success the following year with *Love Story* (1970), a throwback to classic Hollywood schmaltz, about romance and a sudden fatal illness. Drawn from Erich Segal's best-selling novella (Segal also adapted it for the screen), the picture was a monster commercial hit, earning MacGraw an Oscar nomination as Best Actress. The *Love Story* box office was fifty million dollars, an amazing amount for 1970.[21] In comparison, 1968's *Bullitt* had been considered a major hit at nineteen million dollars. *Love Story's* numbers were so ridiculously high, the movie even invited comic commentary, "What can you say about a movie [melodrama with those kind of grosses]? . . . That it caused whole forests to be felled so tons of Kleenex could be produced."[22] MacGraw's rise to Hollywood royalty had also been assisted by a marriage to the flamboyant former actor turned production chief of Paramount, Robert Evans.

Getaway began shooting in Huntsville, Texas, during February 1972, approximately three months prior to McQueen's divorce becoming final. Ironically, both stars (McQueen and MacGraw) had been strongly encouraged to make the picture by their respective spouses. Adams, an ongoing story adviser for her husband, even after their divorce, did not have to push hard. But Evans did. MacGraw was not interested in playing a bank-robbing movie moll. Her husband argued that *Getaway* represented a graduation to adult roles, after the college girl parts of *Goodbye, Columbus* and *Love Story*, though she was then already in her early thirties.

The real reason MacGraw was reluctant to be teamed with McQueen was her fear of what eventually happened—a passionate, messy love affair. In her autobiography, she dated her obsession with the actor to a 1968 screening: "When I first saw him, the movie star 'Steve McQueen,' it was from a seat in the deep, dark Radio City Music Hall. The movie was *Bullitt*. It was one of the very rare times in my life, especially in my grown-up years, when I left the movie theater with my knees knocking for the star. Whatever it is that star is about, Steve had it on screen. And, I was later to find, in a room. It was more than the obvious electric-blue eyes and short sandy hair cut close to a perfect skull. He had a tiger like quality. Something about his short athletic body reminded me of a wild animal, ready at an instant to pounce or attack. I think the essential thing about Steve was that he exuded danger."[23]

If these raw emotions were not an invitation for an affair, here are MacGraw's confessional comments a few pages later in her memoir, after meeting McQueen: "I was obsessed with Steve from the moment he stepped into my world, and there was never enough air for me to breathe to change that feeling. He was very taken with me, too, although I wasn't necessarily his dream lady, physically. I [later] always felt insecure because of his attraction to blonde models and *Playboy* centerfold types, who come at him by the hundreds. (At the memorial service for Steve, his first wife said wryly, 'Steve liked to fuck blondes—

McQueen and young actress Ali MacGraw falling in love during filming of The Getaway *(1972).*

but he married brunettes.') [His second and third wives, MacGraw and Barbara Minty, were brunettes like Adams.]"[24] For all the sexual chemistry that drew McQueen and MacGraw together on the *Getaway* shoot, theirs was the sort of love affair later called "doomed." But first, the actual production of this popular picture merits examination.

Given McQueen's recent collaboration with Peckinpah on *Junior Bonner,* one might assume they simply moved from that picture to *The Getaway.* However, hot new director and sometimes film scholar Peter Bogdanovich was originally slated to direct *Getaway.* But when Bogdanovich wanted to first shoot *What's Up, Doc?* (1972, with Barbra Streisand), a loose remake of the seminal screwball comedy *Bringing Up Baby* (1938, directed by one of Bogdanovich's screen heroes, Howard Hawks), McQueen asked Peckinpah to direct *Getaway.*

Providentially, Peckinpah had long been a fan of the Jim Thompson noir novel from which the film was being adapted. Indeed, years before, the director had planned to do his own adaptation. Couple this with McQueen and Peckinpah's desire to work together again, and one had an excellent foundation upon which to start a movie. Consistent with its noir roots, the novel was set in the 1940s, though Peckinpah gave the film a contemporary setting. Still, Peckinpah, and especially McQueen, were pleased how writer Walter Hill's *Getaway* script "reflected something of [director Raoul] Walsh's *High Sierra.*"[25] In fact, Hill dedicated his screenplay to Walsh. Unlike, however, the doomed love affair of so many noir works, including *High Sierra* and the original *Getaway* novel, Peckinpah wanted an upbeat finale for his bank robbing romantic duo. Moreover, this would complement the director's desire to occasionally pepper the picture with some affectionate parody, such as the winning late inclusion of Slim Pickens's populist "cowboy," so unlike most self-servingly lethal noir characters. A happy *Getaway* conclusion for this modern-day Bonnie and Clyde also reflected the love story playing out before the cameras for McQueen and MacGraw, as life imitated art.

A quick opening synopsis for *Getaway* finds "Doc" McCoy (McQueen) serving a ten-year armed robbery sentence at Huntsville penitentiary. Turned down for parole after four meritorious years, Doc

Sally Struthers and Al Lettieri in a scene from The Getaway.

is near the breaking point, as Peckinpah shows through an efficient opening-credit montage. This has been largely triggered by missing his beautiful young wife Carol (MacGraw). On her next visit, McQueen's character requests that Carol contact the crooked Texas businessman/power broker Jack Benyon (Ben Johnson, fresh from winning a Best Supporting Actor Oscar for Bogdanovich's *The Last Picture Show*, 1971). Doc knows Benyon can arrange an early parole if McQueen's convict will perform yet another bank heist. What is not clear until later is that sexy Carol has also had to both perform sexual favors for Benyon, as well as promise to double cross her husband.

The bank-robbing McCoys then proceed to plan the "job," saddled by two partners brought in by Benyon—Rudy Butler (Al Lettieri) and Frank Jackson (Peckinpah regular Bo Hopkins). Butler has double-crossing plans of his own and executes Hopkins shortly after the robbery. When he attempts to follow suit against Doc, however, McQueen's character gets the better of him, leaving Butler for dead. For the rest of the film, this often scene-chewing villain will be after the McCoys.

Lettieri and his *Getaway* figure deserve a footnote at this point. The part was originally to have gone to Jack Palance (maybe still most frighteningly unforgettable as the hired gunslinger of *Shane*, 1953). But Palance's price was too high, and Peckinpah was impressed with Lettieri's performance in the then not yet released *Godfather* (1972, a gangster who attempts to kill Marlon Brando's title character, before being gunned down by Al Pacino's avenging son in the restaurant.) Lettieri knew the gangster lifestyle, given that his brother was an actual high-profile New York Mafioso, and, if truth be told, Lettieri the actor played the tough guy in real life, too.

Sally Struthers, of *All in the Family* fame, was teamed with Lettieri for much of the shoot—a kidnap victim who becomes his lover. But as someone who also briefly dated him during the production, she had firsthand experience with the actor's dark side: "Al had a lot of problems. He had a terrible drinking problem and a personality problem that came with the drinking. He was so nice and sweet when he was

sober, and he became so evil when he was drunk. He was really scary."[26]
Not surprisingly, there was some real conflict between Lettieri and Mc-
Queen during the making of the film.

Ironically, like many opportunist directors, Peckinpah baited the
two actors, believing it could only help their performances as warring
characters in the picture. Unlike the director's previous collaboration
with McQueen on *Junior Bonner*, where Peckinpah had tried to create an artificially negative aura around the actor playing the heavy (Joe
Don Baker), Lettieri's bad-boy behavior played right into the director's
use of real conflict to stimulate performances.

A final complement to the natural disturbing intensity Lettieri
brings to the part is his frightening appearance, especially as a contrast
to the beautiful couple, McQueen and MacGraw. *The New Yorker* critic
Anthony Lane might have been discussing this very dichotomy when
he wrote, "There is a book to be written on the importance of ugly men
in cinema. So readily does the camera fall into a swoon at the spectacle
of beauty, both male and female, that the need for smelling salts—for
somebody who will jolt us from our silly rapture, and remind us that
the human physiognomy is hardly confined to the spotless—will never
fade from fashion."[27] No matter the greatness of one's hero/antihero, the
scenario is always improved by a memorable heavy.

For all *Getaway*'s violence, much of it precipitated by Lettieri's
character, there are also scenes of quiet poignancy and humor. One
that provides special insight into McQueen addresses Doc and Carol's
first night together, after he has been released from prison. Separated
over four years from his wife, McQueen felt Doc would be so intent
on making love it would play out like a rape. Peckinpah wanted to go
in the opposite direction—an insecure man afraid to sexually perform
again. McQueen invariably fought such "soft" scenes, just as he resisted
the railroad yard/hat sequence in *Junior Bonner*.

In both cases, and elsewhere, Peckinpah prevailed and the pictures
are better for it. Moreover, McQueen is good at these tender scenes. But
for a street kid whose only real "education" involved survival through
playing it tough, showing any emotional vulnerability, be it on film or

in reality, just was not done. Indeed, that was the original catalyst for his minimalist screen persona. Like the film-noir world so often occupied by McQueen's movie idol, Bogart, the actor's painfully neglected childhood had taught him that a desensitized self was less subject to pain.

Following a patient Carol slowly helping Doc find his way back to physical love, after, as McQueen's character tells his wife, "It [prison] does something to you," Doc is entertainingly shown fixing breakfast for Carol. In a largely improvised scene, with little dialogue, McQueen succeeds here by his naturalness with props. With food as a focus, the sequence also taps into McQueen and Peckinpah's proclivity for eating scenes that help define the characters. For example, in contrast to this warm breakfast sequence, with Doc and Carol reconnecting, there is the rib-eating scene between Lettieri's and Struthers's characters. Initially funny, as it briefly turns into a food fight, Lettieri soon becomes angry, with Struther's figure being frightened.

Food can also be a comic distraction. While Doc waits for Carol to buy another getaway car, he sits at a bus stop ravenously devouring a hamburger and a Coke. (The former prisoner who has missed the joys of fast-food takeout perfectly meshes with the chronically underfed young McQueen, who remained chronically hungry the rest of his life.) As he exits the scene, the viewer realizes that the woman next to him on the bus stop bench has been reading a newspaper with a front-page picture of Doc, the bank robber. But comically, she never notices, because she is too intent on finishing the Coke he has left behind!

Whether food related or not, *Getaway* has a great deal of neglected comedy, from an escape that involves Doc and Carol hiding in a dumpster (only to find themselves deposited in a garbage truck), to inspired throwaway lines. An example of the latter occurs when Pickens's character gets the couple across the Mexican border in his wreck of a pickup, with containers of trash in the back. When officials ask Pickens what he is transporting, the modern cowboy deadpans, "Building materials." Even during the shoot-out at an old El Paso hotel, Peckinpah and McQueen manage to include quick comic touches. Doc has just fatally shot one of Johnson's henchmen, causing the dying villain to spray semiautomatic weapon fire around the lobby, including the obliteration of a paperback book rack devoted to cheap sex novels. Peckinpah then immediately cuts to the hotel manager (comic character actor Dub Taylor) diving under a desk, with only his big rear end still sticking out into the line of fire. For a split second the viewer sees protruding from Taylor's back pocket a novel/manual for sex over fifty!

Of course, sometimes the humor is macabre and controversial, sort of anti-comedy to the polite crowd. This is best demonstrated by the suicide of the character playing Struthers's husband (Jack Dodson). Since her character has romantically taken up with their kidnapper (Lettieri), Dodson has become despondent, hanging himself in the hotel bathroom. But this only becomes known through the perspective of Lettieri's gangster. He is yelling at Dodson, telling him his bathroom time is up. It is Sunday morning and a radio evangelist can be heard repeating the phrase, "Receive the Lord." Lettieri opens the bathroom door, looks up without emotion, and then sits down on the toilet— only then does the viewer see Dodson hanging near the shower. Lettieri calmly goes about his "business" while nonchalantly smoking a cigarette and reading a newspaper. Though today this would merely qualify as a basic primer on dark comedy, this was shocking stuff for many 1972 patrons. To illustrate, here is *Life* magazine's take on the sequence: "But the most appalling scene of all will be one he [Peckinpah] personally grafted onto the original script. . . . A bank robber enters a hotel bathroom and discovers a corpse hanging from a water pipe. Barely glancing at the suicide, the robber sits at the toilet. . . . 'I think it's a good scene,' Peckinpah contends. 'It's how a man like that would behave.'"[28] *Life*, not impressed, titled the article "What Price Violence?"

Life notwithstanding, *Getaway* opened to often strong reviews. The *Los Angeles Times* described the film as an "acutely suspenseful and intensely exciting slam-bang diversion directed to a fare-tee-well by Sam Peckinpah . . . [with] Steve McQueen and Ali MacGraw, who generate between them as much electricity as any of the fabled screen teams of the past."[29] The *Los Angeles Herald Examiner* said the film was "punctuated with keenly observed contemporaneity, relentless suspense, and the charged undertone of a taut, dramatic love story between shotgun-toting McQueen and his accomplice and wife, Ali MacGraw."[30] *Cue* said: "[Peckinpah] has exploded another dazzler—one of the best action films seen for some time . . . [and] McQueen is the epitome of 'cool.'"[31] The *London Times* added: "Mr. Peckinpah's flawless timing, his ability to sustain a movement which twists and leaps through such trivial and such enormous accidents . . . [that it] nails one down in a kind of delight at the appalling [violent] adventure."[32]

If there was a common criticism, however, MacGraw's performance was often faulted. *Playboy* wryly observed: "McQueen is marvelous, communicating a wide range of emotions with a minimal effort. But MacGraw seems to belong to another film, as though she were wrenched from the Radcliffe campus of 'Love Story' and dropped into a Texas world of crime without a map." The same review also made the provocative suggestion: "Ali's role might have been better played by Sally Struthers . . . who comes on strong as a smarmy hoodlum's highly cooperative hostage."[33] Along similar lines, the *New Republic* opined: "If you could somehow weave a new leading actress into the master print . . . you would have a first-class crime thriller. All you need is not to have Ali MacGraw . . . Outside of that . . . the picture is smashing."[34]

Despite critics who might fault Peckinpah violence or MacGraw's wooden acting, *Films and Filming*'s take on *Getaway*'s McQueen was fairly universal: "The film gains the strength of this actor's individual star professionalism—the ability to imply by the merest flicker of eyes, or move of facial muscles, the existence of an intense emotional life beneath his public image."[35] For today's student of McQueen, the actor's only disturbing *Getaway* scene is where he smacks MacGraw around, after discovering she has slept with Johnson's character. The violence is bothersome because we now know McQueen was not averse to hitting women in real life. Indeed, the painful catalyst for this *Getaway* spousal abuse—infidelity—almost kept McQueen from taking the part. But Adams, the earlier victim of McQueen's rage after she had an affair, was able to cajole this man she still loved into taking the role.

Again, one has yet another realistically macho component that closely links McQueen to a movie part. The *Hollywood Reporter* believed the best thing about *Getaway* was the slow healing of the wound created by this infidelity—despite it being done to rescue Doc: "McQueen and MacGraw are interesting to watch. . . . For their progressive development of the complicated, touchy relationship between Doc and Carol."[36] Sadly, so many critics were down on MacGraw's *Getaway* acting that the drama of McQueen hitting her was sometimes defused by reviewers using it for comic relief, such as *The New Yorker*'s Pauline Kael suggesting audiences liked the so-so actress being smacked![37]

Peckinpah was so upset by all this negative press that he wrote

(Left to right) McQueen, MacGraw, and director Sam Peckinpah on the set of The Getaway. *Due to a shortage of stunt drivers, actor James Garner, who was visiting the set, was recruited and paid $25 to drive a Volkswagen Bug during the chase scene following the bank robbery.*

MacGraw a personal note: "I was incensed by the reviews. It seems to me they had a personal vendetta against you. I thought you were damn good. . . . You're a much better actress than anyone else gives you credit for, including yourself."[38] Though MacGraw does seem to be sleepwalking through the part, Peckinpah's "vendetta" comment is not without insight—MacGraw's affair with McQueen shocked a lot of people, given she was married, with a two-year-old son, Joshua. Granted, the whole romantic tryst was not confirmed public knowledge. But enough information had leaked out to have wink-wink references in some reviews, such as *Variety*'s bald opening: "'The Getaway' has several commercial things going for it . . . [including] Steve McQueen and Ali MacGraw as stars at a time when public interest has been aroused in some real-life [sexual] situations."[39] Regardless, a touch of scandal seldom hurts the box-office potential of an otherwise quality production, and *Getaway* went on to be Peckinpah's greatest commercial hit, drawing nearly twenty million dollars in the United States alone—great numbers for the early 1970s.

After the completion of *Getaway*, MacGraw went back to her husband, with the now divorced McQueen living in a small rental house in greater Los Angeles's Coldwater Canyon. But the actress soon separated from Evans and accepted the loan of a temporarily vacant house from Candice Bergen, who would become one of MacGraw's closest friends. But MacGraw's passion for McQueen remained, and she was soon renting a house next door to his residence. A troubling insight into the chaos of loving McQueen is provided by the following passage from her memoir: "During my stay in . . . [the Canyon], Steve left for Jamaica . . . [to shoot the film] *Papillon* [1973]. It was a difficult period for me. Bob had forbidden me to take Joshua out of the country, and Steve was the kind of man who could not go more than a couple of weeks without his Old Lady and not feel that he had been abandoned. So I shuttled between Jamaica and my newly rented home with my wonderful baby. I would have preferred to have been with Josh the whole time, but I was scared that Steve would get involved with someone else if I stayed away too long."[40] MacGraw's fear here is just another variation of an article on McQueen's first wife, with a haunting title drawn from an Adams comment, "'A Married Man Should Never Be Left Alone.'"[41]

To paraphrase the amusing New York Yankee legend Yogi Berra, "If you don't know where you're going, you're bound to end up someplace else." McQueen had that sort of power over women—they just followed him, with no thought of the long-term consequences. These same McQueen lovers and/or future wives would have been better served by embracing wit Dorothy Parker's tongue-in-cheek ideals for a male— "someone handsome, ruthless, and stupid." However, McQueen was anything but stupid. Plus, given that star power, where lights seemed to flicker when he entered a room, and one had a sense of his sexual charisma. Of course, the cynical biographer might posit that most of McQueen's lovers would simply fall on the bad side of the bell curve. But that would be too harsh on Adams and MacGraw, two intelligent, cultured women who fell in love with a bad boy.

In MacGraw's case, the depressing scope of their differences was not fully apparent at first, masked as it was by the sexual passion of a new relationship, as well as the excitement of being the star's lover on a major movie production. And *Papillon* was such a production—a throwback to Hollywood's old sense of the epic that *New York Times* critic Vincent Canby confessed to liking so much in his review: "[*Papillon* has] an old-fashioned narrative style to which I'm partial, the kind that seeks to authenticate character and event by telling us a lot more about geography, climate, weather, plant life and architecture then we absolutely need know."[42] *Papillon* director Franklin J. Schaffner, who had won an Oscar for directing the military biography *Patton* (1970), gave this McQueen picture a sweeping scope the actor had not seen since Robert Wise's *The Sand Pebbles* (1966).

Papillon is the Henri Charrière story of various escape attempts from several prison colonies in French Guiana (South America), including the notorious Devil's Island. The title means "butterfly" in French, and is drawn from Charrièrs's butterfly tattoo—an apt metaphor for the fragility of freedom. One is reminded of the poignant close to *All Quiet*

McQueen and Dustin Hoffman in Papillon *(1973). Hoffman based his character in part on the film's screenwriter, the shy Dalton Trumbo.* **Inset:** *Hoffman is framed by the leg of Anne Bancroft in a classic image from the film that made him a star,* The Graduate *(1967).*

on the Western Front (1930), when Lew Ayres's soldier character puts himself in harm's way to touch a passing butterfly, only to be killed. Thankfully, Charrière had a happier fate, eventually escaping on a raft made of dried coconuts.

In the 1920s Charrière had made a living as a Parisian safecracker with a Robin Hood complex, robbing only the government. During the early 1930s he was framed in the murder of a Paris pimp and sentenced to the first of several prisons; he kept escaping. But no one had ever gotten away from Devil's Island. His prison ordeal stretched over thirteen years and included nine escapes. Ultimately, he found freedom in Venezuela, where the colorful character eventually wrote his lengthy best-selling memoir.

With McQueen as arguably the number one international star appropriate for the part, as well as being France's favorite foreign actor, arrangements were quickly made to hire him for the title role at a salary of $1.75 million. And when Dustin Hoffman expressed interest in the picture, another major character, a bookish fellow prisoner named Dega (a composite of several figures in the book) was created. Hoffman's salary was $1.25 million.

Not only had McQueen challenged himself with a physically demanding part (as well as being the first and only time his screen character aged dramatically), but he also faced his greatest acting challenge from a costar. Hoffman represented a new breed of unlikely superstars, one who had extensively honed his skills on the New York stage. Moving to film in the late 1960s, Hoffman had become an overnight phenomenon with *The Graduate* (1967) and *Midnight Cowboy* (1969), two brilliantly different pictures that showcased his range—from a naïve California college graduate to the seedy, streetwise Ratso in New York. Both films earned Hoffman Best Actor Oscar nominations. It was the beginning of an inspired career that so far has brought him two Oscars (for *Kramer vs. Kramer*, 1979, and *Rain Man*, 1988).

One would think this meant trouble for McQueen—the threat of being acted off the screen. But Hoffman struggled with his *Papillon* character and went overboard on various theatrical tricks, such as wearing spectacles with lenses as thick as shot glasses. While the eyeglasses remain in the finished film, Hoffman, courtesy of McQueen, streamlined his characterization. A decade later, during the production of *Tootsie* (1982), Hoffman shared with costar Charles Durning the advice minimalist McQueen had given him: "Less, Dusty. Do less. Just throw that out, you don't need it. Keep it simple." When Durning asked what happened, Hoffman said, "I took his advice. It turned out he was right."[43]

Despite McQueen's sage cinema insight, Hoffman's initial emergence as a leading man with *The Graduate* had dumbfounded McQueen. According to Adams, "Steve couldn't understand the public's fascination with this unconventional looking actor. Time and again after that, Steve would stare at his image in the mirror and say to me, 'Look at that, baby, take a look at that face and that body and tell me the truth. Who would you pick, him or me?' We would then both laugh, although I knew that he was serious."[44] The paradox here is that McQueen's small stature and sometimes simian-like appearance was hardly that of a traditional leading man, either. But McQueen had always been a host to insecurities, and this was simply something else to worry about. Moreover, his salve for this concern, looking in the mirror, was consistent with a man who sometimes asserted his manhood through a nonstop string of affairs.

Despite such apparent shallowness, McQueen was capable of rising to solid material, such as the *Papillon* script, which had been adapted from Charrière's memoir by the talented former blacklisted writer Dalton Trumbo and Lorenzo Semple Jr. (Trumbo also plays a small part in the movie as a prison commandant.) Couple this writing with Schaffner's direction, and one has yet another outstanding McQueen performance, with the actor's best biographer, Marshall Terrill, claiming: "*Papillon* is hands down the best performance of Steve McQueen's twenty-eight-film career."[45]

Terrill might have been drawing from *Films and Filming* critic Gordon Gow, who goes on to describe at length a pivotal *Papillon* scene: "[McQueen] has never acted better than he does as Charrière. . . . The

best sequence in the whole film is . . . [his] first long spell of solitary
confinement, when the actor's personality is merged remarkably with
the gift of the person he portrays, exercising [a McQueen obsession] in
the cell and forcing down unpalatable [rotten] food [and bugs] to keep
up his strength and his will to escape. . . . It is in this episode, too, that
Schaffer brings off his best effects: the overhead shots through the bars
above the [prison] pit, the menacing bat, the droning flies."[46]

At the time of its initial release, however, the picture polarized
reviewers. Film historian Susan Sackett later wrote, "Critics com-
plain about its length (150 minutes) and its pessimistic feeling. [For
example], *Newsweek* wrote: '*Papillon* offers torture as entertainment
but winds up making entertainment a form of torture. . . .' [And] the
Hollywood Reporter called the film 'a long, difficult and grim experience
which does not do back flips to engage the audience.'"[47] But for every
such critical knock there was a period champion. The *Los Angeles Times*
stated: "*Papillon* is an eloquent tribute to the indomitability of the human spirit and a powerful indictment of those institutions dedicated
only to breaking it. . . . [McQueen], aided by Charles Schram's terrific
makeup, certainly does give a persuasive performance of Oscar proportions."[48] The *Los Angeles Herald Examiner* added, "The rewards of
Papillon are two immensely watchable performances by McQueen and
Dustin Hoffman . . . McQueen has probably never been so effective in
a role that demands more character study than action and requires him
to age perceptibly."[49]

Even when publications such as *Variety*, or the aforementioned
Newsweek, found the film full of "brutality," their critics went on to
praise McQueen, with the latter magazine being the most articulate:
"McQueen is marvelous, especially during his extended period of
solitary confinement, transforming himself from defiant, sardonic loner
into a crawling, stammering gray thing, living on insects and labor-
ing with the strength of Hercules to utter a single cogent sentence."[50]
The influential film critic Judith Crist, writing in *New York Magazine*,
also had numerous *Papillon* reservations (such as the extreme length)
but went on to praise "McQueen's emergence as an interesting actor in

repose (rather than as the flip charmer he usually embodies)."[51]

Once again, McQueen, the "great escape" artist, had found an affinity with an unusual screen character: "All my life, I seemed to be looking for something—never knowing what it was—but always there was the sense that I couldn't, and shouldn't, be confined."[52] Surprisingly, the expected *Papillon* Oscar nomination for McQueen did not come. Explanations ranged from having alienating Hollywood insiders over his affair with MacGraw to the old criticism that he was just not popular with his fellow actors/voting members of the Motion Picture Academy because McQueen was too professionally opportunistic. Still, no less a figure than Hoffman observed, "Not only should Steve McQueen have been nominated for *Papillon*, he should have won!"[53] (The Best Actor winner that year was Jack Lemmon for *Save the Tiger*, 1973).

Hoffman's support for McQueen's Oscar consideration is especially significant, given that the two actors eventually had a falling out during *Papillon* and did not speak for the rest of the production, other than in

McQueen in yet another Papillon *escape attempt. Papillon is the French word for butterfly, and in the movie McQueen's character sports a tattoo of a butterfly.*

their scenes together. (The catalyst had been McQueen's demand that some camera-carrying Hoffman guests on the set be removed.)

On a lighter *Papillon* note, a neglected comic challenge for costume personnel was that McQueen loved Jamaica's local cuisine. His constant weight gains necessitated that the actor's ragged prison garb for a starving figure be frequently expanded! One is reminded of the lighting tricks director Francis Ford Coppola had to use to mask the excessive weight of Marlon Brando in *Apocalypse Now* (1979). Brando's role of an errant American officer had originally been offered to McQueen.

Papillon's mixed reviews notwithstanding, the Christmas-released movie went on to be one of the box-office champions of 1974, topped only by *The Sting* (1973) and *The Exorcist* (1973).[54] Coupled with the comparable commercial success of *The Getaway*, McQueen's personal finances had recovered from the double whammy of a divorce and the *Le Mans* debacle. Indeed, when one adds the huge payday McQueen realized with his next picture, *The Towering Inferno* (1974), one might say he was rich like a James Bond villain. McQueen and MacGraw were on the verge of an extended period of dropping out.

10

The Strange Final Years

"I've done everything there is to do but a lot of my life was wasted." [1]
STEVE MCQUEEN

After the completion of *Papillon* (1973) in May 1973, Steve Mc-
Queen and Ali MacGraw moved to a beach house in Trancas, California, a little beyond Malibu. The two were rare celebrities among a
small-town atmosphere of what they called "real people." MacGraw's
divorce from movie mogul Robert Evans was final in June, and Mc-
Queen married his "New York intellectual" on July 13, 1973. For the
superstitious, this would hardly be a lucky date. But given their complete differences in background and tastes, their relationship could have
used any available luck. This was Bullitt meets ballet; a mechanic paired
with a poet; Mr. Blue-Collar versus Ms. Designer Label. The following
story from MacGraw's memoir perfectly captures the contrast: "One
weekend when we were in our favorite apartment in Ventana [a Big Sur
hotel, California], Steve told me excitedly that some of his Hell's Angels
pals were planning a run through Big Sur. He was going to meet them
at the River Inn and 'hang out.' Would I like to come? I preferred to
listen to Mozart in our room high up in the redwoods, and I spent the
afternoon embroidering antique buttons onto the sleeves of an Afghani
ceremonial dancing shirt." [2] Two peas in a pod they were not.

As with McQueen's previous marriage, in which he encouraged
first wife Neile Adams to abandon a budding career, the same request/
demand was made of MacGraw—a huge sacrifice for the superstar
created by *Goodbye, Columbus* and *Love Story*. But again, like Adams,

MacGraw was willing to drop out, at least temporarily, to take care of her husband and the children. The couple had MacGraw's two-year-old son Josh Evans and McQueen's nearly thirteen-year-old son Chad, with the actor's fourteen-year-old daughter Terry frequently visiting on weekends. MacGraw had quickly gone from pampered wealth on the Evans estate to an often harried existence as a mother and wife—an existence exacerbated by a chauvinistic McQueen. MacGraw was paying the price of her husband's neglected childhood, when his mother was never at home. But in the beginning this was simply a new adventure, and MacGraw was all right with the change. Plus, the scandal of the couple's romance had created such ugly headlines that she was only too happy to disappear for a time.

A semblance of the old movie-star life continued when McQueen signed on to be top billed in a picture ultimately coproduced by Twentieth Century-Fox and Warner Brothers, *The Towering Inferno* (1974), an example of what was then being called a new film genre—the "all-star disaster epic" or an "end-of-the-world movie" spectacle. Of course, this type of picture had always existed and might best be demonstrated by a mid-1930s fascination with the phenomenon that included director W. S. Van Dyke's *San Francisco* (1936, chronicling the city's 1906 earthquake and starring Clark Gable, Spencer Tracy, and Jeanette MacDonald), John Ford's *Hurricane* (1937, with Dorothy Lamour, Mary Astor, and Raymond Massey), and Henry King's *In Old Chicago* (1938, with Tyrone Power, Alice Faye, and Don Ameche fighting the Chicago fire of 1871).

This historical perspective notwithstanding, however, *Inferno* producer and codirector Irwin Allen had helped jumpstart this minigenre comeback with the surprise megahit *The Poseidon Adventure* (1972, about a cruise ship capsized by a tidal wave). But others might also date this period rebirth of the disaster epic with *Airport* (1970, sort of a *Grand Hotel* of the sky, chronicling an attempt to safely land a damaged passenger jet). Additional notable all-star variations on this 1970s disaster cycle included *Earthquake*, *Airport 1975* (both 1974), and *The*

Hindenburg (1975). Still, *Inferno* was the best end-of-the-world entry follow-up to *Poseidon*, trading fear of water for fear of fire.

Inferno tells the story of a new futuristic 138-story San Francisco skyscraper and the runaway fire that threatens the lives of the city's elite who were, ironically, celebrating the dedication of the building at a penthouse party. The main players in this high-rise horror film are the fire chief (McQueen), the architect (Paul Newman), the builder (William Holden), a magazine editor (Faye Dunaway), the builder's son-in-law and subcontractor (Richard Chamberlain), the builder's daughter (Susan Blakely), a con artist (Fred Astaire), his intended victim (Jennifer Jones), security chief (O. J. Simpson, more irony), a senator (Robert Vaughn), a public-relations man (Robert Wagner), and his secretary/fiancée (Susan Flannery).

For the time, McQueen signed an amazingly lucrative contract (a million-dollar salary and 7.5 percent of the box-office gross). When the picture became a monster commercial hit, McQueen eventually pocketed more than twelve million dollars! Originally, the script's plum role was the architect, which was first offered to McQueen. But given his blue-collar background, he was more attracted to the part of the fire chief, necessitating the character be built up to equal significance with the architect, a role that went to Newman. Yet, McQueen finally topped his longtime rival in both billing and salary, quite the transition from the Hoosier's mere extra status to Newman's star turn in *Somebody Up There Likes Me* (1956).

The *New York Times*'s positive review effectively defined a performer's limitation in a spectacle film of this sort: "Though the actors are not required to do much except behave well according to type, their presence upgrades a secondary form of movie melodrama."[3] But having said this, both McQueen and Newman clearly anchor the picture and deservedly receive the best notices. The *Los Angeles Times* observed, "McQueen, calm, deadpan, efficient, is the center of the picture, and both he and Newman, rugged and resourceful, remind you what movie stars are and why they can be worth the kingly sums they are paid."[4]

The *Los Angeles Herald Examiner* added, "[McQueen and Newman] invest considerable energy and strength in the film, making the events both matter a lot and seem horrifyingly possible."[5]

Refreshingly, despite McQueen's arbitrary rivalry with Newman, the two superstars got along famously on the shoot. Outtakes during the production document both their kidding around and the occasional prank.[6] The real-life melodrama keyed on Holden and Dunaway. Holden was frustrated by a one-dimensional part, that of a charismatic villain (his character had cut costs on building the skyscraper, with faulty wiring causing the fire). Dunaway frustrated her costars, particularly Holden, by her constant lateness to the set.

In contrast, part of the McQueen/Newman camaraderie was built upon both men doing as many of their *Inferno* stunts as Allen allowed. Providentially, one McQueen action injury (a badly turned ankle) indirectly resulted in some critical praise for the actor. Because of the twisted ankle, several scenes were rewritten so McQueen's character could be seen resting, between heroic bursts of fire-fighting action. These unexpected moments of quiet during the chaos of any disaster movie were later heralded as powerfully realistic. To paraphrase an Alfred Hitchcock axiom about filmmaking: "The best moments are often the result of an accident."

McQueen had also been insightful about taking the role of the fire chief. Besides being closer to the meat-and-potatoes type of guy he was, this figure is the ultimate hero of the film. While the skyscraper fire is technically the fault of an unscrupulous builder (Holden) and his even more nefarious son-in-law (Chamberlain), Newman's screen professional (architect) is also criticized during the movie for contributing to the problem by not doing all his homework. For example, McQueen's chief warns Newman's figure at the end of the film, "You know, they'll keep building them [skyscrapers] higher and higher. And I'll keep eatin' smoke until one of you guys ask us [firemen] how to build 'em." A contrite Newman responds, "Okay, I'm asking." McQueen then triumphantly closes the picture by observing, "You know where to find me. So long, architect."

If that final word was not winning enough, McQueen also served up the movie's most entertaining crack—a line that combined self-deprecating humor with a sacrificially casual courage. McQueen's fire chief is describing on the phone to Newman a potentially suicidal mission to explode huge water tanks on the skyscraper's roof in order to drown the fire. Naturally, it is a mission only the chief can perform. So when Newman innocently asks who will risk it all, McQueen nonchalantly answers, "Oh, they'll find some dumb son-of-a-bitch to bring it [the bomb charge] up." For a picture largely bereft of memorable lines, this one is a real crowd pleaser, and Newman even acts as the set-up man!

Paradoxically, Newman is also saddled with one of *Inferno's* most spoofed observations. Toward the movie's conclusion, after the fire has finally been extinguished, Newman and his lover (Dunaway) are safely at the tower base, and he says of the burned out skyscraper, "Maybe we should leave it this way as a kind of shrine to all the bullshit in the world." For critics of the movie, which received decidedly mixed reviews, this quote was a popular target. To illustrate, *New York Magazine's* Judith Crist responded directly to the actor in her critique, "Not [all the bullshit] in the world, Paul—just in movies co-produced by Twentieth Century-Fox and Warner Bros."[7] Of course, negative notices did not limit themselves to this line. *The New Yorker's* Pauline Kael was the most biting. After noting the picture carries a dedication "to the firefighters of the world," she damned the production with the darkly comic crack, "'Inferno' has opened just in time to capture the Dumb Whore Award of 1974"—a misfire with good intentions.[8]

Not all *Inferno*-directed humor, however, was negative. The *Los Angeles Times* was so bowled over by the epic, it enthusiastically trumpeted, "'Inferno' is $14 million worth of Holy Cow [spectacle]!," and even carried the comedy over to its punning review title: "'Inferno': How to Exceed in Disaster Films."[9] An equally impressed *New York Times* opened its critique with the tongue-in-cheek comment, "'Inferno' is a nearly three-hour suspense film for arsonists, firemen, movie-technology buffs, building inspectors, [and] worry warts."[10]

Other glowing notices often connected the picture to the showmanship of Hollywood's golden age, which meant frequent references to Cecil B. DeMille, director of such spectacle cinema as *The Greatest Show on Earth* (1952) and *The Ten Commandments* (1956). Thus, the *Hollywood Reporter* said, "like . . . DeMille before him, Irwin Allen gives the public the biggest thrills that money can buy," which couples nicely with *Variety's* verdict: "DeMille would be in awe. The box office potential is enormous."[11]

A more sage revenue prediction was never made. Opening during the Christmas holidays of 1974, *Inferno* went on to gross fifty-five million dollars domestically in 1975, second only to that year's *Jaws*.[12] *Inferno* not only far out-grossed such other 1975 hits as *Young Frankenstein* (1974), *The Godfather Part II* (1974), and *Shampoo* (1975), Allen's epic went on to a worldwide box office of two hundred million dollars, making it one of the most commercially successful pictures in movie history. Consequently, even with a split decision on reviews, *Inferno's* revenue returns brought the film an Oscar nomination for Best Picture (losing to *The Godfather Part II*). *Inferno* received a total of eight Academy Award nominations, winning for Best Cinematography, Best Song ("We May Never Love Like This Again"), and Best Film Editing.[13]

I belabor *Inferno's* runaway success because the movie represents a turning point in McQueen's career. After its late 1974 opening, the actor walked away from filmmaking until the little seen screen adaptation of Henrik Ibsen's play, *An Enemy of the People* (1978, which Warner Brothers *never* put into general release). What happened? One explanation has already been noted in the book. Back in the 1960s McQueen had promised, "I want to get some sugar out of this business and run like a thief. I don't want to die with a martini in my hand."[14] The actor's twelve million dollar *Inferno* take was more than a little "sugar."

One could also argue that McQueen had destroyed his Newman as "paper tiger" target. McQueen not only received better billing and pay on *Inferno*, his fire chief figure dominated Newman's architect. Not only that, the actors were best of pals during the shoot. So McQueen had nothing more to prove with regard to catching Newman as some personal high bar of acting. (Still, one wonders if McQueen regretted missing out on the Sundance Kid role, eventually played by Robert Redford, in *Butch Cassidy and the Sundance Kid*. The part had been his for the taking, if he had only accepted a costarring status with Newman, instead of demanding to be top billed. But McQueen's drive to pass Newman was not to be denied.)

Several explanations for McQueen's long post-*Inferno* layoff involved second wife MacGraw. First, while he did not want her acting, McQueen had left the door open by saying maybe the couple could re-team, as they had in *Getaway*. But if he could never find the right property, the actor had an indirect way of keeping her off the screen. Regardless, he seemed less than inclined to accept any part, charging a fifty thousand dollar reading fee to just consider a script.[15] Second, former wife Adams believed that part of McQueen's inactivity was a plan where he "systematically went about destroying Ali's career because of his need to have her in his hip pocket at all times."[16] Conversely, a third perspective claimed McQueen's keeping MacGraw off the screen was a kindness—her horrible reviews for *Getaway* having convinced him she needed protecting. Indeed, MacGraw's notices after their divorce, once she returned to acting, were even more ignominious than her *Getaway* reviews.

Robert Redford, Katherine Ross, and Paul Newman on the set of Butch Cassidy and the Sundance Kid *(1969).*

Though there are probably elements of truth in all these explanations on just why McQueen suddenly dropped out, I am reminded of
a line from the memoir of Mireille Marokvia about the difficulties of
finding truth: "This slice of life . . . is a tragicomic mural on the walls
of a cave . . . memory, like a flashlight, its batteries half spent, conjures
stray images out of the darkness."[17] Besides these multiple possibilities, I
am also a great fan of the hypothesis that suggests going with the easiest
explanation—McQueen simply wanted to take some time off, and it
snowballed into years. After *Getaway* he told a journalist, "I sometimes
hate to go back to work. I want my life as simple as possible. I'm at
an age [early forties] where I'm not as ambitious as I used to be. I've
been surrounded by a whirl of activity for a long time. I just want to be
happy. I don't really care that much. If I feel a film will have something
to say, I'll do it. But now, it seems so fruitless to keep banging away."[18]

Couple this burned-out perspective with a beautiful new wife, a
lovely beach house, and loads of money, and where is the push to get
back in the Hollywood rat race? McQueen's extensive alcohol and
marijuana abuse probably further exacerbated the situation. Any sense
of a work ethic is hard to maintain when one is constantly getting high,
which was frequently McQueen's state during the mid-1970s. Sadly,
the strict conditioning routine the actor maintained for his movie roles
was also dropped. While he had often gained ten to fifteen pounds
between films in the past, his 160 pound ideal weight now ballooned
well past 200. Plus, the scraggly McQueen beard that sometimes briefly
appeared during production lulls now grew to Rip van Winkle proportions. Ironically, the actor was at cross-purposes with *Los Angeles Times*
critic Charles Champlin's then recent passionate explanation as to why
Inferno had received an unlikely Best Picture Oscar nomination: "my
guess is that the response to . . . McQueen figuring things out, doing
[fire chief] things, taking charge, is older and deeper than nostalgia in a
leisure-time, spectator, consumer world . . . [he speaks] . . . to the pleasure of achievement rather more than to the achievement of pleasure . . .
[demonstrating] that it is not entirely old-fashioned for a man to be
proud of his work."[19]

Not surprisingly, the McQueen-MacGraw love nest by the sea had turned into a nightmare for her, as an often stoned McQueen watched television by the hour. They even had their bedroom wired "so that she could listen to classical music on the stereo while he watched television."[20] Moreover, he seemed to have no interest in the outside world, either culturally or socially. As the superstar said at the time, "I like to eat at six, go for a ride on my motorcycle, and go to sleep."[21] The couple fought constantly, and sometimes the disagreements turned ugly. "Our worst fight resulted in Steve inadvertently backhanding me on the forehead, breaking open the skin next to my eyebrow," MacGraw later wrote. "Both of us were so shocked by the incident that it actually served to quiet us down for a while. After that encounter Steve was so upset that he decided that every time we had an argument it would be 'safer' for him to go into town to spend the night . . . there were times when Steve would get so angry that I was afraid of him, at least for the instant."[22]

Adams described an even more disturbing McQueen and MacGraw argument, though the incident is presented in a darkly comic manner: "[My children] Terry and Chad were sitting in front of the TV watching a show, trying to wait out the argument. Then he [Chad] heard Steve angrily say, 'Ali, you need to cool off, goddamn it!' and a second later, he saw something come flying past the window from above and into the pool down below. It was not a small object. . . . Then Terry said, 'I think it's Ali. I think Dad just threw her off the porch!' And he had! Ali kept swimming around. . . . Chad told me he could see she was really angry. . . . Steve called to the children and told them to get to bed. And by the time they woke up the next day, everything was all right again."[23]

Paradoxically, the stormy relationship between McQueen and MacGraw was probably the catalyst for the actor finally choosing such an offbeat project as his return to pictures, the aforementioned Ibsen adaptation, *An Enemy of the People.* In 1971 McQueen had joined a film production partnership called First Artists, which at that time also included Newman, Sidney Poitier, and Barbra Streisand. The idea was increased creative control and more profits, sort of an updated version of 1919's United Artists, whose original members were Charlie Chaplin, Douglas Fairbanks, Mary Pickford, and D. W. Griffith. However, the now semiretired McQueen was being pressured by First Artists to fulfill his two-picture obligation to the company. The actor decided to start with *Enemy*.

Yet, why would McQueen pick what is essentially an obscure art-house story—an idealistic scientist goes against a tourist-conscious town over the dangers of a polluted water system? Like the actor's decision to drop out at the beach, there are several explanations. First, given that he initially came across the Ibsen play among MacGraw's many books of the "classics," one production hypothesis is that he was trying to impress his "New York intellectual" wife. Second, one could also argue that the maverick McQueen was always walking away from sure things, such as the *Dirty Harry* franchise, and embracing offbeat projects such as the William Faulkner adaptation of *The Reivers*. In fact, during McQueen's hiatus, he had already turned down pivotal roles in such soon-to-be classics as *Apocalypse Now* (1979) and *Close Encounters of the Third Kind* (1977). Even before that, McQueen had said no to Gene Hackman's Popeye Doyle role in *The French Connection* (1971, for which Hackman won a Best Actor Oscar), simply because McQueen did not do cop roles after *Bullitt* (1968).

A third and most often cited reason for McQueen doing *Enemy* was simply to shaft First Artists.[24] If the production company was going to force his hand, he would do something decidedly noncommercial. But a funny thing happened on the way to the making of *Enemy*; McQueen became immersed in the project, and the most professional of productions evolved. Had he changed his mind about payback against First Artists, or had one of the earlier motives been true, such as impressing MacGraw? Again, there is no definitive answer. But he truly made an honest effort on the film.

Most obviously, the movie is peppered with talent, including a screenplay taken from a translation by the great playwright Arthur Miller to a cast that included one of celebrated director Ingmar Bergman's seminal actresses, Bibi Andersson. McQueen's performance as

Doctor Thomas Stockman is not without merit, but his limited range and the movie's canned theater nature pales in comparison to a stage production anchored by the presence of a theatrical actor in the lead, such as the late 1990s *Enemy* tour that featured Ian McKellen as Stockman. The most sympathetically insightful take on McQueen's performance is found in film historian Arthur Knight's *Hollywood Reporter* review: "[McQueen] lends a quiet dignity. Although lacking the voice and authority to sustain Ibsen's intense confrontation scenes, it is by no means a bad performance. It nevertheless lacks the sweep and stature to make it a memorable one."[25] The critique is reminiscent of McQueen's notices from his one starring role on Broadway, where he had difficulty handling and projecting a wordy part. But McQueen had gone on to turn himself into an accomplished screen actor of often poignant minimalism, defining himself through actions more than words.

Unlike Knight's balanced assessment, other reviews of McQueen's work on *Enemy* tended to be overly harsh on the actor's attempt to stretch himself. The *Los Angeles Herald Examiner* compared his performance to two of cinema history's most famous misfires, before turning the actor's longtime association with Westerns into a comic negative: "Think of cocky Clark Gable as the tragic [title character] 'Parnell,' or Gregory Peck playing Captain Ahab as if he were Abraham Lincoln . . . [McQueen] speaks in the same casual, laconic style he uses as a drawling cowpoke, so most of his dialogue ends up sounding like 'Yup' or 'Nope.'"[26] (One should also add that McQueen's long hair and full beard made him nearly unrecognizable in his *Enemy* role.)

A year after the actor's death (1980), the *Los Angeles Times* critic Kevin Thomas did a revisionist piece on the film that sounded more Knight-like: "[It] is a decent, solid presentation of a modern classic. . . . Ironically, it proves a far more notable valedictory to McQueen's career than his final two films . . . 'Tom Horn' and the [*sic*] 'The Bounty Hunter' [both 1980, with the latter's title being *The Hunter*]."[27] Though one might negate this perspective as pure sentimentality linked to McQueen's death, more than twenty-five years later this same sympathetically "sincere" take on *Enemy* is to be found in the film fan bible, *Leonard Maltin's 2007 Movie Guide*.[28]

Regardless of one's take on the picture, however, it was ultimately a failure for McQueen. Like most of Hollywood, he measured a movie's success purely at the box office. Warner Brothers, the distributor for this First Artists production, never got a handle on how to market *An Enemy of the People*—a title many people believed sounded like a Western. Consequently, the film never went into general release, though there were various test marketings and aborted advertising campaigns, with McQueen even doing a University of California at Los Angeles lecture on "The Genius of Ibsen."

Paradoxically, if *Enemy* was at all inspired as a way to impress Mac-Graw, the film's production further contributed to the unraveling of the McQueens' marriage. With their home being extensively remodeled at the time, the actor rented a large suite in the Beverly Wilshire Hotel during the shoot, spending nearly fifty thousand dollars on a redecoration project. "After we divorced I was told by more than one friend who stayed at the hotel that Steve's room, right next to the pool, was the scene of a constant parade of models and starlets," MacGraw later confessed in her memoir. "Sensing that, I never set foot in that hotel apartment. But the truth also was that I was secretly relieved to have him out of the house, to be alone with the boys [son Josh and stepson Chad] as I worked on remodeling our home."[29]

The Wilshire suite was where McQueen met his third wife, fashion model Barbara Minty, twenty-four years his junior. He had seen her in a Club Med advertisement, and he set up a phony movie audition for a part in *Tom Horn*. Ironically, given McQueen's long one-sided rivalry with Newman, Minty initially thought the meeting was with New-man. Minty later revealed more confusion in her combination memoir/McQueen biography when the star that greeted her at the door "had long hair, sported a beard and looked exactly like . . . the character he portrayed in *An Enemy of the People* [then in production]. Frankly, to me he looked more like a San Pedro Beach bum than an international movie star. In fact, it didn't even dawn on me that he was my first crush on *Wanted: Dead or Alive*. . . . [But after that first meeting, she told her agent], 'I'm going to marry that man! I just love him!'"[30]

Despite this romantic sense of destiny, Minty's initial impressions of McQueen's Wilshire Hotel suite match the girl-magnet description previously cited in MacGraw's book. Of course, even in a sea of sexy film groupies, Minty's *Cosmopolitan* cover-girl beauty stood out. Another long-legged brunette, twenty-four-year-old Minty bore a striking resemblance to MacGraw, though this latest model was more a full-figure girl. Though only six years older than the star's daughter, Terry, Minty had a great deal in common with McQueen, starting with a love of the outdoors and living the simple rustic life. (She already had an Idaho getaway home near where he was interested in building a cabin.) Also, like McQueen's semiretired tendencies, Minty was even then scaling back her successful modeling career.

The actor's 1977 meeting with Minty was fortuitous, since this was also the year his marriage to MacGraw hit the proverbial "wall." Divorce was a frequent topic of conversation, and the arguments continued. When McQueen's ex-wife Adams threw a big eighteenth birthday party for daughter Terry in June 1977, McQueen turned up with Chad and stepson Josh, but no MacGraw—they were battling again. Still, the childlike, child-orientated McQueen had forged a good relationship with Josh. Indeed, after he filed for divorce from MacGraw in November 1977, she rented another house near the couple's Trancas, California, beach residence in order that Josh could continue to have regular contact with McQueen.

The alleged final catalyst for the couple's split was MacGraw's decision to take a part in director Sam Peckinpah's *Convoy* (1978). Though this broke McQueen's rule about working, she believed that the marriage was in trouble, and she was anxious for a nest egg, given her prenuptial agreement with McQueen. But he probably just used *Convoy* as a "last straw." Their relationship had turned ugly, and he had begun to shower a great deal of attention on Minty.

Still, McQueen's relationships with past wives remained complicated. By 1978 Minty had moved into his beach house. Yet, in March of that year, he had a romantic rendezvous with Adams in Las Vegas, where she was making a comeback in a revival of *Can Can*. He even proposed they get back together! But she was much more content just remaining friends. Adams recalled that McQueen asked her, "'Hey, why can't you and me and Ali and Barbara all live together under one roof?' I just shook my head and he laughed at the thought as if he were telling a joke on himself. 'Can you imagine that? Ooooweee!'"[31] If this were not surprising enough, McQueen and MacGraw had a similar tryst in June 1978 after the disastrous critical opening of *Convoy*, with MacGraw again convinced they could work as a couple. But the almost immediate return of their arguments soured any new hopes.

Minty seemed to have won McQueen by default, if winning is the proper term for becoming the partner of a womanizer. But while she was nearly half his age, Minty had been around the block. In fact, the model had previously been the girlfriend of another famous Hollywood player, Warren Beatty, who maintained a suite at the Beverly Wilshire Hotel, too, on the same floor as McQueen![32] Given McQueen's competitive nature in sexual conquests, his initial interest in Minty just might have been driven by taking her away from Beatty.

Regardless, something worked between McQueen and the young model. Insiders later claimed she did not have the passion of the actor's first two wives. But given McQueen's volatile nature, maybe that was a good thing. Consequently, she was much more content to just let him play leader, and do as much, or as little, as he wished. As one of McQueen's biographers noted of Minty, "She had no desire to change the world; she merely wanted to make her portion of it comfortable."[33] Having such a young beauty come into McQueen's life also energized him. He tried to stop smoking and managed to get back in shape, though the beard and junk-food habits (especially mashed potatoes) continued. More importantly, he came back to mainstream movies with his final two films, the aforementioned *Tom Horn* and *The Hunter*.

Tom Horn was a real Western hero—the cavalry scout who captured Geronimo—and was a pioneering frontier Pinkerton agent before joining Teddy Roosevelt's Rough Riders in the Spanish American War. But he came to a tragic end when his hired-gun association with a Wyoming cattlemen's association resulted in a trumped-up murder charge and his 1903 hanging. More than seventy years after Horn's death, he was suddenly a hot property, with two major Hollywood stars interested in making biography films of his life. The same day McQueen announced his plans to do *Tom Horn*, Robert Redford and United Artists issued a statement about a comparable picture, to be called *Mr. Horn*.[34]

Redford and company soon dropped out, but McQueen's germination period on the project stretched out over eighteen months. There were questions about how much of Horn's life would be covered, and if Geronimo would figure prominently in the story. More importantly, there were differences on the budget. This was McQueen's final First Artists production, with Warner Brothers again distributing. But certain key personnel at the two companies were not on good terms, and Warners balked at funding a picture of the scope the actor had originally envisioned. McQueen might have fought this, but he was more interested in finally fulfilling his First Artists obligation.

Ultimately, the actor's picture focuses on Horn's last three years in the turn-of-the-century West. He has essentially become a hired assassin for cattlemen, ridding them of a sizable rustling problem. But as in many revisionist end-of-the-West stories, such as director Don Siegel's *The Shootist* (1977, with John Wayne), once civilization arrives, the violent men who made it possible become an embarrassment. Consequently, they have to die. The perennial outsider/loner McQueen had always been attracted to these edgy characters that time had passed by. This had been the case in so many of his signature movies, from his first screen Western, *The Magnificent Seven* (1960), to his definitive quasi-Western detective film, *Bullitt* (1968, in which he might be called a noir cowboy).

There is a brutal matter-of-fact honesty about how McQueen brings Horn to life. *The New Yorker* described the transformation eloquently: "Steve McQueen is fifty now, and he is a wonderfully worn-looking old-soldier cowpoke. . . . His looks and his outfit—his long, dust-thick hair, a pulled-down big Stetson . . . his high cheekbones and seamed, indrawn face—are part of an effortless, intensely visual performance that does not rely excessively on the dazzling, lopsided McQueen grin. He is the best sight in a picture stuffed with vivid Western scenes and faces."[35]

The *New York Times's* Janet Maslin movingly added, "McQueen lends Horn a grace and resignation that stays understated even when the film turns clumsily emphatic. And the sadness he brings to the role is quietly, effectively pervasive. He seems at once on a grander and smaller scale than the rest of the movie, offering tiny, pared-down gestures against those grand landscapes. And even when the . . . [movie] does little to aggrandize his character, he rises to heroic stature."[36]

Tom Horn also boasted some wonderful character actors, including Richard Farnsworth (whom McQueen had once fired from *Wanted: Dead or Alive*), and Slim Pickens (whose improvisations had been so comically creative at the conclusion of *The Getaway*). Paradoxically, Pickens's character inspires Horn's best serious line. About to be hanged, McQueen's character tells his friend, the reluctant sheriff, "You keep your nerve, Sam [Pickens], 'cause I'm going to keep mine." But like McQueen's ready wit, Horn also makes several amusing observations, from his brief explanation of a past incarceration, "for the invasion of Mexico," to a more drawn-out story involving prizefighter Gentleman Jim Corbett. A tongue-in-cheek Corbett asks Horn if he wants a bout. McQueen's character responds, "If I win this fight, then am *I* the champion of the world?"

"You're not big enough," says Jim.

"Well then, what're you pickin' on a little feller like me for?" Horn comically inquires.

Interestingly, *Tom Horn* also featured Minty's parents, Gene and Wilma, as extras. When McQueen and Minty had visited them in their Oregon home just prior to the shoot, McQueen had invited the couple to the Patagonia, Arizona, location to be part of the production. While Wilma simply played one of the anonymous town locals, Gene had a more prominent part as a sheriff at Horn's execution. The film's direc-

McQueen as the title character of Tom Horn *(1980). McQueen conducted extensive research to play his role, even meeting with famed Western writer Louis L'Amour.*

tor, William Wiard, wanted one or two imposing extras to accompany
McQueen and Pickens on the march to the gallows. Given that Gene
was six-feet tall and weighed in at 220 pounds, he more than fit the
bill. (Gene's parents had been big *Wanted: Dead or Alive* fans, and it was
through her paternal grandparents that Barbara had developed a childhood crush on McQueen.)

Of course, the fresh-faced boyish Josh Randall of *Wanted* was now
the weathered and wrinkled Horn. To paraphrase novelist George
Orwell, "The face you have at fifty is the face you deserve," which was
McQueen's age at the time of *Tom Horn*'s release. From the volatile
stress of a childhood in the streets, to an adulthood often spent in the
desert wind and sun of dirt bike racing, McQueen had not aged well,
while his older rival, Newman, looked "forever young," like he had
made some *Dorian Gray* arrangement, where only his picture in the
closet aged. The deep creases in McQueen's countenance looked like a
road map of Indiana, tracing every trauma, real or imagined, he had experienced through his rough-and-tumble life. Wearing these extra years
also explains his tendency to frequently hide behind a beard. But as the
previous *Tom Horn* notices suggest, this world-weary appearance merely
adds a naturalism to McQueen's low-key performance. The *Hollywood
Reporter*'s equally positive *Horn* review opened with a summary of this
fact: "[The role] fits his persona like a well-worn saddle . . . an Old West
gunman who understands triggers but not trickery."[37]

Despite this praise, not all critics were on board about the delights
of *Horn*. The most damning rebuke came from *Variety*, which faulted
the film on almost every level, from production values and direction to
a mediocre "walking through the part" job from McQueen.[38] Naturally,
this would have been upsetting to the actor, given *Variety*'s special status
in the entertainment community. But there would have been added
angst attached to this panning, given the extra work McQueen had put
into the production. While the actor had been a bear for details on all
his work since *Wanted*, he had topped himself on *Horn*. Starting with
a preproduction campout at his subject's grave, McQueen had passionately thrown himself into every aspect of the production. In fact, he had

even attempted to take a director's credit, too, but the Guild awarded that title to Wiard. This was Wiard's first feature, after directing such popular television shows as *M.A.S.H.* and *The Rockford Files.* Counting McQueen, there had been a total of five directors on *Horn*. The actor was often too much the perfectionist.

To the movie's credit, the maliciousness of *Variety's* review seemed an aberration compared to most other *Horn* notices. Indeed, *Variety's* critique was such a mirror opposite of the *Hollywood Reporter's* same day glowing review, that the *Los Angeles Times* was moved to do a follow-up article on the contrast.[39]

During the *Horn* shoot McQueen and Minty could have lived in either a luxurious mansion or a grandiose hotel in nearby Tucson, Arizona. According to Minty, "That wasn't going to cut it for Steve. He opted for us to live in a 20-foot Winnebago for three months. I thought it sounded like a hoot and I was game for the new adventure. . . . Steve didn't live in a Winnebago because he wanted to get into character or see what it was like to live in the Old West—he just loved the serenity of the desert. We had all the privacy we needed and the nights were still and quiet."[40] But while Minty's book suggests she was always there with her autumnal cowboy, she frequently left to fly to California modeling assignments. The less-than-monogamous McQueen occasionally strayed, after what he viewed were acts of desertion.

The three-month shoot started in January 1979, and McQueen had respiratory problems throughout. The actor frequently voiced concerns over bronchitis and pleurisy. In fact, he was already suffering from the yet undiagnosed mesothelioma, a rare form of cancer that led to his death. Though McQueen's June 1979 move from his Trancas Beach house to Santa Paula, California (the "Antique Plane Capital of the World"), is credited to his new fascination with biplanes, another contributing factor was escaping the damp sea air.

Horn was in theaters by the time of the move, and while the notices were often strong, the box office was disappointing. One should note that another mitigating problem was that the Western's time as a popular genre had now passed. Even the watershed end-of-the-West saga *The Shootist*, with sterling reviews and the archetypal cowboy, John Wayne, had fared poorly on ticket sales. But as McQueen biographer Christopher Sandford later wrote, "within ten years *Horn* would be rediscovered as a masterpiece of myth-debunking and a powerful starting point for the modern, deglamourized Western—notably Clint Eastwood's *Unforgiven* [1992]."[41] But one might add that *Horn*'s mix of violence and adherence to a dying Western code is also reminiscent of McQueen's work with Sam Peckinpah.

Of course, by the time of *Horn*'s release, McQueen was busy working on getting his pilot's license and becoming a new citizen, with Minty, of Santa Paula. The small town, forty miles north of their beach home, had a population of approximately twenty thousand residents. McQueen immediately embraced the place because it reminded him of Slater, Missouri, where he had had occasional periods of stability in a largely rootless childhood. Ironically, given his impending death, he was fond of saying he wanted to die in Santa Paula.

McQueen and his prized period toys in The Hunter *(1980), an underrated spoof of the actor's action persona.*

Unable to initially find a house, McQueen and Minty set up housekeeping in a hangar at the Santa Paula airport! They carved a living space out of an assortment of collectibles the actor was forever stockpiling. "It was as if Steve bought everything that was missing from his childhood, that he couldn't afford when he was growing up," Minty observed.[42] While the majority of McQueen's treasures were salted away in a Ventura County, California, warehouse, the couple's airport "apartment" featured a cross-section of these artifacts. A partial list of his favorite antiques included: 140 vintage motorcycles, automobiles, biplanes, toys, cash registers, guns, knifes, framed film posters, slot machines, signs, clocks, telephones, furniture, jukeboxes, and whatever else might catch his attention at a secondhand store or a swap meet. Eventually, McQueen brought his whole collection to the airport. "Soon the hangar took on the look of a museum," one McQueen biographer noted. "Surrounded by this awesome display, he felt completely comfortable. He was in no hurry to find suitable quarters but the search was begun."[43] In McQueen's final film, *The Hunter*, he even surrounds his title character with just these sorts of items, especially focusing on the period toys. One of the actor's favorite jokes at the time was telling Minty, "You're the youngest thing I have."

Besides flying old biplanes, similar to what his pilot father would have used to barnstorm across America, McQueen relished dressing up like an ace from yesteryear, from wearing goggles to a leather flying jacket. *Peanut's* World War I flyer Snoopy had nothing on McQueen. Consequently, the actor was overjoyed to receive his pilot's license in July 1979, especially since McQueen's dyslexia had caused him to flunk his first two written exams! The performer's natural athletic skills made him an excellent aviator. Minty also earned a pilot's license, though she kept her flying repertoire fairly traditional, while her husband mastered several acrobatic stunts. For McQueen, it was like taking the joys of motorcycling into the air.

Also in July 1979 McQueen bought a small fifteen-acre ranch just outside of Santa Paula, only three miles from the airport. The four-bedroom Victorian house had been built in 1896 and needed extensive restoration, in part because McQueen wanted to return the home to all its turn-of-the-century glory, and then some. At the same time, the actor would be gifted with a new local friend and adviser, Grady Ragsdale Jr., who would become McQueen's foreman/general troubleshooter, and later biographer.[44]

Conveniently, with the mess of remodeling under way, McQueen's next and final film, *The Hunter*, necessitated going to Chicago for its late summer and early fall shoot. Additional production work in Los Angeles kept him and Minty away from Santa Paula, except for weekends in their hangar digs, until mid-October. McQueen hated leaving his lifetime of collectibles, but that was undoubtedly tempered by the countless antiques included in *The Hunter*, all of which became the actor's property upon the film's completion. In true McQueen fashion, his character even observes at one point, "New things are no good."

For what would be his last movie, McQueen had come full circle. Once again he was playing a bounty hunter. Though the story had a contemporary setting, *Hunter* was a quasi-Western, with even an opening history lesson dating the profession to an 1872 Supreme Court ruling. Through an ongoing Old West loophole, bounty hunters can track down criminals without the legal restrictions of search warrants and extradition papers. McQueen's character, based upon real-life bounty hunter Ralph "Papa" Thorson (who has a cameo as a bartender), is largely a roguish figure, forever leaving on another assignment. But his home life is anchored by the beautiful young Kathryn Harrold, whose age and appearance remind one of Minty.

McQueen's hunter is also often a mirror of the man, from his obsession with antiques and a young lover to being a figure who has decidedly slowed down. Part of the picture's charm is how McQueen affectionately parodies his no-nonsense action persona, particularly in a chase on foot over several Chicago rooftops, where, at one point, he has to stop and back up, in order to get enough running speed to jump from one building to another. Also like the real McQueen, the actor's "Papa" does not care what he looks like, frequently wearing a ratty old bathrobe and glasses, as he plays with an army of vintage toys. (Michael

Douglas seems to have borrowed the look and attitude for his underrated performance in *Wonder Boys*, 2000).

Giving McQueen's hunter certain traits that were atypical to the star's persona, however, really upset some critics. Thorson was both a classic music lover and a crummy driver, traits then played for comic effect by McQueen. Given the actor's fame as a celebrated racer and star of the classic *Bullitt* chase scene, being a challenged driver generated the most adverse criticism. *Variety*'s review stated, "McQueen may have felt that the time had come to revise his persona a bit but what's involved here is desecration. Given [the] star's rep . . . as a terrific driver, someone thought it might be cute to make him a lousy one here but seeing him crash stupidly into car after car throughout the film runs the gag into the ground."[45]

Reviewing cracks about McQueen's bad-driving Thorson also generated frequent condescending comparisons to the car-crashing comedy *The Blues Brothers* (another 1980 movie shot in Chicago), such as the *Hollywood Reporter*'s comment, "[McQueen] drives with a ruthless ineptitude that would do credit to 'The Blues Brothers.'"[46] What these dissenting critics seemed to have missed, however, is that *Hunter* is also

The real-life character upon which The Hunter *is based, bounty hunter Ralph "Papa" Thorson, had a cameo in the film playing a bartender.*

a *comedy*. Yet, the picture's reviews, be they good, bad, or indifferent, make "action" the optimum word, such as "action adventure" or "action-melodrama." There is plenty of movement in this movie, such as a chase that continues on a Chicago El train and culminates with a car taking a dive into the Chicago River from a high-rise parking garage. Still, the accent is on comedy. Examples range from a Bigfoot-sized figure Thorson captures at the beginning of the picture (so large that he comically dwarfs the 1952 Chevy convertible that McQueen's character drives), to two crazy dynamite-throwing brothers that lead Thorson on a merry combine-driving chase through a Nebraska cornfield.

McQueen's ongoing spoof of his tough-guy persona should have been a sufficient comedy clue. But he further embellishes it with broad actions, such as fainting at the hospital after his pregnant girlfriend starts to deliver their baby in the parking lot, and comic lines, such as his definition of what a stun gun does: "Ruins their [the felons'] day." Plus, despite some critics complaining that McQueen had not honored his persona, such journalistic malcontents seem to have had no historical awareness of how the actor often followed a stereotypical action picture such as *Bullitt* with a comedy, such as *The Reivers* (1969). Thus, moving from *Horn* to *Hunter* was a standard modus operandi for McQueen.

The reviews for *Hunter* were sharply divided. The *New York Times* called the film "exceptionally clumsy, [and] unpleasant," while the *Los Angeles Times* said, "'The Hunter' is a lackluster reminder that Steve McQueen is a charismatic star but that even stars need something to shine in."[47] In contrast, *Playboy* observed, "McQueen is what you mean when you call a man cool, yet *The Hunter* has some charmingly unheroic human touches. I especially liked his ineptitude behind the wheel of a car—he's not a very good parker . . . [the picture] has pace, humor, humanity and reel after reel of pure physical excitement."[48] *Newsweek* added, "McQueen, as usual, breezes through his part with cool and witty grace," while *US Magazine* enthused, "At 50, the actor's settled into a graceful middle-age. Although the lopsided smile and intense

One chase scene from The Hunter *took McQueen to the top of a Chicago elevated train.*

blue eyes remain unchanged, youthful cockiness has been replaced by a seasoned authority."[49]

The closing line for the *US Magazine* review was, "[*The Hunter*] satisfies—until the next [McQueen film]." But there would be no more movies for the actor. The health problems that had plagued him on the production of *Horn* persisted during this final shoot: shortness of breath, chronic colds, and tiredness. In December 1979, shortly after *Hunter* wrapped, McQueen found out his right lung had a massive tumor—he had a terminal case of mesothelioma. This rare cancer was normally caused by asbestos inhalation, a substance McQueen had been constantly in contact with by way of his asbestos-treated, flameproof automobile-racing uniforms. Worse yet, like many drivers, his nose and mouth were also covered with an asbestos-treated cloth inside his helmet during races. In addition, the military tanks McQueen drove and worked on during his years in the marines were also insulated with asbestos.

Spending his final Christmas at Cedars-Sinai Hospital in Los Angeles, McQueen learned more about mesothelioma and how it had spread throughout his body, including the lining of the stomach and nodules in his neck and chest. Despite receiving a death sentence from his doctors (only twenty-four mesothelioma cases had ever been studied), McQueen vowed to beat the cancer. But at the same time, he kept the diagnosis secret from the public and most of his friends and family, including his children, Terry and Chad. But Terry "read" between the lines, while Chad bought his father's explanation that everything was okay. McQueen also began to put his proverbial "house in order," marrying the beautiful, loyal Minty on January 16, 1980, at the couple's Santa Paula ranch.

Evangelist Billy Graham, who ministered to McQueen late in the actor's life, writes in the foreword to *Steve McQueen: The Final Chapter*, "It was also interesting to me that Steve had accepted Christ some weeks before he even knew he was ill. Otherwise, people might have thought it was a deathbed decision."[50] Of course, that oversimplifies. McQueen had always hated hospitals, and just as fervently believed he would never reach old age. Couple this with his persistent poor health throughout 1979, and McQueen's religious conversion probably had a lot to do with the actor feeling something was not right. Being born again was undoubtedly also influenced by Minty's devout belief.

"If the ancient Greeks were right that it is the manner of one's death as much as the substance of one's life's that determines its ultimate meaning," then McQueen's final months might be hotly contested along radically different lines.[51] That is, there are some who might interpret the actor's sudden embrace of Christ, and a controversial cancer treatment soon to be addressed, as a cop out to McQueen's tough-guy loner nature, which also doubled as his screen persona. Conversely, when the traditional medical profession essentially said, "Go home and die," it makes perfect sense that the antiheroic actor would have fought this Establishment death sentence. McQueen's rallying of diverse forces to fight his cancer was consistent with what any former street kid would do when threatened—take whatever action is necessary.

McQueen covers his nose and mouth with an asbestos-treated cloth before a 1971 film automobile race.

Rumors about McQueen's condition began to surface in the tabloids almost from the beginning. But a second visit to Cedars-Sinai in February 1980 was the catalyst for increased speculation in the scandal sheets. The actor's inoperable cancer had spread even more. In March the *National Enquirer* broke a story about McQueen's fight against cancer, a diagnosis he was still denying publicly. Indeed, the actor hoped that by attending a premier of *Horn* later that month he could undercut the validity of the cancer story.

McQueen and Minty did make the opening of the picture, with McQueen looking relatively healthy. But the effort put him in bed for a week. Sadly, he also believed that the movie could have been better. Interestingly, he saw this revisionist Western as a metaphor for modern Hollywood: "[Horn] is totally used by his employers and is eventually framed for murder. It's very applicable to the way some people, especially in the film business and in politics, use people they feel are lower than they are, or 'unacceptable,' for anything more than a dirty job. It happens every day."[52] The premier attendance did not stop the media frenzy. And McQueen's next medical decision, to begin a metabolic treatment under the supervision of a Doctor William Donald Kelley, eventually fanned the tabloid fires all the more.

Kelley advocated fighting the cancer with a special diet, vitamin supplements, and detoxification. But Kelley's training was in orthodontia, not medicine! Moreover, his controversial cancer claims and business dealings had been investigated by an army of government agencies, including the Food and Drug Administration, the Federal Bureau of Investigation, and the Internal Revenue Service. Even Kelley's book on his medical theories had been banned by a Texas court for being misleading. Not surprisingly, given this background, McQueen's eventual treatment by Kelley took place in Mexico, where medical guidelines were more lax. The setting was a former health spa turned clinic called Plaza Santa Maria, a half-hour drive south of San Diego. The actor checked in at the end of July 1980. A media circus was about to begin, with Kelley soon appearing on Tom Snyder's popular late night television program, *The Tomorrow Show*.

Between July and his November 7, 1980, death, McQueen traveled back and forth between his Santa Paula home and Kelley's clinic. Ironically, the actor's death came as a result of a blood clot in the heart after surgery to remove a tumor in his stomach so large that he had looked pregnant during the last stages of his illness. Opinions continue to differ on Kelley's treatment. Adams had these thoughts about the subject after the actor's funeral: "Steve used to say, 'Life is a scam, baby.' In the end, the greatest scam had been perpetrated on him in Mexico. He had unknowingly and bravely brought it about in his quest and fight for hope and life."[53] While most with memories of the event embraced this perspective, others, such as McQueen's gifted biographer Marshall Terrill, who also assisted Minty in the writing of her book, noted, "His [Kelley's] work is now considered by some in the medical field a major breakthrough in cancer treatment."[54]

Regardless, an iconic actor had died, a man-child forever in search of a home he had been denied as a youngster. I am reminded of a critical assessment on the writing of Horton Foote, the author who adapted his play, *The Traveling Lady*, for McQueen's film, *Baby, the Rain Must Fall* (1965). The author/critic might just as well have been speaking of McQueen when he observed, "The theme that obsesses him is the myth of home, a safe place that exists only as a wish or an idealized memory."[55] After an often troubled life, and an equally troubled death, one can only hope that McQueen has somehow now found his way to a "safe place."

Epilogue

*"[Steve McQueen] comes out of the tradition of
Gable, Bogie, Cagney and even me. He's a stunner."*[1]

EDWARD G. ROBINSON

While writing a book on Steve McQueen's early idol, James Dean, I came across the following overview on the star of *Rebel without a Cause* (1955), "He has been cussed, discussed, loved and hated."[2] This would also effectively double as a summation for McQueen. As I suggested early in the book, while Dean was often an angst poser, McQueen was the proverbial real deal—a poster-child victim of a dysfunctional family. How McQueen went from a "mean streets" hustling kid to the Golden Globe's World Film Favorite Male in 1966 and 1969 is an amazing turn of events.[3] Yet, an even greater legacy for McQueen the man was his ongoing compassion for young people, especially all the time and money he poured into the Boys Republic, an institution for troubled youngsters that had helped turn the actor's life around. The plaque honoring him in the Boys Republic McQueen Center represents a tribute he undoubtedly would have placed ahead of any acting awards or racing trophies: "Steve McQueen came here as a troubled boy but left here as a man. He went on to achieve stardom in motion pictures but returned to this campus often to share of himself and his fortune. His legacy is hope and inspiration to those students here now, and those yet to come."

To the very end, McQueen used his resources to help underprivileged youth. Part of his last film, *The Hunter* (1980), was shot in the Kenmore slum section of Chicago. McQueen had known similar tough neighborhoods and struggling families. He contacted an area church and asked the priest what he could do financially. McQueen soon had a figure and immediately wrote out a check for the amount. Before handing over the money, however, he had his producer match it. This generosity had also occurred on numerous other McQueen shoots, such as the large checks written to a Taiwan orphanage by the actor and director Robert Wise during the production of *The Sand Pebbles* (1966). Indeed, like the actor's ongoing commitment to the Boys Republic, McQueen would financially support this orphanage for the rest of his life.

McQueen also went an additional charitable mile on *Hunter* after asking a young extra, Karen Wilson, why she was not in school. When the girl responded she really needed the money, McQueen did some research. The teenage Karen, living in squalor with her family, was also the main caretaker for a local abused child. An impressed McQueen and his soon-to-be third wife, Barbara Minty, visited Karen's mother and said, "We'd like to take Karen back with us to California, [and] put her in a good school so that she has a chance to get out of here."[4] Karen's mother consented to the couple becoming the girl's legal guardians. They then placed Karen in a private California boarding school, while she spent weekends with the McQueens. She graduated from this exclusive high school before the actor's 1980 death. The young woman has since gone on to a happy West Coast life—a married mother of four who also works for a Los Angeles escrow company.

Of course, for all these youth-orientated good deeds born of McQueen's neglected childhood, the actor's Achilles' heel was his womanizing, sometimes turning violent with his first two wives. Again, the roots probably go back to a promiscuous mother who was just not there, either physically or emotionally, for a son whose father had left when McQueen was a baby. Thus, to describe the actor's problems in a relationship, one might borrow the poetic insights of another artist, painter/writer Joe Andoe, on his similar difficulties with women: "While I had huge Viking hammers, she required fine delicate Swiss watch tools and somebody with the motor skills to use them correctly."[5] I like the analogy both for its applicable poignancy and the fact that the machine-obsessed McQueen also often saw things in mechanical terms.

The good news on McQueen's relationships with women was that he seemed to have turned a corner by the end of his life. First, he had recognized that there was a problem: "When you think about how you've treated some women, you feel terrible; you feel sick inside."[6] Second, despite his earlier failings with his first two wives (Neile Adams and Ali MacGraw), they still continued to be friendly with the troubled actor and remained pro-McQueen advocates after his death. Third, his longtime girlfriend and eventual widow, Minty, finally brought out a softer side of the actor with regard to relationships. Part of this transition was probably the result of an older man finally finding a soul mate who was a much younger woman. While the actor's marriage to Minty was still a work in progress at the time of his death, their union might have eventually mirrored that of Charlie Chaplin and Oona O'Neill— in which another much older iconic womanizer finally found marital happiness.

Naturally, the celebration of great accomplishments in the arts, as was the case with McQueen, do not necessitate, nor should they, that we admire the ethics of a gifted performer. As a biographer I have frequently experienced what Robert A. Caro once labeled the profession's "dark-side," the proverbial skeletons in the closet.[7] Still, it is comfortingly bittersweet to find that one's troubled hero had begun to move beyond certain problems at the time of his death that had haunted him since childhood. Regardless of one's view on whatever progress McQueen had made over any private demons, "We have certainly made heroes of far lesser men."[8]

For most of us, however, the simple proof of McQueen's greatness lies in all the brilliant pieces of time preserved in his movies. His period of screen stardom was relatively short, largely limited to the 1960s and 1970s, with much of the latter decade spent in reclusive semiretirement. But as noted earlier in the book, he had often conducted his life in a fast-forward mode, just as he raced automobiles and motorcycles. I am reminded of the famous passage from Jack Kerouac's novel *On the Road* (1957), something I committed to memory for a high school lit class back when the world was young: "The only people that interest me are the mad ones, the ones who are mad to live, mad to talk, desirous of everything at the same time, the ones that never yawn or say a commonplace thing . . . but burn, burn, burn like roman candles across the night."[9] For much of his life, this was also McQueen.

McQueen's raw energy was a part of the 1950s Beat Generation that embraced *On the Road* as a bible. In fact, while the book was originally written in 1951, it was born of several late 1940s cross-country driving adventures by Kerouac at approximately the same time McQueen had set out on his own personal odyssey to discover America and himself. Art in this time was about stream of consciousness, whether in the way Jackson Pollock poured a painting or Kerouac composed a book on a single massive roll of paper. This naturalness also describes McQueen's approach to performing. Pop-culture critic Gary Giddins puts this in perspective: "McQueen exemplified film acting as a force of will . . . that crossed Bogart's wariness with Mitchum's reticence. . . . [McQueen] bet everything on presence, and won the bet. Robert Mitchum is said to have described McQueen's acting as boring, perhaps sensing a poacher in his own backyard. They have in common animal naturalness, often characterized as cool. In their best roles, they act as though acting were beneath them."[10] (Appropriately, McQueen spent much of the 1950s living in the capital of the Beat Generation, New York's Greenwich Village.)

Fittingly, in acclaimed writer Leonard Michaels's short story, "In the Fifties," he discusses McQueen and Kerouac almost simultaneously. Michaels's equally stream-of-consciousness style insightfully zeroes in with comic flippancy on McQueen's nervous energy over a choice of careers. After meeting the actor at a party, he wrote, "[McQueen] became famous in a TV series about a cowboy with a rifle [*Wanted: Dead or Alive*]. He said he didn't know which he liked best, acting or driving a racing car. I thought he was a silly person and then realized he thought I was."[11] Whatever McQueen's links to the Beats, he was certainly on the same page with the movement's general antiestablishment foundation and a personalized lifestyle that embraced everything from slang-oriented expression and mind-altering drugs to being "desirous of everything at the same time."

Of course, a Beat sensitivity is hardly crucial to an appreciation of McQueen. Indeed, his loner nature, like Dean before him, forever suggests he belongs to a party of one. And, as noted earlier, he remains an iconic figure because of his movies, starting with the signature motorcycle action of *The Great Escape* (1963) to the car-chase thrills of *Bullitt* (1968). But there are numerous other memorable movies, beginning with his title character in *Papillon* (1973), a part which moved the normally caustic critic David Thomson to write, "McQueen is very touching as the man who defies solitary confinement, madness, and aging and becomes a wistful genius of survival. In the last hour of that film, he had moments of inspired, heroic craziness."[12] Suddenly, the actor who always kidded about a lack of range was giving an acting clinic.

The Magnificent Seven (1960) both established McQueen as a screen star and was an early demonstration of the actor's laconic minimalism—an actor who often defined his character through his physical interaction with various props, from his cowboy hat to his shotgun. The movie also operates as a pioneering example of the self-referential phenomenon, a Western that has its characters periodically examine the roots of the genre. Moreover, the often privately witty McQueen was able to shine here comedically, too. For example, when McQueen's character is asked why seven gunslingers took on the task of defending a poor village for the most modest of pay, he likened it to a naked man who suddenly jumped on a cactus, "He said it seemed to be a good idea at the time."

Personally, I am drawn to several under-the-radar McQueen pictures, such as the poignant period comedy *The Reivers* (1969) and the moving character study collaboration with director Sam Peckinpah, *Junior Bonner* (1972). Previous kudos notwithstanding, McQueen's title character in *Bonner* is arguably his greatest performance, as Peckinpah effectively toys with the actor's tough-guy persona, especially the scenes that feature McQueen's screen parents (Robert Preston and Ida Lupino). McQueen was also undoubtedly inspired by working with Lupino, an actress who had costarred with Humphrey Bogart in McQueen's favorite film, *High Sierra* (1941). Though *Bonner* is a contemporary rodeo movie, the picture also sentimentally celebrates the spirit of the old West, chronicling the story of a father and son who are refugees from an earlier time.

Even the sometimes critically maligned final movie, *Hunter* (1980), is not without a great deal of charm—a comic character study of yet another McQueen bounty hunter. Like a well-defined literary character, this also brought a certain symmetry to the actor's career, since McQueen had first arrived as a performer with his television bounty hunter on *Wanted*. Beyond that, however, his *Hunter* character also represents a fascinating final snapshot of a still evolving McQueen, bravely spoofing his age and his action hero persona. Plus, he has entertainingly peppered the part with footnotes of his real life, from an obsession with the vintage toys he never had as a child, to a beautiful young lover more than a little reminiscent of his third wife. The bittersweet promise of a future that was not to be is all there in *Hunter*, from his professional character-actor potential to a more stable, secure personal life.

One might draw a McQueen metaphor from one of the actor's later-in-life comic observations. His frequent antique shopping revealed that sellers increased the price when they realized he was *Steve McQueen*. Thus, his frequent warning to friends and/or family shopping with him was, "Remember, don't let them add the movie star tax."[13] But the real "movie star tax" for celebrities such as McQueen was the threatened loss of a private life, which helps explain the actor's bearded, long-haired reclusiveness near the end. Still, considering his less-than-stable beginnings, McQueen navigated stardom's slippery slopes as well as most of his contemporaries. Yet, it was often a roller-coaster existence. Given McQueen's Charles Dickens-like childhood, and his meteoric rise in the movies with a simultaneous racing career, his life story rivals those of his movie narratives. Then, top this off with a rare form of terminal cancer, and McQueen the man would have been justified in echoing his dying line from *Sand Pebbles*, "What the hell happened?" Yet, like a Hemingway hero, while life ultimately destroyed him, as it will destroy us all, McQueen did not let it defeat him.

For me, a most telling image of the actor occurs early in *Hunter*. McQueen has broken into the house of the latest bond-jumping felon he has been hired to capture. Suddenly, in the midst of this dangerous situation, he takes time to get down on his hands and knees to check out a toy train set on the floor. Like this character, McQueen's often unorthodox life was always lived on his own terms, but with the underlying insecurity of the lost child he perceived himself to be. When one factors this little-boy-scared-of-the-dark component into his tough-guy minimalist screen persona of saying little and doing much, the movie McQueen has an added poignancy. This McQueen mask had allowed him to perform "the great escape" from both a hardscrabble life and personal fear that Henry David Thoreau once described as leading most men "to live lives of quiet desperation." Not surprisingly, it also en-

McQueen's defiance as the title character of Papillon *is effectively captured in this publicity photograph.*

hanced his art. As critic Andrew Sarris said of McQueen, "Some people are so numb from pain they're just blocks of wood. But he was very expressive. You can feel his pain."[14]

This fear factor also provides possible insight into his fondness for speed, both as a professional racer, and simply in living life fast and on the edge—"the great escape" again. McQueen never felt he would live a long life, and like many with that fear, such as Mickey Mantle, star of the New York Yankees, the actor squeezed as much self-destructive living into one life as was humanly possible. To apply a pertinent fractured comic axiom from Mantle's celebrated manager, Casey Stengel, to McQueen: "There's a time in every man's life and I've had plenty of them." Still, I think the actor might have embraced a paraphrased pop-culture panacea on film as art from *New York Times* critic Holland Cotter: "[Movie art] ended up being my thing, not a thing just to look at but to read like a map or a book; not just something to feel safe with but something to get lost in, confused by; a world with lines and colors [both a diversion and a haven]."[15] Or, as novelist Michael Chabon once said of old movie fans, which also described McQueen, "[They] climbed into a movie as into a time machine or a bottle of whiskey and set the dial for 'never come back.'"[16]

For the student of McQueen, the ongoing gift of this "There's a time" crack, is that we will always have the films. But the McQueen capstone for me is his humility and honesty: "I have to be careful because I'm a limited actor. I mean my range isn't very great. There's a whole lot of stuff I can't do, so I have to find characters and situations that feel right. Even then, when I've got something that fits, it's a hell of a lot of work. I'm not a serious actor. There's something about my shaggy-dog eyes that makes people think I'm good. I'm not all that good."[17]

But for most of us, McQueen was just "that good." Born to be unimportant, he built his hard-fought legend on persevering defiance, such as his signature line from *Papillon*, "I'm still here, you bastards." Ultimately, we would like to believe the dream his widow had about this often troubled man, shortly after McQueen's death: "'It's okay honey,' I heard Steve's voice say. 'Don't worry, I'm fine. Nothing hurts, I'm young again and I'm so happy. Be happy and go on with your life.' . . . [then] he was gone."[18]

Filmography

Like many actors who came of age during the 1950s, Steve Mc-
Queen also did a great deal of television early in his career, including
the popular Western series *Wanted: Dead or Alive*. While the series was
in production his screen career began to take off, and he only did spo-
radic small-screen work after *Wanted*.

July 1956   *Somebody Up There Likes Me* (Metro-Goldwyn-Mayer, 110 minutes)
                Director: Robert Wise. Screenplay: Ernest Lehman, from Rocky Graziano's
                autobiography, written with Rowland Barber. Stars: Paul Newman, Pier
                Angeli, Everett Sloane, Eileen Heckart, Sal Mineo, an uncredited Steve
                McQueen.

July 1958   *Never Love a Stranger* (United Artists, 91 minutes)
                Director: Robert Stevens. Screenplay: Harold Robbins, Richard Day, from
                Robbins's book. Stars: John Drew Barrymore, Lita Milan, Robert Bray,
                Steve McQueen.

September 1958   *The Blob* (Paramount, 85 minutes)
                Director: Irvin S. Yeaworth Jr. Screenplay: Theodore Stimanson, Kate
                Phillips, from an Irvine H. Millgate story. Stars: Steven McQueen, Aneta
                Corseaut, Earl Rowe, Olin Howlin, Steven Chase.

February 1959   *The Great Saint Louis Bank Robbery* (United Artists, 86 minutes)
                Directors: Charles Guggenheim, John Stix. Screenplay: Richard T. Hef-
                fron. Stars: Steve McQueen, David Clarke, Graham Denton, Molly Mc-
                Carthy, James Dukas.

December 1959   *Never So Few* (MGM, 124 minutes)
                Director: John Sturges. Screenplay: Millard Kaufman, from the Tom T.
                Chamales novel. Stars: Frank Sinatra, Gina Lollabrigida, Peter Lawford,
                Steve McQueen, Richard Johnson, Paul Henreid, Brian Donlevy, Dean
                Jones, Charles Bronson.

October 1960   *The Magnificent Seven* (United Artists, 128 minutes)
                Director: John Sturges. Screenplay: William Roberts, from *The Seven
                Samurai* screenplay (Japan, 1954). Stars: Yul Brynner, Steve McQueen,
                Eli Wallach, Horst Buchholz, James Coburn, Charles Bronson, Robert
                Vaughn, Brad Dexter, Vladimir Sokoloff, Rosenda Monteros.

July 1961   *The Honeymoon Machine* (MGM, 87 minutes)
                Director: Richard Thorpe. Screenplay: George Wells, from Lorenzo
                Semple's play *The Golden Fleecing*. Stars: Steve McQueen, Brigid Bazlen,
                Jim Hutton, Paula Prentiss, Dean Jagger, Jack Weston, Jack Mullaney,
                Marcel Hillaire.

June 1962   *Hell Is for Heroes* (Paramount, 90 minutes)
                     Director: Don Siegel. Screenplay: Robert Pirosh, Richard Carr, from a
                     Robert Pirosh story. Stars: Steve McQueen, Bobby Darin, Fess Parker,
                     Nick Adams, Bob Newhart, Harry Guardino, James Coburn.

October 1962   *The War Lover* (Columbia, 105 minutes)
                     Director: Philip Leacock. Screenplay: Howard Koch, from John Hersey's
                     novel. Stars: Steve McQueen, Robert Wagner, Shirley Anne Field, Gary
                     Cockrell.

August 1963   *The Great Escape* (United Artists, 168 minutes)
                     Director: John Sturges. Screenplay: James Clavell, W. R. Burnett, from
                     Paul Brickhill's novel. Stars: Steve McQueen, James Garner, Richard At-
                     tenborough, James Donald, Charles Bronson, Donald Pleasence, James
                     Coburn, John Leyton.

November 1963   *Soldier in the Rain* (United Artists, 87 minutes)
                     Director: Ralph Nelson. Screenplay: Maurice Richlin, Blake Edwards,
                     from William Goldman's novel. Stars: Jackie Gleason, Steve McQueen,
                     Tuesday Weld, Tony Bill, Tom Poston, Ed Nelson.

December 1963   *Love with the Proper Stranger* (Paramount, 100 minutes)
                     Director: Robert Mulligan. Screenplay: Arnold Schulman. Stars: Natalie
                     Wood, Steve McQueen, Edie Adams, Herschel Bernardi, Tom Bosley,
                     Harvey Lembeck.

January 1965   *Baby, the Rain Must Fall* (Columbia, 93 minutes)
                     Director: Robert Mulligan. Screenplay: Horton Foote, from his play *The
                     Traveling Lady*. Stars: Lee Remick, Steve McQueen, Don Murray, Paul Fix,
                     Josephine Hutchinson, Ruth White.

October 1965   *The Cincinnati Kid* (MGM, 102 minutes)
                     Director: Norman Jewison. Screenplay: Ring Lardner Jr., Terry Southern,
                     from Richard Jessup's novel. Stars: Steve McQueen, Edward G. Robinson,
                     Ann-Margret, Karl Malden, Tuesday Weld, Joan Blondell, Rip Torn, Jack
                     Weston, Cab Calloway, Jeff Corey, Theo Marcuse.

June 1966   *Nevada Smith* (Paramount, 131 minutes)
                     Director: Henry Hathaway. Screenplay: John Michael Hayes, inspired
                     from the Nevada Smith character in Harold Robbins's novel *The Car-
                     petbaggers*. Stars: Steve McQueen, Karl Malden, Brian Keith, Suzanne
                     Pleshette, Arthur Kennedy, Janet Margolin, Howard Da Silva, Raf Vallone,
                     Pat Hingle, Martin Landau, Paul Fix.

December 1966   *The Sand Pebbles* (Twentieth Century-Fox, 193 minutes)
                     Director: Robert Wise. Screenplay: Richard Anderson, from Richard
                     McKenna's novel. Stars: Steve McQueen, Richard Attenborough, Richard
                     Crenna, Candice Bergen, Marayat Andriane, Mako, Larry Gates, Charles
                     Robinson, Simon Oakland, Gavin McLeod, Joseph di Reda.

June 1968   *The Thomas Crown Affair* (United Artists, 102 minutes)
                     Director: Norman Jewison. Screenplay: Alan R. Trustman. Stars: Steve
                     McQueen, Faye Dunaway, Paul Burke, Jack Weston, Yaphet Kotto, Biff
                     McGuire, Astrid Heeren, Nikita Knatz.

October 1968   *Bullitt* (Warner Brothers, 114 minutes)
Director: Peter Yates. Screenplay: Alan R. Trustman, Harry Kleiner, from Robert L. Pike's novel *Mute Witness*. Stars: Steve McQueen, Robert Vaughn, Jacqueline Bisset, Don Gordon, Robert Duvall, Simon Oakland, Norman Fell, Carl Reindel, Felice Orland, Vic Tayback.

December 1969   *The Reivers* (National General, 111 minutes)
Director: Mark Rydell. Screenplay: Irving Ravetch, Harriet Frank Jr., from William Faulkner's novel. Stars: Steve McQueen, Sharon Farrell, Will Geer, Rupert Crosse, Mitch Vogel, Burgess Meredith, Clifton James, Juana Hernandez, Dub Taylor, Allyn Ann McLerie, Diane Shalet, Diane Ladd, Ellen Geer.

June 1971   *Le Mans* (National General, 106 minutes)
Director: Lee H. Katzin. Screenplay: Harry Kleiner. Stars: Steve McQueen, Siegfried Rauch, Elga Anderson, Ronald Leigh-Hunt, Fred Haltiner, Luc Merenda, 45 Le Mans drivers.

July 1971   *On Any Sunday* (Cinema 5, 189 minutes)
Director/Screenplay: Bruce Brown. Stars: Steve McQueen, Mert Lawwill, Malcolm Smith, Gene Romero, Jim Rice, Dick Mann, Whitney Martin.

August 1972   *Junior Bonner* (ABC-Cinerama, 103 minutes)
Director: Sam Peckinpah. Screenplay: Jeb Rosebrook. Stars: Steve McQueen, Robert Preston, Ida Lupino, Joe Don Baker, Barbara Leigh, Mary Murphy, Ben Johnson, Matthew Peckinpah, Rod Hart.

December 1972   *The Getaway* (National General, 122 minutes)
Director: Sam Peckinpah. Screenplay: Walter Hill, from Jim Thompson's novel. Stars: Steve McQueen, Ali MacGraw, Ben Johnson, Sally Struthers, Al Lettieri, Slim Pickens, Richard Bright, Jack Dodson, Dub Taylor, Bo Hopkins.

December 1973   *Papillon* (Allied Artists, 150 minutes)
Director: Franklin J. Schaffner. Screenplay: Dalton Trumbo, Lorenzo Semple Jr., from Henri Charrière's book. Stars: Steve McQueen, Dustin Hoffman, Victor Jory, Don Gordon, Anthony Zerbe, Robert Deman, Woodrow Parfrey, Bill Mumy, George Coulouris, Ratna Assan, Dalton Trumbo, Vic Tayback.

December 1974   *The Towering Inferno* (Twentieth Century-Fox/Warner Brothers, 165 minutes)
Dialogue Director: John Guillermin. Action Director: Irwin Allen. Screenplay: Stirling Silliphant, from Richard Martin Stern's novel *The Tower*, and the Frank M. Robinson/Thomas Scortia novel *The Glass Inferno*. Stars: Steve McQueen, Paul Newman, Faye Dunaway, William Holden, Fred Astaire, Susan Blakely, Richard Chamberlain, Jennifer Jones, O. J. Simpson, Robert Vaughn, Robert Wagner, Susan Flannery, Don Gordon, Sheila Mathews, Maureen McGovern.

March 1978   *An Enemy of the People* (Warner Brothers, 103 minutes)
Director: George Schaefer. Screenplay: Alexander Jacobs, from Arthur Miller's translation/adaptation of Henrik Ibsen's play. Stars: Steve

McQueen, Charles Durning, Bibi Anderson, Eric Christmas, Michael
Cristofer, Richard A. Dysart.

March 1980   *Tom Horn* (Warner Brothers, 98 minutes)
Director: William Wiard. Screenplay: Thomas McGuane, Bud Shrake,
from the autobiography *Life of Tom Horn, Government Scout and Inter-
preter, Written by Himself.* Stars: Steve McQueen, Linda Evans, Richard
Farnsworth, Billy Green Bush, Slim Pickens, Peter Canon, Elisha Cook.

July 1980   *The Hunter* (Paramount, 117 minutes)
Director: Buzz Kulik. Screenplay: Ted Leighton, Peter Hyams, from Chris-
topher Keane's book and the life of Ralph "Papa" Thorson. Stars: Steve
McQueen, Eli Wallach, Kathryn Harrold, LeVar Burton, Ben Johnson,
Richard Venture, Tracey Walter, Ralph "Papa" Thorson, Taurean Blacque,
Christopher Keane.

Additional Film Material

"AMC Backstory: 'The Towering Inferno.'" Disk 2 of 1974's *The Towering Inferno* Special
Edition DVD, Twentieth Century Fox Home Entertainment, 2006.
Crenna, Richard. Voice-over on 1966's *The Sand Pebbles* DVD, Cinema Classics Collection,
2007.
Jewison, Norman. Voice-over on 1968's *The Thomas Crown Affair* DVD, MGM Home
Entertainment, 2005.
Steve McQueen: The Essence of Cool. Extra feature 1968's *Bullitt* DVD,
Warner Brothers Entertainment, 1996.

Notes

Preface

1. Paul Duncan, ed., *McQueen* (Los Angeles: Taschen, 2007), 37.

2. Fernanda Eberstadt, "The Unexpected Fantasist," *New York Times Magazine*, August 26, 2007.

3. Jack Kerouac, *On The Road: The Original Scroll,* Howard Cunnell, ed. (1957; reprint, New York: Viking, 2007).

4. Holland Cotter, "On My Own Road," *New York Times*, September 2, 2007.

5. Casey St. Charnez, *The Complete Films of Steve McQueen* (1984; reprint, New York: Citadel Press, 1992), 254.

6. Duncan, ed. *McQueen*, 46.

7. Wes D. Gehring, *James Dean: Rebel with a Cause* (Indianapolis: Indiana Historical Society Press, 2005).

8. Kurt Vonnegut Jr., *Slaughterhouse-Five* (1969; reprint, New York: Dell, 1974), 43.

9. Gehring, *Carole Lombard: The Hoosier Tornado* (Indianapolis: Indiana Historical Society Press, 2003), 213.

Prologue

1. Joyce Haber, "McQueen Plays Rodeo Role Next," *Los Angeles Times*, June 29, 1971.

2. Christopher Sandford, *McQueen: The Biography* (2001; reprint, New York: Taylor Trade Publishing, 2003), 7.

3. George Eells, "Steve McQueen . . . Rugged, Tormented, Thrill-happy," *Look*, October 11, 1960, p. 47.

4. Marcus Winslow Jr., interview with author, July 23, 2004. See also, Wes D. Gehring, *James Dean: Rebel with a Cause* (Indianapolis: Indiana Historical Society Press, 2005).

5. Marshall Terrill, *Steve McQueen: Portrait of an American Rebel* (1993; reprint, London: Plexus Publishing, 2005), 3.

6. Hedda Hopper, original draft of her Steve McQueen profile, June 28, 1959, Steve McQueen files, Margaret Herrick Library, Academy of Motion Picture Arts and Sciences, Beverly Hills, California.

7. Tim Brooks and Earle Marsh, *The Complete Directory to Prime Time Network TV Shows, 1946–Present* (New York: Ballantine Books, 1979), 804.

8. William J. Felchner, "The Best of Steve McQueen," *Big Reel*, July 1995, p. 148.

9. Sandford, *McQueen*, 83.

10. *Variety* review, quoted in Neile McQueen Toffel, *My Husband, My Friend* (New York: Antheneum, 1986), 84.

11. Ibid.

12. Vernon Scott, "Moving Over: Television's Steve McQueen Co-stars in New Movie," *Newark Evening News*, April 29, 1959.

13. Joseph Finnigan, "Hollywood: McQueen Survives 'Blob,'" *Newark Evening News*, July 21, 1963.

14. Roderick Mann, "Steve McQueen: A Reservoir of Violence," *New York World Telegram and the Sun*, February 19, 1966.

15. Terrill, *Steve McQueen*, 42.

16. Sandford, *McQueen*, 85.

17. Marie Torre, "Hero on 'Wanted' a [Method] Studio Alumnus," *New York Herald Tribune*, November 26, 1958.

18. Joe Hyams, "Feudin' & Fussin': Steve McQueen Talks Back," *New York Herald Tribune*, April 18, 1959.

19. William R. Nolan, *McQueen* (New York: Congdon and Weed, 1984), 30.

20. Norman Jewison, *This Terrible Business Has Been Good to Me: An Autobiography* (New York: Saint Martin's Press, 2004), 103.

21. Nolan, *McQueen*, 37.

22. *Wanted: Dead or Alive* review, *Variety*, September 10, 1958.

23. Ibid., September 28, 1960.

24. Terrill, *Steve McQueen*, 238.

25. Toffel, *My Husband, My Friend*, 86.

26. Erskine Johnson, "Sharp Shadow Again," *Los Angeles Mirror*, October 28, 1958.

27. John Kehoe, "Steve McQueen," *Biography Magazine*, July 2001, p. 116.

28. Earl Wilson, "Sluggin' Steve," *New York Post*, undated, in McQueen files, Herrick Library.

29. Earl Wilson, "That's Earl," *Newark Evening News*, August 30, 1959.

30. "So He Got a Horse!" *TV Guide*, May 30, 1959, p. 13.

31. Sidney Skolsky, "Hollywood Is My Beat, *Hollywood Citizen News*, January 28, 1960.

32. Earl Wilson, "Steve McQueen's Reforming; He's Hot as a Firecracker," *Los Angeles Mirror*, November 1, 1960.

33. Hyams, "Feudin' & Fussin.'"

34. "'Sometimes Wild Roles' Easy for Tight-Lipped Steve," *Los Angeles Herald Examiner*, June 30, 1968.

35. Randall Riese, *The Unabridged James Dean: His Life From A to Z* (Chicago: Contemporary Books, 1991), 92.

36. "Steve McQueen," *Los Angeles Times*, May 12, 1959.

37. Penina Spiegel, *McQueen: The Untold Story of a Bad Boy in Hollywood* (Garden City, NY: Doubleday and Company, 1986), 103.

Chapter 1

1. Christopher Sandford, *McQueen: The Biography* (2001; reprint, New York: Taylor Trade Publishing, 2003), 13.

2. See "William McQueen," "Julian Crawford," and "Victor L. Crawford," http:www.familysearch.org/eng/search/IGI/individual_record.

3. William F. Nolan, *Steve McQueen: Star on Wheels* (New York: Berkley Publishing, 1972), 21.

4. Nolan, *McQueen* (New York: Congdon and Weed, 1984), 6–7.

5. Neile McQueen Toffel, *My Husband, My Friend* (New York: Atheneum, 1986), 93.

6. See Wes D. Gehring, *Red Skelton: The Mask behind the Mask* (Indianapolis: Indiana Historical Society Press, 2008), and *Irene Dunne: First Lady of Hollywood* (Lanham, MD: Scarecrow Press, 2003).

7. George Eells, "Steve McQueen . . . Rugged, Tormented, Thrill-happy," *Look*, October 11, 1960, p. 49.

8. Marc Pachter, "The Biographer Himself: An Introduction," in Pachter, ed., *Telling Lives: The Biographer's Art* (Philadelphia: University of Pennsylvania Press, 1985), 14.

9. Claire Tomalin, quoted in Thomas Mallon's review, "Thomas Hardy's English Lessons," *New York Times*, January 28, 2007.

10. May Okon, "Wanted—To Be Somebody," *New York News*, February 5, 1967.

11. Sandford, *McQueen*, 16.

12. Penina Spiegel, *McQueen: The Untold Story of a Bad Boy in Hollywood* (Garden City, NY: Doubleday and Company, 1986), 9.

13. Toffel, *My Husband, My Friend*, 51–52.

14. Sandford, *McQueen*, 27.

15. See Wes D. Gehring, *James Dean: Rebel with a Cause* (Indianapolis: Indiana Historical Society Press, 2005), 39.

16. Andy Webster, "The Escape Artist," *Premiere*, September 1999, p. 104.

17. Ibid., 105.

18. David Hoppe, "Steve McQueen's Indiana Legacy," *Arts Indiana Magazine* (Winter 2001): p. 23.

19. See note 2.

20. David L. Smith, *Hoosiers in Hollywood* (Indianapolis: Indiana Historical Society Press, 2006), 102.

21. Steve McQueen, "Steve McQueen Skirted 8-Ball," *Newark Evening News*, August 31, 1963.

22. Toffel, *My Husband, My Friend*, 87.

23. Sandford, *McQueen*, 18.

24. See note 2.

25. Smith, *Hoosiers in Hollywood*, 102.

26. McQueen, "Steve McQueen Skirted 8-Ball."

27. For example, see Marshall Terrill, *Steve McQueen: Portrait of an American Rebel* (1993; reprint, London: Plexus Publishing, 2005), 6.

28. Nolan, *Steve McQueen*, 11.

29. Lennie La Guire, "Steve McQueen Lives on at Boys Republic," *Los Angeles Herald Examiner*, December 11, 1981.

30. Eudora Welty, foreword to *To the Lighthouse*, by Virginia Woolf (1927, reprint, New York: Harvest Book, 1981), vii.

Chapter 2

1. Andy Webster, "The Escape Artist," *Premiere*, September 1999, p. 88.

2. William Nolan, *Steve McQueen: Star on Wheels* (New York: Berkley Publishing, 1972), 24.

3. George Eells, "Steve McQueen . . . Rugged, Tormented, Thrill-happy," *Look*, October 11, 1960, p. 49.

4. Wes D. Gehring, *Red Skelton: The Mask behind the Mask* (Indianapolis: Indiana Historical Society Press, 2008).

5. Terrence Rafferty, "Cops and Rabbis: 'The Yiddish Policeman's Union,'" *New York Times*, May 13, 2007.

6. Neile McQueen Toffel, *My Husband, My Friend* (New York: Atheneum, 1986), 12.

7. Christopher Sandford, *McQueen: The Biography* (2001; reprint, New York: Taylor Trade Publishing, 2003), 40.

8. Johanna Neuman, "Military Archives Spotlight the Stars," *Indianapolis Star*, June 10, 2005.

9. William F. Nolan, *McQueen* (New York: Congdon and Weed, 1984), 14.

10. Ibid., 26.

11. Bruce Bahrenburg, "McQueen 'of the Times,'" *Newark Evening News*, December 25, 1966.

12. Sheilah Graham, "Steve McQueen Delves Deep Issues," *Hollywood Reporter*, July 5, 1966.

13. Ed Bark, "McQueen Haunted by Loneliness," *Indianapolis Star*, March 31, 1998, E-5.

14. Webster, "Escape Artist," 104.

15. Vernon Scott, "Steve McQueen: Non-conformist with a Cause," *TV Time Sunday Supplement*, July 31, 1966.

16. "McQueen Meets the Press—Again and Again and Again," *Los Angeles Times*, June 30, 1968.

17. Joseph Finnegan, "For a Chap Who Once Played 'Blob,' Steve McQueen Has Done Right Well," *Louisville Courier Journal*, July 21, 1963.

18. For example, see Wanda Hale's "Film Talk: The Real McQueen," *New York Daily News*, December 19, 1966.

19. Terrence Rafferty, "The Real McQueen," *GQ*, April 1999, p. 88.

20. Sandford, *McQueen*, 50.

21. Louella Parsons, "Steve McQueen: A Rebel Is Anchored," *Pictorial TV View*, July 3, 1966.

22. James Wolcott, "The Real McQueen," *Vanity Fair*, September 2000, p. 349.

23. Nolan, *Steve McQueen*, 28.

24. Penina Spiegel, *McQueen: The Untold Story of a Bad Boy in Hollywood* (Garden City, NY: Doubleday and Company, 1986), 42.

25. Robert Johnson, "TV's Angry Young Star," *Saturday Evening Post*, January 14, 1961, p. 60.

26. "Steve McQueen," in *Current Biography 1966*, ed. Charles Moritz (New York: H. W. Wilson Company, 1966), 256.

27. Peter Bunzel, "The Bad Boy's Breakout," *Life*, July 12, 1963, p. 66.

28. Martin Sheen, introduction to *James Dean: American Icon*, by David Dalton (New York: Saint Martin's Press, 1984), 7.

29. David Thomson, "Look Out, He's Dangerous," *London Independent*, August 1, 1999.

30. Johnson, "TV's Angry Young Star," 27.

31. Foster Hirsch, *A Method to Their Madness: A History of the Actors Studio* (New York: W. W. Norton, 1984), 294.

32. Lee Strasberg, *A Dream of Passion: The Development* (Boston: Little, Brown and Company, 1987), 57.

33. Norman Jewison, *This Terrible Business Has Been Good to Me* (New York: Saint Martin's Press, 2004), 103.

34. Bunzel, "Bad Boy's Breakout," 66.

Chapter 3

1. Penina Spiegel, *McQueen: The Untold Story of a Bad Boy in Hollywood* (Garden City, NY: Doubleday and Company, 1986), 91.

2. Eli Wallach, *The Good, the Bad, and Me* (New York: Harcourt, 2005), 205–6.

3. Christopher Sandford, *McQueen: The Biography* (2001; reprint, New York: Taylor Trade Publishing, 2003), 64.

4. William F. Nolan, *McQueen* (New York: Congdon and Weed, 1984), 23.

5. *Hatful of Rain* review, *Variety*, July 3, 1956.

6. Marshall Terrill, *Steve McQueen: Portrait of an American Rebel* (1993; reprint, London: Plexus Publishing, 2005), 29.

7. Neile McQueen Toffel, *My Husband, My Friend* (New York: Atheneum, 1986), 46.

8. Wes D. Gehring, *James Dean: Rebel with a Cause* (Indianapolis: Indiana Historical Society Press, 2005).

9. "Lee Strasberg," in *Current Biography 1960*, Charles Moritz, ed. (New York: H. W. Wilson Company, 1960), 406.

10. William Bast, *James Dean: A Biography* (New York: Ballantine Books, 1956), 66.

11. Spiegel, *McQueen*, 76.

12. Toffel, *My Husband, My Friend*, 47.

13. David L. Smith, *Hoosiers in Hollywood* (Indianapolis: Indiana Historical Society Press, 2006), 104.

14. Spiegel, *McQueen*, 91.

15. Malachy McCoy, *Steve McQueen: The Unauthorized Biography* (Chicago: Henry Regnery Company, 1974), 89.

16. Andy Webster, "The Escape Artist," *Premiere*, September 1999, p. 88.

17. Peer J. Oppenheimer, "A Paradox Named Steve McQueen," *Hollywood Citizen News*, December 15, 1962.

18. Nolan, *McQueen*, 66.

19. Candice Bergen, *Knock Wood* (1984; reprint, New York: Ballantine Books, 1985), 166.

20. William Nolan, *Steve McQueen: Star on Wheels* (New York: Berkley Publishing, 1972), 36.

21. Tim Brooks and Earle Marsh, *The Complete Directory to Prime Time Network TV Shows, 1946–Present* (New York: Ballantine Books, 1979), 804.

Chapter 4

1. *Never So Few* review, *Variety*, December 9, 1959.

2. Kitty Kelley, *His Way: The Unauthorized Biography of Frank Sinatra* (New York: Bantam Books, 1986), 256.

3. Michael Freedland, *All the Way: A Biography of Frank Sinatra* (New York: Saint Martin's Press, 1997), 259.

4. William Nolan, *Steve McQueen: Star on Wheels* (New York: Berkley Publishing, 1972), 41.

5. Neile McQueen Toffel, *My Husband, My Friend* (New York: Atheneum, 1986), 90.

6. Bosley Crowther, *Never So Few* review, *New York Times*, January 22, 1960.

7. Freedland, *All the Way*, 259.

8. Kay Proctor, "'The 7' Delights in Action," *Los Angeles Examiner*, November 24, 1960.

9. For example, see "Tony Quinn Loses 'Magnificent' Suit against Brynner," *Variety*, November 30, 1965.

10. Malachy McCoy, *Steve McQueen: The Unauthorized Biography* (Chicago: Henry Regnery Company, 1974), 80.

11. Andy Webster, "The Escape Artist," *Premiere*, September 1999, p. 89.

12. Eli Wallach, *The Good, the Bad, and Me* (New York: Harcourt, 2005), 205.

13. Robert Johnson, "TV's Angry Young Star," *Saturday Evening Post*, January 14, 1961, pp. 27, 58.

14. McCoy, *Steve McQueen*, 86–87.

15. Johnson, "TV's Angry Young Star," 58.

16. Jhan Robbins, *Yul Brynner: The Inscrutable King* (New York: Dodd, Mead and Company, 1987), 95.

17. Wallach, *The Good, the Bad, and Me*, 205.

18. Philip French, *Westerns: Aspects of a Movie Genre* (1973; reprint, New York: Viking Press, 1974), 32.

19. Quoted in Casey St. Charnez, *The Complete Films of Steve McQueen* (1984; reprint, New York: Citadel Press, 1992), 42.

20. Charles Stinson, "'Magnificent Seven' Magnificent Western," *Los Angeles Times*, November 25, 1960.

21. "Healthy Transplant," *Newsweek*, October 31, 1960.

22. *The Magnificent Seven* review, *Variety*, October 5, 1960.

23. James Power, "Sturges Production Let Down by Story," *Hollywood Reporter*, October 5, 1960.

24. *Magnificent Seven* review, *Variety*.

25. Dick Williams, *The Magnificent Seven* review, *Los Angeles Mirror*, November 19, 1960.

26. Harvey Pack, "Steve McQueen Starring in 'Magnificent Seven,'" *Brooklyn Eagle*, October 30, 1960.

27. Michael Sragow, "A Breakout Summer Feat: 'The Great Escape,'" *Los Angeles Times*, June 6, 2003.

28. Jean-Pierre Coursodon (with Pierre Sauvage), *American Directors, Volume II* (New York: McGraw-Hill Book Company, 1983), 348.

29. William F. Nolan, *McQueen* (New York: Congdon and Weed, 1984), 47.

30. Raymond Strait, *James Garner* (New York: Saint Martin's Press, 1985), 185.

31. Alan Hamilton, "His Stunts Thrilled but Even Steve McQueen Could Not Match the Derring-Do of the Real Great Escapes," *London Times*, March 17, 2004.

32. Marshall Terrill, *Steve McQueen: Portrait of an American Rebel* (1993; reprint, London: Plexus Publishing, 2005), 84.

33. *The Great Escape* review, *Variety*, April 17, 1963.

34. Peter Bunzel, "The Bad Boy's Breakout," *Life*, July 12, 1963, p. 63.

35. Terrill, *Steve McQueen*, 85.

36. Philip K. Scheuer, "'The Great Escape' Is Top Suspense Thriller," *Los Angeles Times*, July 2, 1963.

37. James Powers, "'The Great Escape' Great Adventure," *Hollywood Reporter*, April 17, 1963.

38. *Great Escape* review, *Variety*.

39. Judith Crist, "From Stalag: 'The Big Escape,'" *New York Herald Tribune*, August 8, 1963.

40. John G. Mitchell, "Stirring Epic Told Vividly," *New York Journal American*, August 8, 1963.

41. Bosley Crowther, *The Great Escape* review, *New York Times*, August 8, 1963.

42. Pauline Kael, *I Lost It at the Movies* (Boston: Little Brown and Company, 1965), 206.

43. Crist, "From Stalag."

44. Powers, "'Great Escape' Great Adventure."

45. Cobbett Steinberg, *Reel Facts: The Movie Book of Records* (New York: Vintage Books, 1978), 349.

46. Tom Carson, "Toy Story," *Esquire*, May 2001, p. 54.

Chapter 5

1. Diane Daniels, "Is It Neile's Turn to Run Now?" *Movie TV Secrets*, July 1965, p. 66.

2. Peer J. Oppenheimer, "A Paradox Named Steve McQueen," *Hollywood Citizen News*, December 15, 1962.

3. Grady Ragsdale Jr., *Steve McQueen: The Final Chapter* (Ventura, CA: Vision House, 1983), 72.

4. Neile McQueen Toffel, *My Husband, My Friend* (New York: Atheneum, 1986), 177.

5. Marshall Terrill, *Steve McQueen: Portrait of an American Rebel* (1993; reprint, London: Plexus Publishing, 2005), 49.

6. Roderick Mann, "Steve McQueen: A Reservoir of Violence," *New York World Telegram*, February 19, 1966.

7. See Wes D. Gehring, *James Dean: Rebel with a Cause* (Indianapolis: Indiana Historical Society Press, 2005).

8. Paul Hendrickson, "JD: The Legend That Won't Go Away," *Philadelphia Inquirer*, July 22, 1973.

9. Malachy McCoy, *Steve McQueen: The Unauthorized Biography* (Chicago: Henry Regnery Company, 1974), 105.

10. Hyman Goldberg, "Steve McQueen: Show-Biz Wheel!" *New York Mirror Magazine*, June 17, 1962, p. 8.

11. Robert Johnson, "TV's Angry Young Star," *Saturday Evening Post*, January 14, 1961, p. 59.

12. Ernest Hemingway, *Death in the Afternoon* (1932; reprint, New York: Scribner, 2003), 2.

13. Casey St. Charnez, *The Complete Films of Steve McQueen* (1984; reprint, New York: Citadel Press, 1992), 250.

14. Peter Bunzel, "The Bad Boy's Breakout," *Life*, July 12, 1963, p. 65.

15. Mann, "Steve McQueen."

16. George H. Jackson, "Acting Wins Over Racing," *Los Angeles Herald Examiner*, November 25, 1962.

17. William Nolan, *Steve McQueen: Star on Wheels* (New York: Berkley Publishing, 1972), 64.

18. Steve McQueen, "Motorcycles: What I Like in a Bike—and Why," *Popular Science*, November 1966, pp. 77–80.

19. Herbert Shuldiner, "Candid Interview with Steve McQueen: 'I like to ride flat out,'" ibid., 80.

20. Ragsdale, *Steve McQueen*, 84.

21. See Gehring, *James Dean.*

22. John Gilmore, *Laid Bare: A Memoir of Wrecked Lives and the Hollywood Death Trip* (Los Angeles: Amok Books, 1997).

23. *My Husband, My Friend* review, *Variety*, January 7, 1986.

24. See Penina Spiegel, *McQueen: The Untold Story of a Bad Boy in Hollywood* (Garden City, NY: Doubleday and Company, 1986).

25. Jim Cheng, "1970s Game-Show Fixture Reilly Dies," *USA Today*, May 29, 2007, p. 4-D.

26. Bosley Crowther, *The Honeymoon Machine* review, *New York Times*, August 24, 1961; Kate Cameron, "Loew's State Has Howling Comedy Show," *New York Daily News*, August 24, 1961.

27. Lowell E. Redelings, "'Honeymoon' Amusing Film," *Hollywood Citizen News*, August 3, 1961.

28. *The Honeymoon Machine* review, *Motion Picture Exhibitor*, July 12, 1961; *The Honeymoon Machine* review, *Independent Film Journal*, July 15, 1961.

29. *The Honeymoon Machine* review, *Variety*, July 5, 1961," and "'The Honeymoon Machine': Light, Bright, and Packed with Laughs," *New York Journal American*, August 24, 1961.

30. Constance Littlefield, "'Honeymoon Machine' Top Comedy," *Los Angeles Examiner*, August 3, 1961.

31. St. Charnez, *Complete Films of Steve McQueen*, 54.

32. Mona Simpson, "Proximity to Darkness: As a Writer, Leonard Michaels Sought Out Tragedy," *New York Times*, June 10, 2007.

33. Stuart M. Kaminsky, *Don Siegel: Director* (New York: Curtis Books, 1974), 159–60.

34. Terrill, *Steve McQueen*, 69.

35. Philip K. Scheuer, "'The Great Escape' Is Top Suspense Thriller," *Los Angeles Times*, July 2, 1963.

36. Audrey Kearns, "War Is Hell, Even for Film Heroes," *Hollywood Citizen News*, May 31, 1962.

37. Kaminsky, *Don Siegel*, 163–64.

38. Jean-Pierre Coursodon (with Pierre Sauvage), *American Directors, Volume II* (New York: McGraw-Hill Book Company, 1983), 338.

39. McCoy, *Steve McQueen*, 110.

40. Eugene Archer, *Hell Is for Heroes* review, *New York Times*, July 12, 1962.

41. James Powers, "Blanke-Siegel Film Is Well Handled," *Hollywood Reporter*, May 23, 1962.

42. George H. Jackson, "'Hell for Heroes' Gripping Film," *Los Angeles Examiner*, May 31, 1962; *Hell Is for Heroes* review, *Variety*, May 30, 1962.

43. St. Charnez, *Complete Films of Steve McQueen*, 59.

44. Hazel Flynn, "Acting Best Thing about 'War Lover,'" *Hollywood Citizen News*, November 23, 1962.

45. *War Lover* review, *Variety*, October 24, 1962.

46. John L. Scott, "McQueen and Wagner Team in 'War Lover,'" *Los Angeles Times*, November 23, 1962.

47. *The War Lover* review, *Variety*.

48. Flynn, "Acting Best Thing about 'War Lover.'"

49. Hedda Hopper, "Steve McQueen: They Hate Him and He Loves It," *Chicago Tribune*, June 10, 1962.

50. McCoy, *Steve McQueen*, 100.

Chapter 6

1. Marshall Terrill, *Steve McQueen: Portrait of an American Rebel* (1993; reprint, London: Plexus Publishing, 2005), 111.

2. Cobbett Steinberg, *Reel Facts: The Movie Book of Records* (New York: Vintage Books, 1978), 407–8.

3. "Steve McQueen: A Brentwood Retreat Suited to the Dynamic Star," *Architectural Digest*, April 1994, p. 239.

4. Neile McQueen Toffel, *My Husband, My Friend* (New York: Atheneum, 1986), 110.

5. Mamie Van Doren (with Art Aveilhe), *Playing the Field: My Story* (New York: G. P. Putnam's Sons, 1987), 204.

6. Suzanne Finstad, *Natasha: The Biography of Natalie Wood* (New York: Harmony Books, 2001), 246.

7. Ibid., 247.

8. "A Married Man Should Never Be Left Alone," *Modern Screen*, March 1966, p. 22.

9. Bruce Bahrenburg, "McQueen 'of the Times,'" *Newark* (NJ) *Evening News*, December 25, 1966.

10. Barbara McQueen (with Marshall Terrill), *Steve McQueen: The Last Mile* (Dearfield, IL: Dalton Watson Fine Books, 2007).

11. David Thomson, "Look Out, He's Dangerous," *London Independent*, August 1, 1999.

12. Peter Bart, "On McQueen's Cycles," *New York Times*, January 24, 1965.

13. Christopher Sandford, *McQueen: The Biography* (2001; reprint, New York: Taylor Trade Publishing, 2003), 161.

14. Toffel, *My Husband, My Friend*; Cynthia Lennon has done two memoirs, with the first one being most recommended: *A Twist of Lennon* (1978; reprint, New York: Avon Books, 1980).

15. Steinberg, *Reel Facts*, 350.

16. See Wes D. Gehring, *Leo McCarey: From Marx to McCarthy* (Lanham, MD: Scarecrow Press, 2005).

17. Penina Spiegel, *McQueen: The Untold Story of a Bad Boy in Hollywood* (Garden City, NY: Doubleday and Company, 1986), 166.

18. Wanda Hale, *Soldier in the Rain* review, *New York Daily News*, November 29, 1963.

19. Although *Hell Is for Heroes* (1962) screenwriter Robert Pirosh later had a major falling out with McQueen, he was one of several writers to credit the actor with witty additions to the script.

20. William Faulkner, *The Reivers* (New York: Random House, 1962).

21. *Soldier in the Rain* review, *Variety*, November 19, 1963.

22. Bosley Crowther, "'Soldier in Rain' Fails to Be Very Funny," *New York Times*, November 29, 1963.

23. Archer Winsten, "'Soldier in the Rain' at Palace," *New York Post*, November 29, 1963.

24. "An Honest Soldier," *Newsweek*, December 2, 1962.

25. Mandel Herbstman, *Soldier in the Rain* review, *Film Daily*, November 19, 1963, and *Soldier in the Rain* review, *Motion Picture Herald*, November 27, 1963.

26. "The Real McQueen," *Newsweek*, January 6, 1964, p. 42.

27. *Love with the Proper Stranger* review, *Saturday Review*, January 4, 1964.

28. "'Love with the Stranger' [*sic*] Is a Smash Box Office Entry," *Hollywood Reporter*, December 19, 1963.

29. Steve McQueen Clipping Files, Margaret Herrick Library, Academy of Motion Picture Arts and Sciences, Beverly Hills, California.

30. "New York, New York," *Time*, December 27, 1963.

31. Murray Schumach, "Bronx Is Re-created for Film on Italians," *New York Times*, April 20, 1963.

32. "Talk with a Star," *Newsweek*, January 6, 1964.

33. Ian Johnson, *Love with the Proper Stranger* review, *Films and Filming*, October 1964.

34. William Peper, "'Rain' Slows to a Drizzle," *New York World Telegram and Sun*, January 14, 1965.

35. Bosley Crowther, *Baby the Rain Must Fall* review, *New York Times*, January 14, 1965; Judith Crist, "Must Fall: Up from Here On," *New York Herald Tribune*, January 14, 1965.

36. Toffel, *My Husband, My Friend*, 122.

37. Terrill, *Steve McQueen*, 102.

38. "'Baby Rain Must Fall' Dreary Tale of Drifter," *Los Angeles Times*, January 29, 1965.

39. Allen Eyles, *Baby, the Rain Must Fall* review, *Films and Filming*, July 1965.

40. Howard Thompson, *The Cincinnati Kid* review, *New York Times*, October 28, 1965, p. 48.

41. Judith Crist, *The Cincinnati Kid* review, *New York Herald Tribune*, October 28, 1965, p. 15.

42. "Busted Flush," *Newsweek*, November 8, 1965.

43. Dale Monroe, "Poker Game, Gals Highlight Drama," *Hollywood Citizen News*, November 8, 1965.

44. Hollis Alpert, "The Professionals," *Saturday Review*, November 6, 1965.

45. *The Cincinnati Kid* review, *Variety*, October 20, 1965.

46. "'Cincinnati Kid' A Sharp Card," *New York Journal American*, October 28, 1965, p. 17.

47. Norman Jewison, *This Terrible Business Has Been Good to Me* (New York: Saint Martin's Press, 2005), 104.

48. Allen Eyles, *The Cincinnati Kid* review, *Films and Filming*, January 1966.

49. Quoted in Jean-Pierre Coursodon (with Pierre Sauvage), *American Directors, Volume II* (New York: McGraw-Hill Book Company, 1983), 151.

50. John G. Cawelti, *The Six-Gun Mystique* (Bowling Green, OH: Bowling Green University Popular Press, 1971).

51. Allen Eyles, *Nevada Smith* review, *Films and Filming*, October 1966.

52. *Nevada Smith* review, *Motion Picture Herald*, June 8, 1966.

53. Vincent Canby, *Nevada Smith* review, *New York Times*, June 24, 1966.

54. Eyles, *Nevada Smith* review.

Chapter 7

1. Steve McQueen's dying line from *The Sand Pebbles*.

2. Bosley Crowther, *The Sand Pebbles* review, *New York Times*, December 21, 1966.

3. "James Coburn," in *Current Biography 1999*, Clifford Thompson, ed. (New York: H. W. Wilson Company, 1999), 139–40.

4. Arthur Marcede, "Steve McQueen: 'I Must Be Free to Live in My Own Way,'" *TV Rapid Movie Guide*, December 1966, p. 38.

5. Neile McQueen Toffel, *My Husband, My Friend* (New York: Atheneum, 1986).

6. Candice Bergen, *Knock Wood* (1984; reprint, New York: Ballantine Books, 1985), 166.

7. Malachy McCoy, *Steve McQueen: The Unauthorized Biography* (Chicago: Henry Regnery Company, 1974), 155.

8. Patricia Bosworth, *Marlon Brando* (New York: Viking, 2001), 30.

9. Ibid., 33.

10. Richard Crenna voice-over on 1966's *The Sand Pebbles* DVD, Cinema Classics Collection, 2007.

11. Ernest Hemingway, *For Whom the Bell Tolls* (New York: Charles Scribner's Sons, 1940), 471.

12. Casey St. Charnez, *The Complete Films of Steve McQueen* (1984; reprint, New York: Citadel Press, 1992), 129.

13. Crowther, *Sand Pebbles* review.

14. George H. Jackson, "A Massive Film Saga," *Los Angeles Herald Examiner*, December 29, 1966.

15. James Powers, "'Sand Pebbles' Has All the Elements," *Hollywood Reporter*, December 21, 1966.

16. Arthur Knight, "Unsentimental Gentleman," *Saturday Review*, December 21, 1966.

17. See Abe Greenberg, "Steve McQueen Captures Taipei," *Hollywood Citizen News*, April 22, 1966.

18. Cobbett Steinbert, *Reel Facts: The Movie Book of Records* (New York: Vintage Books, 1978), 407.

19. See Bosley Crowther, *Grand Prix* review, *New York Times*, December 22, 1966.

20. McCoy, *Steve McQueen*, 158.

21. See St. Charnez, *Complete Films of Steve McQueen*, 134.

22. Norman Jewison, *This Terrible Business Has Been Good to Me* (New York: Saint Martin's Press, 2005), 161.

23. Christopher Sandford, *McQueen: The Biography* (2001; reprint, New York: Taylor Trade Publishing, 2003), 198.

24. Marshall Terrill, *Steve McQueen: Portrait of an American Rebel* (1993; reprint, London: Plexus Publishing, 2005), 147.

25. John Mahoney, "Mirisch 'Crown' Flashy," *Hollywood Reporter*, June 19, 1968.

26. Penina Spiegel, *McQueen: The Untold Story of a Bad Boy in Hollywood* (Garden City, NY: Doubleday and Company, 1986), 202.

27. Norman Jewison voice-over on 1968's *The Thomas Crown Affair* DVD, MGM Home Entertainment, 2005.

28. Penelope Gilliatt, "What Is Your Robbery Trying to Say?" *The New Yorker*, July 13, 1968.

29. *The Thomas Crown Affair* review, *Motion Picture Exhibitor*, June 19, 1968.

30. Judy Klemesrud, "Steve McQueen: Phi Beta Hubcap," *New York Times*, August 4, 1968.

31. *The Thomas Crown Affair* review, *Variety*, June 19, 1968.

32. Reed Porter, "'Thos. Crown Affair' Glossy, Mod Love-in," *Hollywood Citizen News*, June 28, 1968.

33. David Rider, *The Thomas Crown Affair* review, *Films and Filming*, April 1969.

34. *The Thomas Crown Affair* review, *Motion Picture Herald*, June 19, 1968.

35. *The Thomas Crown Affair* review, *Time*, July 12, 1968; Archer Winsten, "'Thomas Crown Affair' in Triple Bow," *New York Post*, June 27, 1968.

36. Charles Champlin, "'Thomas Crown Affair' at Grauman's," *Los Angeles Times*, June 28, 1968.

37. Klemesrud, "Steve McQueen."

38. See *Steve McQueen: The Essence of Cool*, extra feature, *Bullitt* DVD, Warner Brothers Entertainment, 1996.

39. Charles Champlin, "'Bullitt' at the Pix Theater," *Los Angeles Times*, December 20, 1968.

40. John Mahoney, "W 7's 'Bullitt' Superb," *Hollywood Reporter*, October 16, 1968.

41. Terrill, *Steve McQueen*, 168.

42. Spiegel, *McQueen*, 222.

43. Kevin Thomas, "Bad Boy McQueen Does Switch to Play Cop Role," *Los Angeles Times*, March 27, 1968.

44. Spiegel, *McQueen*, 212.

45. David Lamb, "The Movies . . . Steve McQueen Cutting the Mustard, Learning to Like Cops," *Los Angeles Herald Examiner*, May 12, 1968.

46. Richard Schickel, "Crime Flick with a Taste of Genius," *Life*, November 22, 1968; "Cop Art," *Time*, November 8, 1968.

47. *Bullitt* review, *Cue*, October 26, 1968; Nadine M. Edwards, "Exciting Suspense in McQueen Film," *Hollywood Citizen News*, December 20, 1968; *Bullitt* review, *Variety*, October 16, 1968.

48. Allan Hunter, *Faye Dunaway* (New York: Saint Martin's Press, 1986), 62–63.

Chapter 8

1. Nat Freedland, *The Reivers* review, *Entertainment World*, November 21, 1969.

2. "Southern Reconstruction," *Time*, January 5, 1970.

3. Wanda Hale, "McQueen Starred in Film of Comic Faulkner Novel," *New York News*, December 21, 1969.

4. Andrea Maletz, "'The Reivers': Faulknerian and McQueenian Charm," *Boston after Dark*, January 7, 1970.

5. Roland Gelatt, "Down Memory Lane," *Saturday Review*, January 3, 1970.

6. Margaret Tarratt, *The Reivers* review, *Films and Filming*, January 1971.

7. Malachy McCoy, *Steve McQueen: The Unauthorized Biography* (Chicago: Henry Regnery Company, 1974), 182.

8. *The Reivers* review, *Variety*, November 26, 1969.

9. John Mahoney, "How Long Since You've Seen a Movie for Fun? Here's One," *Hollywood Reporter*, November 26, 1969.

10. Marshall Terrill, *Steve McQueen: Portrait of an American Rebel* (1993; reprint, London: Plexus Publishing, 2005), 180.

11. Penina Spiegel, *McQueen: The Untold Story of a Bad Boy in Hollywood* (Garden City, NY: Doubleday and Company, 1986), 234.

12. S. K. Oberbeck, "Yoknapatawpha Boy," *Newsweek*, January 5, 1970.

13. "Americana," *The New Yorker*, December 27, 1969, p. 47.

14. *The Reivers* review, *Motion Picture Exhibitor*, December 3, 1969; *The Reivers* review, *Cue*, December 27, 1969.

15. William F. Nolan, *McQueen* (New York: Congdon and Weed, 1984), 91.

16. See Casey St. Charnez, *The Complete Films of Steve McQueen* (1984; reprint, New York: Citadel Press, 1992), 163.

17. Neile McQueen Toffel, *My Husband, My Friend* (New York: Atheneum, 1986), 199.

18. Ibid., 192.

19. McCoy, *Steve McQueen*, 188.

20. *Le Mans* review, *Playboy*, September 1971.

21. James Powers, "Cinema Center's 'Le Mans' Tense Auto Race Spectacle," *Hollywood Reporter*, June 15, 1971.

22. See Wes D. Gehring, *Charlie Chaplin: A Bio-Bibliography* (Westport, CT: Greenwood Press, 1983).

23. Christopher Sandford, *McQueen: The Biography* (2001; reprint, New York: Taylor Trade Publishing, 2003), 251, 252.

24. See Leonard Maltin, *Leonard Maltin's 2006 Movie Guide* (New York: Signet Book, 2005).

25. Marc Santora, "A First Lady Receives Her Goodbye," *New York Times*, July 15, 2007.

26. Toffel, *My Husband, My Friend*, 226–32.

27. For example, see the *Le Mans* ad, *Indianapolis News*, June 29, 1971.

28. Howard Thompson, *Le Mans* review, *New York Times*, June 24, 1971.

29. Winfred Blevins, *Le Mans* review, *Los Angeles Herald Examiner*, June 17, 1971.

30. *Le Mans* review, *Variety*, June 16, 1971.

31. *Le Mans* review, *Boxoffice*, July 5, 1971.

32. See Vincent Canby, *McCabe & Mrs. Miller* review, *New York Times*, June 25, 1971; Roger Greenspun, *Klute* review, *New York Times*, June 24, 1971.

33. David Elliott, "Eastwood and Siegel Classic Combination," *Indianapolis News*, July 3, 1971.

34. "In Brief: Current Movies," *Indianapolis Star*, July 4, 1971.

35. Terrill, *Steve McQueen*, 204.

36. Vincent Canby, "Bruce Brown's Documentary Studies the Motorcyclist's View of Racing," *New York Times*, July 29, 1971.

37. *On Any Sunday* review, *Variety*, July 21, 1971.

38. *Le Mans* review, *Cue*, June 27, 1971.

39. Jeremy McCarter, "Miller's Tales," *New York Times*, July 15, 2007.

Chapter 9

1. Marshall Terrill, *Steve McQueen: Portrait of an American Rebel* (1993; reprint, London: Plexus Publishing, 2005), 212.

2. Garner Simmons, *Peckinpah: A Portrait in Montage* (New York: Limelight Editions, 1998), 153.

3. Malachy McCoy, *Steve McQueen: The Unauthorized Biography* (Chicago: Henry Regnery, 1974), 204.

4. Christopher Sandford, *McQueen: The Biography* (2001; reprint, New York: Taylor Trade Publishing, 2003), 273.

5. Simmons, *Peckinpah*, 148.

6. Marshall Fine, *Bloody Sam: The Life and Films of Sam Peckinpah* (New York: Donald Fine, 1991), 219.

7. Penina Spiegel, *McQueen: The Untold Story of a Bad Boy in Hollywood* (Garden City, NY: Doubleday and Company, 1986), 287.

8. Sidney Poitier, *The Measure of a Man* (2000; reprint, San Francisco: Harper, 2001).

9. Fine, *Bloody Sam*, 200.

10. Joseph A. Gomez, "Sam Peckinpah and the 'Post-Western,'" *American Classic Screen* (Spring 1980): 33.

11. Archer Winsten, "'Junior Bonner' at 3 Theaters," *New York Post*, August 3, 1972.

12. Kathleen Carroll, *Junior Bonner* review, *New York Daily News*, August 3, 1972.

13. *London Times* review quoted in Casey St. Charnex, *The Complete Films of Steve McQueen* (1984; reprint, New York: Citadel Press, 1992), 184.

14. Vincent Canby, *Junior Bonner* review, *New York Times*, August 3, 1972.

15. Simmons, *Peckinpah*, 151–52.

16. Sam Peckinpah, "Playboy Interview: Sam Peckinpah," *Playboy*, April 1972, pp. 74, 192.

17. *Junior Bonner* review, *Variety*, June 14, 1972; Andrew Sarris, *Junior Bonner* review, *Village Voice*, September 28, 1972.

18. Roger Greenspun, *The Magnificent Seven Ride!* Review, *New York Times*, August 3, 1972.

19. Sandford, *McQueen*, 245.

20. Frank Miller, *Leading Men: The 50 Most Unforgettable Actors of the Studio Era* (San Francisco: Chronicle Books, 2006), 147.

21. Cobbett Steinberg, *Reel Facts: The Movie Book of Records* (New York: Vintage Books, 1978), 352.

22. Susan Sackett, *Box Office Hits* (New York: Billboard Books, 1990), 210.

23. Ali MacGraw, *Moving Pictures* (New York: Bantam Books, 1991), 87–88.

24. Ibid., 92.

25. Simmons, *Peckinpah*, 156.

26. Terrill, *Steve McQueen*, 235.

27. Anthony Lane, "Hot Stuff," *The New Yorker*, July 30, 2007, p. 91.

28. P. F. Kluge, "What Price Violence?" *Life*, August 11, 1972, p. 49.

29. Kevin Thomas, "Ali and Steve in 'Getaway,'" *Los Angeles Times*, December 18, 1972.

30. Ray Lloyd, "MacGraw, McQueen in 'The Getaway,'" *Los Angeles Herald Examiner*, December 19, 1972.

31. *The Getaway* review, *Cue*, December 23, 1972.

32. Dilys Powell, "Savage Escape," *London Times*, January 28, 1973.

33. *The Getaway* review, *Playboy*, March 1973.

34. *The Getaway* review, *New Republic*, February 10, 1973, p. 35.

35. Margaret Tarratt, *The Getaway* review, *Films and Filming*, March 1973.

36. Lee Reynolds, "First Artists' 'The Getaway,'" *Hollywood Reporter*, December, 13, 1972.

37. Pauline Kael, *The Getaway* review, *The New Yorker*, December 23, 1972.

38. Fine, *Bloody Sam*, 232.

39. *The Getaway*, review, *Variety*, December 13, 1972.

40. MacGraw, *Moving Pictures*, 101.

41. "A Married Man Should Never Be Left Alone," *Modern Screen*, March 1966, p. 22.

42. Vincent Canby, *Papillon* review, *New York Times*, December 17, 1973.

43. Terrill, *Steve McQueen*, 262.

44. Neile McQueen Toffel, *My Husband, My Friend* (New York: Atheneum, 1986), 172.

45. Terrill, *Steve McQueen*, 257.

46. Gordon Gow, *Papillon* review, *Films and Filming*, April 1974.

47. Sackett, *Box Office Hits*, 232.

48. Kevin Thomas, *Papillon* review, *Los Angeles Times*, December 1973.

49. Ray Loynd, "'Papillon' Captures Physical Travails," *Los Angeles Herald Examiner*, December 18, 1973.

50. *Papillon* review, *Variety*, December 12, 1973; "Stuck on an Island," *Newsweek*, December 17, 1973.

51. Judith Crist, "No Butterfly, McQueen," *New York Magazine*, December 24, 1973, p. 68.

52. Paul Duncan, ed., *McQueen* (Los Angeles: Taschen, 2007), 150.

53. Terrill, *Steve McQueen*, 268.

54. Steinberg, *Reel Facts*, 353.

Chapter 10

1. Paul Duncan, ed., *McQueen* (Los Angeles: Taschen, 2007), 170.

2. Ali MacGraw, *Moving Pictures* (New York: Bantam Books, 1991), 108.

3. Vincent Canby, *The Towering Inferno* review, *New York Times*, December 20, 1974.

4. Charles Champlin, "'Inferno': How to Exceed in Disaster Films," *Los Angeles Times*, December 15, 1974.

5. Richard Cuskelly, "Irwin Allen and His 'Towering Inferno,'" *Los Angeles Herald Examiner*, December 15, 1974.

6. "AMC Backstory: 'The Towering Inferno,'" disk 2 of 1974's *The Towering Inferno* Special Edition DVD, Twentieth Century Fox Home Entertainment, 2006.

7. Judith Crist, *The Towering Inferno* review, *New York Magazine*, January 3, 1975.

8. Pauline Kael, *The Towering Inferno* review, *The New Yorker*, December 30, 1974.

9. Champlin, "'Inferno.'"

10. Canby, *Towering Inferno* review.

11. John H. Dorr, *The Towering Inferno* review, *Hollywood Reporter*, December 16, 1974; *The Towering Inferno* review, *Variety*, December 18, 1974.

12. Cobbett Steinberg, *Reel Facts: The Movie Book of Records* (New York: Vintage Books, 1978), 353.

13. Susan Sackett, *Box Office Hits* (New York: Billboard Books, 1990), 234.

14. For example, see Casey St. Charnez, *The Complete Films of Steve McQueen* (1984; reprint, New York: Citadel Press, 1992), 249.

15. Christopher Sandford, *McQueen: The Biography* (2001; reprint, New York: Taylor Trade Publishing, 2003), 330–31.

16. Neile McQueen Toffel, *My Husband, My Friend* (New York: Atheneum, 1986), 281.

17. Mireille Marokvia's *Sins of the Innocent: A Memoir* review, *New York Times*, September 6, 2006.

18. Marshall Terrill, *Steve McQueen: Portrait of an American Rebel* (1993; reprint, London: Plexus Publishing, 2005), 283–84.

19. Charles Champlin, "Critic at Large: Popularizing the Work Epic," *Los Angeles Times*, March 6, 1975.

20. Penina Spiegel, *McQueen: The Untold Story of a Bad Boy in Hollywood* (Garden City, NY: Doubleday and Company, 1986), 296.

21. St. Charnez, *Complete Films of Steve McQueen*, 252.

22. MacGraw, *Moving Pictures*, 111.

23. Toffel, *My Husband, My Friend*, 282.

24. Several seminal McQueen texts suggest this reason, including Terrill's definitive *Steve McQueen*.

25. Arthur Knight, *An Enemy of the People* review, *Hollywood Reporter*, August 28, 1978.

26. Michael Sragow, "We Saw the 'Enemy' and It Isn't McQueen," *Los Angeles Herald Examiner*, August 3, 1980.

27. Kevin Thomas, "'Enemy of the People': A Memory of Steve McQueen," *Los Angeles Times*, October 20, 1981.

28. Leonard Maltin, *Leonard Maltin's 2007 Movie Guide* (New York: Signet Book, 2006), 397.

29. MacGraw, *Moving Pictures*, 112.

30. Barbara McQueen (with Marshall Terrill), *Steve McQueen: The Last Mile* (Deerfield, IL: Dalton Watson Fine Books, 2007), 33.

31. Toffel, *My Husband, My Friend*, 286.

32. Terrill, *Steve McQueen*, 316.

33. Spiegel, *McQueen*, 317.

34. "Redford, McQueen Announce Horn Films," *Hollywood Reporter*, March 3, 1977.

35. Roger Augeel, "Easy Rider," *The New Yorker*, June 2, 1980.

36. Janet Maslin, *Tom Horn* review, *New York Times*, May 23, 1980.

37. Robert Osborne, *Tom Horn* review, *Hollywood Reporter*, March 28, 1980.

38. "*Tom Horn*: McQueen Blows It," *Variety*, April 2, 1980.

39. An untitled *Los Angeles Times* column on *Tom Horn*, with only a July 1980 citation, Steve McQueen Files, Margaret Herrick Library, Academy of Motion Picture Arts and Sciences, Beverly Hills, California.

40. McQueen, *Steve McQueen*, 123.

41. Sandford, *McQueen*, 392.

42. McQueen, *Steve McQueen*, 160.

43. Grady Ragsdale Jr., *Steve McQueen: The Final Chapter* (Ventura, CA: Vision House, 1983), 22–23.

44. Ibid.

45. "*The Hunter*: Another Summer Big-Star Misfire," *Variety*, July 30, 1980.

46. Arthur Knight, *The Hunter* review, *Hollywood Reporter*, July 28, 1980.

47. Vincent Canby, "Film: 'The Hunter,' Tracking Fugitives," *New York Times*, August 1, 1980; Charles Champlin, "Drawing a Bead on 'Hunter,'" *Los Angeles Times*, August 1, 1980.

48. *The Hunter* review, *Playboy*, October 1980.

49. David Ansen, "An Undying Breed," *Newsweek*, August 11, 1980, p. 69; Stephen Schaefer, "Bounty Hunter McQueen: An American Classic," *Us Magazine*, August 5, 1980, p. 61.

50. Billy Graham, foreword, in Ragsdale, *Steve McQueen*, 10.

51. Jonathan Rosen, "Prisoner of War," *New York Times*, May 27, 2007.

52. Ragsdale, *Steve McQueen*, 98.

53. Toffel, *My Husband, My Friend*, 323.

54. Terrill, *Steve McQueen*, 403.

55. Alex Witchell, "His Kind of Town: Horton Foote," *New York Times Magazine*, August 19, 2007.

Epilogue

1. Paul Duncan, ed., *McQueen* (Los Angeles: Taschen, 2007), 91.

2. Frank Friedrichsen, "The Short Tragic Life of Jimmy Dean," *Movie Star Parade*, December 1955, p. 42.

3. Cobbett Steinbert, *Reel Facts: The Movie Book of Records* (New York: Vintage Books, 1978), 173, 175.

4. Barbara McQueen (with Marshall Terrill), *Steve McQueen: The Last Mile* (Deerfield, IL: Dalton Watson Fine Books, 2007), 188.

5. Amy Finnerty, "Color Me Bad: Joe Andoe's Memoir…," *New York Times*, August 19, 2007.

6. Duncan, ed., *McQueen*, 76.

7. William Zinsser, ed., *Extraordinary Lives: The Art and Craft of American Biography* (Boston: Houghton Mifflin Company, 1986), 217.

8. Marshall Terrill, *Steve McQueen: Portrait of an American Rebel* (1993; reprint, London: Plexus Publishing, 2005), 441.

9. Jack Kerouac, *On the Road: The Original Scroll*, Howard Cunnell, ed. (1957; reprint, New York: Viking, 2007).

10. Gary Giddins, *Natural Selection: Gary Giddins on Comedy, Film, Music, and Books* (New York: Oxford University Press, 2006), 166.

11. Leonard Michaels, *The Collected Stories* (New York: Farrar, Straus and Giroux, 2007), 124.

12. David Thomson, *The New Biographical Dictionary of Film* (New York: Alfred A. Knopf, 2003), 588.

13. Grady Ragsdale Jr., *Steve McQueen: The Final Chapter* (Ventura, CA: Vision House, 1983), 42.

14. Duncan, ed., *McQueen*, 116.

15. Holland Cotter, "On My Own Road," *New York Times*, September 2, 2007.

16. Michael Chabon, *Wonder Boys* (New York: Picador, 1995), 251.

17. Casey St. Charnez, *The Complete Films of Steve McQueen* (1984; reprint, New York: Citadel Press, 1992), 251.

18. McQueen, *Steve McQueen*, 233.

Select Bibliography

Special Collections

Steve McQueen Clipping Files. Beech Grove Public Library, Beech Grove, IN.

Steve McQueen Clipping Files. Margaret Herrick Library, Academy of Motion Picture Arts and Sciences, Beverly Hills, CA.

Steve McQueen Clipping Files. Performing Arts Library, New York Public Library at Lincoln Center, New York, NY.

Individual Clipping files for each of McQueen's films at both the Academy Library and New York's Performing Arts Library. These files were also supplemented by the microfilm "Tombs" (dead newspaper) section of New York City's Main Library at Fifth Avenue and Forty-second Street.

Books

Bast, William. *James Dean: A Biography*. New York: Ballantine Books, 1956.

Bergen, Candice. *Knock Wood*. 1984. Reprint, New York: Ballantine Books, 1985.

Bosworth, Patricia. *Marlon Brando*. New York: Viking, 2001.

Brooks, Tim, and Earle Marsh. *The Complete Directory to Prime Time Network TV Shows, 1946–Present*. New York: Ballantine Books, 1979.

Cawelti, John G. *The Six-Gun Mystique*. Bowling Green, OH: Bowling Green University Popular Press, 1971.

Chabon, Michael. *Wonder Boys*. New York: Picador, 1995.

Claxton, William. *Steve McQueen*. Los Angeles: Taschen, 2004.

Coursodon, Jean-Pierre (with Pierre Sauvage). *American Director, Volume II*. New York: McGraw-Hill Book Company, 1983.

Doren, Mamie Van (with Art Aveilhe). *Playing the Field: My Story*. New York: G. P. Putnam's Sons, 1987.

Duncan, Paul, ed. *McQueen*. Los Angeles: Taschen, 2007.

Faulkner, William. *The Reivers*. New York: Random House, 1962.

Fine, Marshall. *Bloody Sam: The Life and Films of Sam Peckinpah*. New York: Donald Fine, 1991.

Finstad, Suzanne. *Natasha: The Biography of Natalie Wood*. New York: Harmony Books, 2001.

Freeland, Michael. *All the Way: A Biography of Frank Sinatra*. New York: St. Martin's Press, 1997.

French, Philip. *Westerns: Aspects of a Movie Genre*. 1973. Reprint, New York: Viking Press, 1974.

Gehring, Wes D. *Carole Lombard: The Hoosier Tornado*. Indianapolis: Indiana Historical Society Press, 2003.

———. *Charlie Chaplin: A Bio-Bibliography*. Westport, CT: Greenwood Press, 1983.

———. *The Charlie Chaplin Murder Mystery*. Indianapolis: New Century Press, 2006.

———. *Irene Dunne: First Lady of Hollywood*. Lanham, MD: Scarecrow Press, 2003.

———. *James Dean: Rebel with a Cause*. Indianapolis: Indiana Historical Society Press, 2005.

———. *Leo McCarey: From Marx to McCarthy*. Lanham, MD: Scarecrow Press, 2005.

———. *Red Skelton: The Mask behind the Mask*. Indianapolis: Indiana Historical Society Press, 2008.

Giddins, Gary, *Natural Selection: Gary Giddins on Comedy, Film, Music, and Books*. New York: Oxford University Press, 2006.

Gilmore, John. *Laid Bare: A Memoir of Wrecked Lives and the Hollywood Death Trip*. Los Angeles: Amok Books, 1997.

Hemingway, Ernest. *Death in the Afternoon*. 1932. Reprint, New York: Scribner, 2003.

———. *For Whom the Bell Tolls*. New York: Charles Scribner's Sons, 1940.

Hirsch, Foster. *A Method to Their Madness: A History of the Actors Studio*. New York: W. W. Norton, 1984.

Hunter, Allan. *Faye Dunaway*. New York: St. Martin's Press, 1986.

"James Coburn." In *Current Biography 1999*. Edited by Clifford Thompson. New York: H. W. Wilson Company, 1999.

Jewison, Norman. *This Terrible Business Has Been Good to Me*. New York: St. Martin's Press, 2004.

Kael, Pauline. *I Lost It at the Movies*. Boston: Little Brown and Company, 1965.

Kaminsky, Stuart M. *Don Siegel: Director*. New York: Curtis Books, 1974.

Kelley, Kitty. *His Way: The Unauthorized Biography of Frank Sinatra*. New York: Bantam Books, 1986.

Kerouac, Jack. *On the Road: The Original Scroll*. 1957. Reprint, Howard Cunnell, ed. New York: Viking, 2007.

Lennon, Cynthia. *A Twist of Lennon*. 1978. Reprint, New York: Avon Books, 1980.

McCoy, Malachy. *Steve McQueen: The Unauthorized Biography*. Chicago: Henry Regnery Company, 1974.

MacGraw, Ali. *Moving Pictures*. New York: Bantam Books, 1991.

McQueen, Barbara (with Marshall Terrill). *Steve McQueen: The Last Mile*. Deerfield, IL: Dalton Watson Fine Books, 2007.

Maltin, Leonard, ed. *Leonard Maltin's 2006 Movie Guide*. New York: Signet Books, 2005.

———, ed. *Leonard Maltin's 2007 Movie Guide*. New York: Signet Books, 2006.

Michaels, Leonard. *The Collected Stories*. New York: Farrar, Straus and Giroux, 2007.

Miller, Frank. *Leading Men: The 50 Most Unforgettable Actors of the Studio Era*. San Francisco: Chronicle Books, 2006.

Nolan, William F. *McQueen*. New York: Congdon and Weed, 1984.

———. *Steve McQueen: Star on Wheels*. New York: Berkley Publishing, 1972.

Poitier, Sidney. *The Measure of a Man*. 2000. Reprint, San Francisco: Harper, 2001.

Ragsdale, Grady, Jr. *Steve McQueen: The Final Chapter*. Ventura, CA: Vision House, 1983.

Robbins, Jhan. *Yul Brynner: The Inscrutable King*. New York: Dodd, Mead and Company, 1987.

Sackett, Susan. *Box Office Hits*. New York: Billboard Books, 1990.

Sandford, Christopher. *McQueen: The Biography*. 2001. Reprint, New York: Taylor Trade Publishing, 2003.

Simmons, Garner. *Peckinpah: A Portrait in Montage*. New York: Limelight Editions, 1998.

Smith, David L. *Hoosiers in Hollywood*. Indianapolis: Indiana Historical Society Press, 2006.

Spiegel, Penina. *McQueen: The Untold Story of a Bad Boy in Hollywood*. Garden City, NY: Doubleday and Company, 1986.

St. Charnez, Casey. *The Complete Films of Steve McQueen*. 1984. Reprint, New York: Citadel Press, 1992.

Steinberg, Cobbett. *Reel Facts: The Movie Book of Records*. New York: Vintage Books, 1978.

"Steve McQueen." In *Current Biography 1966*. Edited by Charles Moritz. New York: H. W. Wilson Company, 1966.

Strait, Raymond. *James Garner.* New York: St. Martin's Press, 1985.

Strasberg, Lee. *A Dream of Passion: The Development.* Boston: Little, Brown and Company, 1987.

Terrill, Marshall. *Steve McQueen: Portrait of an American Rebel.* 1993. Reprint, London: Plexus Publishing, 2005.

Thomson, David. *The New Biographical Dictionary of Film.* New York: Alfred A. Knopf, 2003.

Toffel, Neile McQueen. *My Husband, My Friend.* New York: Atheneum, 1986.

Vonnegut, Kurt, Jr. *Slaughterhouse-Five.* 1969. Reprint, New York: Dell, 1974.

Wallach, Eli. *The Good, the Bad, and Me.* New York: Harcourt, 2005.

Zinsser, William, ed. *Extraordinary Lives: The Art and Craft of American Biography.* Boston: Houghton Mifflin Company, 1986.

Shorter Works

Alpert, Hollis. "The Professionals." *Saturday Review,* November 6, 1965.

"Americana." *The New Yorker,* December 27, 1969.

Ansen, David. "An Undying Breed." *Newsweek,* August 11, 1980.

Augeel, Roger. "Easy Rider." *The New Yorker,* June 2, 1980.

Bullitt review. *Cue,* October 26, 1968.

Bunzel, Peter. "The Bad Boy's Breakout." *Life,* July 12, 1963.

"Busted Flush." *Newsweek,* November 8, 1965.

Carson, Tom. "Toy Story." *Esquire,* May 2001.

"Cop Art." *Time,* November 8, 1968.

Crist, Judith. "No Butterfly, McQueen." *New York Magazine,* December 24, 1973.

———. *The Towering Inferno* review. *New York Magazine,* January 3, 1975.

Daniels, Diane. "Is It Neile's Turn to Run Now?" *Movie TV Secrets,* July 1965.

Eells, George. "Steve McQueen . . . Rugged, Tormented, Thrill-happy." *Look,* October 11, 1960.

Eyles, Allen. *Baby, The Rain Must Fall* review. *Films and Filming,* July 1965.

———. *The Cincinnati Kid* review. *Films and Filming,* January 1966.

———. *Nevada Smith* review. *Films and Filming,* October 1966.

Felchner, William J. "The Best of Steve McQueen." *Big Reel,* July 1995.

Fredrichsen, Frank. "The Short Tragic Life of Jimmy Dean." *Movie Star Parade,* December 1955.

Freedland, Nat. *The Reivers* review. *Entertainment World,* November 21, 1969.

Gehring, Wes D. Interview Marcus Winslow Jr., July 23, 2004.

———. "James Dean: 50 Years after His Death." *USA Today Magazine,* May 2005.

———. "The Populist Films of Robert Redford." *USA Today Magazine,* May 1999.

———. "Reassembling the Dust: The Art of Biography." *USA Today Magazine,* March 2003.

———. "Reel World: When McQueen Was King." *USA Today Magazine,* September 2007.

Gellatt, Roland. "Down Memory Lane." *Saturday Review,* January 3, 1970.

The Getaway review. *Cue,* December 23, 1972.

The Getaway review. *New Republic,* February 10, 1973.

The Getaway review. *Playboy,* March 1973.

Gilliatt, Penelope. "What Is Your Robbery Trying to Say?" *The New Yorker,* July 13, 1968.

Goldberg, Hyman. "Steve McQueen: Show-Biz Wheel!" *New York Mirror Magazine,* June 17, 1962.

Gomez, Joseph A. "Sam Peckinpah and the 'Post-Western.'" *American Classic Screen* (Spring 1980).

Gow, Gordon. *Papillon* review. *Films and Filming*, April 1974.

"Healthy Transplant." *Newsweek*, October 31, 1960.

Herbstman, Mandel. *Soldier in the Rain* review. *Film Daily*, November 19, 1963.

"An Honest Soldier." *Newsweek*, December 2, 1962.

The Honeymoon Machine review. *Independent Film Journal*, July 15, 1961.

The Honeymoon Machine review. *Motion Picture Exhibitor*, July 12, 1961.

Hoppe, David. "Steve McQueen's Indiana Legacy." *Arts Indiana Magazine* (Winter 2001).

Hopper, Hedda. Original draft of a Steve McQueen profile, June 28, 1959. In the "Steve McQueen Files," Margaret Herrick Library, Academy of Motion Picture Arts and Sciences, Beverly Hills, CA.

The Hunter review. *Playboy*, October 1980.

Johnson, Ian. *Love with the Proper Stranger* review. *Films and Filming*, October 1964.

Johnson, Robert. "TV's Angry Young Star." *Saturday Evening Post*, January 14, 1961.

Kael, Pauline. *The Getaway* review. *The New Yorker*, December 23, 1972.

———. *The Towering Inferno* review. *The New Yorker*, December 30, 1974.

Kehoe, John. "Steve McQueen." *Biography Magazine*, July 2001.

Kluge, P. F. "What Price Violence?" *Life*, August 11, 1972.

Knight, Arthur. *An Enemy of the People* review. *Hollywood Reporter*, August 28, 1978.

———. "Unsentimental Gentleman." *Saturday Review*, December 21, 1966.

Lane, Anthony. "Hot Stuff." *The New Yorker*, July 30, 2007.

Lane, Conrad. "Henry Hathaway: The Toughest Director Living." *Films of the Golden Age* (Fall 1999).

Le Mans review. *Box Office*, July 5, 1971.

Le Mans review. *Cue*, June 27, 1971.

Le Mans review. *Playboy*, September 1971.

"Lee Strasberg." In *Current Biography 1960*. Edited by Charles Moritz. New York: H. W. Wilson Company, 1960.

Love with the Proper Stranger review. *Saturday Review*, January 4, 1964.

McQueen, Steve. Family background at http:www.familysearch.org/Eng/search/IGI/individual-record.

———. "Motorcycles: What I Like in a Bike–and Why." *Popular Science*, November 1966.

Nevada Smith review. *Motion Picture Herald*, June 8, 1966.

Maletz, Andrea. "'The Reivers': Faulknerian and McQueenian Charm." *Boston After Dark*, January 7, 1970.

Marcede, Arthur. "Steve McQueen: 'I Must Be Free to Live in My Own Way.'" *TV Guide Movie Guide*, December 1966.

"A Married Man Should Never Be Left Alone." *Modern Screen*, March 1966.

"New York, New York." *Time*, December 27, 1963.

Oberbeck, S. K. "Yoknapatawpha Boy." *Newsweek*, January 5, 1970.

Pachter, Marc. "The Biographer Himself: An Introduction." In *Telling Lives: The Biographer's Art*. Edited by Marc Pachter. Philadelphia: University of Pennsylvania Press, 1985.

Peckinpah, Sam. "Playboy Interview: Sam Peckinpah." *Playboy*, April 1972.

Rafferty, Terrence. "The Real McQueen." *GQ*, April 1999.

"The Real McQueen." *Newsweek*, January 6, 1964.

The Reivers review. *Cue*, December 27, 1969.

The Reivers review. *Motion Picture Exhibitor*, December 3, 1969.

Rider, David. *The Thomas Crown Affair* review. *Films and Filming*, April 1969.

Schaefer, Stephen. "Bounty Hunter McQueen: An American Classic." *US Magazine*, August 5, 1980.

Schickel, Richard. "Crime Flick with a Taste of Genius." *Life*, November 22, 1968.

Sheen, Martin. Introduction to *James Dean: American Icon*, by David Dalton. New York: St. Martin's Press, 1984.

Shuldiner, Herbert. "Candid Interview with Steve McQueen: 'I like to ride flat out . . . .'" *Popular Science*, November 1966.

Soldier in the Rain review. *Motion Picture Herald*, November 27, 1963.

"Southern Reconstruction." *Time*, January 5, 1970.

"Steve McQueen: A Brentwood Retreat Suited to the Dynamic Star." *Architectural Digest*, April 1994.

"Stuck on an Island." *Newsweek*, December 17, 1973.

"Talk with a Star." *Newsweek*, January 6, 1964.

Tarratt, Margaret. *The Getaway* review. *Films and Filming*, March 1973.

———. *The Reivers* review. *Films and Filming*, January 1971.

The Thomas Crown Affair review. *Motion Picture Exhibitor*, June 19, 1968.

The Thomas Crown Affair review. *Motion Picture Herald*, June 19, 1968.

The Thomas Crown Affair review. *Time*, July 12, 1968.

Webster, Andy. "The Escape Artist." *Premiere*, September 1999.

Wolcott, James. "The Real McQueen." *Vanity Fair*, September 2000.

Newspapers (see additional citations in Notes)

Brooklyn (NY) Eagle, 1960.

Chicago Tribune, 1962.

Hollywood Citizen News, 1960, 1961, 1962, 1965, 1966, 1968.

Hollywood Reporter, 1960, 1962, 1963, 1966, 1968, 1969, 1971, 1972, 1974, 1977, 1980.

Indianapolis News, 1971.

Indianapolis Star, 1971, 1998, 2005.

London Times, 1973, 2004.

Los Angeles Examiner, 1960, 1961, 1962, 1966.

Los Angeles Herald Examiner, 1962, 1968, 1971, 1972, 1973, 1974, 1980, 1981.

Los Angeles Mirror, 1958, 1960.

Los Angeles Times, 1959, 1960, 1962, 1963, 1965, 1968, 1971, 1972, 1973, 1974, 1975, 1980, 1981, 2003.

Newark (NJ) Evening News, 1959, 1963, 1966.

New York Daily News, 1961, 1963, 1966, 1972.

New York Herald Tribune, 1959, 1963, 1965.

New York Journal American, 1961, 1963, 1965.

New York News, 1969.

New York Post, 1958, 1963, 1968, 1972.

New York Times, 1960, 1961, 1962, 1963, 1965, 1966, 1968, 1971, 1972, 1973, 1974, 1980, 2006, 2007.

New York World Telegram, 1966.

New York World Telegram and the Sun, 1965, 1966.

Philadelphia Inquirer, 1973.
Pictorial TV View, 1966.
TV Time Sunday Supplement, 1966.
USA Today, 2007.
Variety, 1956, 1958, 1959, 1960, 1961, 1962, 1963, 1965, 1968, 1969, 1971, 1972, 1973, 1974,
       1980, 1986.
Village Voice, 1972.